ISBN 978-1-330-84211-9
PIBN 10112575

English
Français
Deutsche
Italiano
Español
Português

www.forgottenbooks.com

Mythology Photography **Fiction**
Fishing Christianity **Art** Cooking
Essays Buddhism Freemasonry
Medicine **Biology** Music **Ancient
Egypt** Evolution Carpentry Physics
Dance Geology **Mathematics** Fitness
Shakespeare **Folklore** Yoga Marketing
Confidence Immortality Biographies
Poetry **Psychology** Witchcraft
Electronics Chemistry History **Law**
Accounting **Philosophy** Anthropology
Alchemy Drama Quantum Mechanics
Atheism Sexual Health **Ancient History**
Entrepreneurship Languages Sport
Paleontology Needlework Islam
Metaphysics Investment Archaeology
Parenting Statistics Criminology
Motivational

TO MY MOTHER

PREFACE

In the following pages modern Chinese history, from the constitutional point of view, is treated as a continuous development since the inception of reform in 1898 under the Emperor Kuang Hsü. It was only gradually that China was brought to a realization of the necessity for change in her political structure. During the years prior to 1898, it became apparent to a few in the country that the Chinese house must be repaired if it was to remain standing. The "Hundred Days" of reform in 1898 marked the attempt to patch up, without seriously altering, the existing structure. The fundamental nature of the alterations necessary, however, was not appreciated at that time. With the failure of the reform movement came a reaction against change. This reaction against the 'new' culminated in the Boxer uprising. The disastrous termination of the anti-foreign movement brought a deeper realization of the need for radical reforms. The reforms undertaken involved the introduction of a measure of representative government into China. But although committed to the idea of change, the rulers of China were not prepared to move rapidly enough to satisfy the radical element in the reform party and revolution resulted. The revolutionary ideas marked a decided break with the past. Since the revolution of 1911, the history of China has been the attempt to find a middle ground, suited to the needs of the country, between the old traditional life of the State, and the new conceptions of governmental relationships brought to the East from the West. No change, whether in the nature of progression or retrogression, stands by itself, but each links itself naturally with the antecedent and the subsequent condition. That fact of itself justifies the attempt to trace the threads of constitutional development in modern China. The endeavor is further justified by the outstanding importance to the world of the Far Eastern question which cannot be divorced from the internal history of China.

The material for the first two chapters has been drawn largely from such authoritative secondary works as H. B. Morse's "International Relations of the Chinese Empire," Smith's "China in Convulsion," and "China under the Empress Dowager," by Bland and Backhouse (1910 edition). The succeeding chapters have been written from a study of the documents, and from knowledge of the situation gained during residence in China. Where the interpretation of a fact or event has been given in the form of a quotation, it has been because the words quoted have expressed the point of view of the present writer.

It is impossible here to make more than a general acknowledgment of the aid given by friends both in China and the United States in the preparation of this study. Grateful acknowledgment is due, however, to the aid given and suggestions made by Professors W. W. Willoughby and W. F. Willoughby, and Professor Henry Jones Ford, who read and criticised the entire manuscript; to Dr. S. K. Hornbeck who read and gave valuable suggestions as to the first half of the book; and to Professor E. S. Corwin. The writer is under a further debt of gratitude to his wife for her aid in the gathering of materials, in the preparation of the manuscript, and in the reading of the proofs of the book.

HAROLD MONK VINACKE.

Oxford, Ohio, 8 August, 1920.

CONTENTS

CHAPTER I

For generations prior to the end of the nineteenth century China had been politically in a state of suspended animation. Life had continued but there had been little growth and to the casual observer, almost no perceptible decay in her institutions. Dynasties rose and fell without seriously affecting the political organization of the country. One barbarian rule after another was imposed on the "sons of Han," yet, after the conquest, the conquerors ruled according to the accepted customs and traditions. Then, within a period of less than twenty years, the whole political system was outwardly and rather ostentatiously changed. The form of a constitutional monarchy was substituted for the paternal despotism of the past, and, almost immediately, the limited monarchy gave way to a republic. Political change does not come unheralded in any country, certainly not in a State ruled by custom and tradition as China had for so long been. But it is not easy to show why any change comes in the life of a nation, and it is not always profitable to undertake such a task. In order to follow the course of modern constitutional or political development in China, however, it is necessary: (1) to appreciate the conditions which created the necessity for reform and change; and (2) to discover why those conditions led to a change in the political structure instead of a simple change of dynasty. This understanding can be best gained by means of a brief description of the organization of the government under the Manchus, together with a discussion of some of the new problems the Empire had to face during the last years of Manchu rule.

At the head of the governmental organization stood the Emperor. In theory he wielded the absolute power of life and death over his subjects. In him were vested all of the prerogatives of government: executive, legislative, and judicial. The Imperial Mandates had the force of law; the Emperor was the highest court of judicial appeal in the land, the stroke of the "vermillion pencil" being final; he had the absolute power of appointment and dismissal. In short, he was the typical despot of the Oriental Court. Practically, however, he was limited in the use of his powers by the strength of custom over the minds of the people; by the laws established by his predecessors; and because he could enforce his will only so far as his agents were willing to carry out his commands. The Emperor ruled as the "Son of Heaven," but if he was unable to preserve order in the Empire, or if he failed to respect the customs of the people, it was felt that he had exhausted the "mandate of Heaven," and the people held themselves justified in deposing him. "The Chinese confer on their Emperor absolute power, but argue that when they are oppressed it does not proceed from the absolute power of the Emperor, but rather from a want of proper appreciation of his high duties, and that when the Emperor is thus guilty, they are under no obligation to countenance or obey him."[1]

Assisting the Emperor in the performance of his extensive duties was, at first, the Grand Secretariat (Nei Ko); to which was added about 1730 the Grand Council (Kun Ki-chu). It was the duty of the Grand Secretariat to deliberate on matters connected with the government of the realm; to find out the will of the Emperor and to see that it was proclaimed throughout the Empire. The Grand Council, which usually

[1] Jernigan, "China in Law and Commerce," p. 56.

consisted of five members, gradually displaced the Grand Secretariat, becoming the actual Privy Council of the Emperor.[2]
Its duties also were to deliberate and advise on the affairs of
the State in the presence of the Emperor. While the advice of
the Grand Council was always sought, it was not always followed, the Throne having the final decision of every question.
The actual administration of the affairs of the nation was not,
however, carried on by the council but was in the hands of
the six Boards (increased to seven by the creation of the
Tsungli Yamen,[3] or Foreign Board, in 1861) i.e. the Boards
of Civil Office, Revenue, Rites, War, Punishment, and Works.

Before passing on to the provincial system one branch of
the central administration deserves especial mention. The
only body in the Empire with the right directly to criticise
the Emperor was the Censorate. The duty of the Censors
was to criticise, and "this duty they exercised without fear,
though not always without favor."[4] No question affecting
the interest of the State was too great, and none too small for
their scrutiny. The scope of their work can be judged from
the name, "The All Examining Court." Thus the Censorate,
says Williams, had "the care of manners and customs, the investigation of all public offices within and without the capital,
the discrimination between the good and bad performance of

[2] Membership in the Grand Secretariat continued to be the
highest honor attainable, however, although in later years, when
it had been superseded by the Grand Council, it had come to be
a mere Court of Archives. Morse, Trade and Administration,
pp. 42-43.

[3] The Tsungli Yamen (Foreign Board), dealing with the problems of foreign intercourse, the most pressing questions of the
day, was gradually increased in size and power until, in 1876,
its membership included all of the members of the Grand Council, and none who were not at least President or Vice-president
of a Board. Morse, Trade and Administration, p. 42.

[4] Morse, "Trade and Administration of China," p. 46.

their business, and between the depravity and uprightness of the officers employed in them."[5]   It was largely through the Censors that the Emperor was able to keep in touch with public sentiment throughout his domains, and because they did give an expression, albeit imperfect, to public opinion they constituted one of the few effective checks on the exercise of the Imperial power.   But the effectiveness of the check was greatly lessened by the fact that the Censorate did not act as an organic whole, but that each member acted independently of the others.[6]   Thus the censors lost the force that goes with united action.   It was also lessened by the fact that in the later days of the Dynasty, under the Empress Tzu Hsi, criticism of the Government was liable to subject the critic to severe punishment for his temerity.   In spite of the limitations of the Censorate, however, it is important to note that there was a way by which the sovereign could keep informed of the actions of his officials and could be reminded of his own obligations to the people.

While the power of the Emperor was supreme its exercise was delegated to his personal representatives throughout the Empire.   For administrative purposes the provinces were grouped into viceroyalties.   In two of the provinces, Chihli

[5] Williams, "The Middle Kingdom," vol. I, p. 430.   In theory and practice the action of the censorate often differed.   In theory the Censors held before the Emperor the ideals of government set forth by Confucius and his followers.   In practice it was unfortunately often true, as Weale says (Reshaping of Far East, p. 220) that the "Censorate stands, censoring those acts which are not acceptable because no bribe had been paid."   But even in the last years of the Manchu rule there were Censors who put their duty before even their lives.   Men were always to be found of the type of Wu K'o-tu who committed suicide as the highest protest against the act of Tzu Hsi (the Empress Dowager) in not providing the proper heir for the Emperor T'ung Chih.

[6] See Colquhoun, "China in Transformation," p. 287.

and Szechuan, the Viceroy had only the administration of the one province. In all other cases he had supervision over two or more. In addition to the Viceroy each province had a Governor, except where the Viceroy himself exercised direct control. Both Viceroy and Governor were responsible to the Crown and had the right of directly petitioning the Emperor.[7] Both were honorary members of the Censorate and had the right of criticism that went with membership in that body.

Subject only to the final supervision of the Emperor and the central administration, these highest provincial officials exercised as absolute a power in the government of their provinces as the Emperor did over the whole country. As Morse says: "The Provinces are satrapies to the extent that so long as the tribute and matriculations are duly paid, and the general policy of the central administration followed, they are free to administer their own affairs in detail as may seem best to their own provincial authorities."[8] From this it follows that the administration of the laws, and the carrying out of the Imperial orders varied from province to province in accordance with the interests and the initiative of the Governor or Viceroy. This was true as late as 1900, when Yuan Shih-kai in Shantung, and Liu K'un-yi in the Liang-Kiang, refused to carry out the anti-foreign policy of the Court, while in other parts of the Empire foreigners were being murdered and their property destroyed.

So long as he sent in his apportionment of the Imperial revenue, then, and did not come openly into conflict with the policy of the central government, the Governor of each province exercised an absolute control over the territory assigned to him. His power was limited only by his fear of the removal power of the Emperor, and by his ability to have his will

[7] In position the Governor ranked with, but after the Viceroy.
[8] "Trade and Administration," p. 46.

carried out in the province. He was directly responsible to the Emperor for the maintenance of peace and order in his province, and because of this responsibility, he was careful, in most cases, not to take any action antagonistic to the desires and interests of the people. In order that he might not be able to establish himself so firmly in his post as to be tempted to set up an independent rule, a Governor or Viceroy was commonly appointed for a term of three years, with the possibility of one renewal, after which he would be transferred to another province. Li Hung-chang provided one of the notable exceptions to the rule, being maintained as Viceroy of Chihli province for over twenty years. A high provincial official was never appointed to a post in his native province.

Assisting the Governor in the actual administration was the provincial treasurer, who was the head of the civil service, as well as the chief fiscal agent of the province; the provincial judge, who was the final (provincial) court of appeal; the salt comptroller; and the grain intendent. These four officials constituted the deliberative and executive council of the provincial government, and, with the Governor and the Viceroy, formed the general provincial administration residing at the capital of the province.

For administrative purposes each province was divided into Hsien, Chow or T'ing; several Hsien together formed a department or prefecture; and two or more Prefectures would be united in a Circuit. Thus the largest subdivision was the Circuit and the smallest the Hsien. "The unit for administrative purposes within the province is the Hsien or *Dis*-triet;—two or three or more (up to five or six) *D*istricts collectively form a Fu or Prefecture; and two or more Prefectures are placed under the jurisdiction of a Taotai. . . . The Chow and the T'ing proper are a superior kind of Hsien, being component parts of a Fu; the Chihli-chow and Chihli-

T'ing are an inferior kind of Fu, both having as direct a relation to the provincial government as a Fu, but the latter distinguished from the Fu by having no Hsien subordinated to it."[9]

All the provincial officials, down to the Hsien magistrate, were appointed directly by the central government. The Prefeet exercised the delegated authority of the Governor in his prefecture, and was held responsible for its share of the revenue of the province, as well as for the maintenance of order in his jurisdiction. However, he dealt more with the external relations of his Fu than with its internal administration, and was rather a channel of communication than an executive officer. He acted as the court of appeal from the Hsien's court.

The Hsien (district magistrate) was the foundation of the administrative system. He was the lowest official appointed by the central government and in many ways was the most important officer of the administration. His work brought him into direct touch with the people and thus he came to personify the power of government to the mass of the population. In the transference of responsibility it all came ultimately to the Hsien. Just as the Governor was responsible for his province, so the magistrate was responsible for the proper exercise of all of the prerogatives of government in his district. An enumeration of some of his functions will serve to show his importance. He was police magistrate, deciding ordinary police cases; and was court of first instance in civil and criminal cases. In addition to being the agent of the provincial government and the Imperial administration in collecting taxes and the grain tribute, he was the registrar of land, the famine commissioner, and the representative of the Board of Works in the oversight of public buildings, etc. In fact everything

[9] Morse, p. 52.

pertaining to the conduct of government came under his charge.[10]   He alone had no one on whom he could shift the responsibility for his acts.

This delegation of responsibility is well illustrated by the specimen proclamation given by Parker: "The magistrate has had the honor to receive instructions from the prefect, who cites the directions of the Taotai, moved by the Treasurer and the Judge, recipients of the commands of their Excellencies the Viceroy and Governor, acting at the instance of the Foreign Board, who have been honored with his Majesty's commands."

"Politically the government of China turns on the reciprocal duty of parents and children. The Emperor is the head of the government but the family is its base, and it is not from the central head at Peking, but from the family unit that the building of the governmental fabric proceeds. In the family life may be seen the larger life of the Empire, and it is the family unit that gives the semblance of unity to the Empire."[11]   The family was the social unit, just as the Hsien was the administrative unit of the Empire. And the family organization was based on the custom and tradition of centuries. This being so, the magistrate was able to perform his duties, and carry out the Imperial commands only so far as they did not come into conflict with the custom and tradition of his district. The greatest objection to a new law or tax, or to any innovation was that it had not been in existence before. "In the administration of the affairs of the Empire,"

[10] "In Chinese official documents the district magistrate is frequently referred to as the father and mother of his people. And as the head of a household can make it happy or unhappy according to his disposition, so the rule of a good or bad magistrate promotes order or disorder among the people of his district." Jernigan, p. 35.

[11] Jernigan, p. 34.

says Jerningan,[12] "the principle is recognized that laws are the particular institution of the legislator, while customs are the institution of a nation in general, and that nothing tends more to produce a revolution than an attempt to change a custom by a law."

The village itself was organized, entirely apart ,from the general administration, on the basis of the family. The several families united in a village organization selected one of their number to serve as the village headman (Tipao).[13]   He acted as the intermediary between the Hsien and the village. Because of the pressure this semi-political organization could bring to bear on him, it was possible to force the magistrate to adjust his execution of the law to the customs of the locality.[14]

[12] Jernigan, p. 33.

[13] Morse says (Trade and Administration, p. 60), that the headman was nominated by the magistrate from among the village elders, "but dependent upon the good will of his constituents." On the other hand, Jernigan (p. 34), finds that the Tipao was selected by the families, but that "it is sometimes required, after the headman of a village has been selected, that he receive the confirmation of the district magistrate."   This latter view is more nearly correct, although the selection of the Tipao varied in different localities.

[14] The pressure that the Tipao could bring to bear on the magistrate may be understood, when the extent to which the magistrate was forced to rely on these extra-official functionaries for the administration of his district, is considered. "The Tipao," says Morse, "acts as constable, and is responsible for the good conduct and moral behavior of every one of his constituents; he is also responsible for the due payment of land tax and tribute," etc. (p. 60).   Since this village headman was not known to the official administrative system he could not be fully controlled by it.   And since the magistrate could not conduct the work of his district except through the Tipao, who represented the people, it can be seen how powerful an influence the village could exert on the administration.

Applying this to the actual administration of the Empire, remembering that the customs and traditions of one Hsien were by no means identical with those of any other Hsien in the Empire, it is clear that the carrying out of the law would vary from province to province, and from Hsien to Hsien. not only with the personnel of the official hierarchy, but with the difference in habits and customs.

More than any other country, the old China was governed by the class of scholars, the literati. Membership and preferment in the official system was based on a series of examinations open to all classes. Beginning with the district examinations, a candidate passed through the prefectural examination, and that of the province, finally coming to the Metropolitan examination in Peking. Success in these examinations gave admission to a distinct class in the state, the literati, the class given the highest place in the popular esteem. Such success meant even more than individual prestige. It threw its reflected light on the whole village from which the successful candidate had come, so that frequently the inhabitants of a village would unite to give a promising student every possible opportunity to prepare himself for the examinations, and his progress would be watched with interest by all the villagers. There was no national system of education, but a man who had established himself in the opinion of his fellows as a scholar would gather a few disciples around him and impart his knowledge to them. As the whole plan of education was based on the Confucian Classics, it was possible for one teacher to conduct a student through the entire curriculum, thus fitting him for examination. Fortunate was the village which had an able expounder of the Classics!

This system would seem to promise an unusually intelligent administration. But while examination was the basis of official preferment, the practice of buying and selling office had grown up. So that the most successful candidate had to be prepared to satisfy the demands of those who had the bestowal of patronage, or could influence its bestowal, if he could hope to leave the class of "expectant"[15] officials, or to reach any very high place in the government. Furthermore, the education necessary to compete in the examinations was not always calculated to fit a man for the actual duties and responsibilities of public administration.

From this brief review of the administrative system of the Chinese Empire as it existed under the Manchu regime, it will be seen that two principles must be borne in mind in discussing the reasons for the changes after 1898: first, that of responsibility, each higher official holding his immediate inferior absolutely responsible for the condition of the territory under his jurisdiction; and, second, the variation in the administration due to the differences in local customs, and to the willingness and ability of the men administering the laws.

While trade between China and European countries had been carried on by Europeans for many years, it was not until 1842 that China may be said to have been opened in reality to foreign intercourse. The traders, before that year, had been confined to one port, Canton, and had not been permitted to reside there throughout the year. No official communication was permitted between the States of the West because of the Chinese conception of lordship over the "outer barbarians." From 1842 until the end of the century, however, step by step, China was driven from her position of isolation and forced into the family of nations. This meant also that she was forced, in practice if not in theory, to recognize the

---

[15] "Expectant" officials were those who had passed the examinations, thus qualifying for an official post, but who had not yet received an appointment. In other words, they constituted the official "waiting list."

modern legal principle of the equality of nations in their dealings with one another.

Back of each step taken by the European countries in their application of pressure to China lay the desire at first to develop trade and later to exploit the "Middle Kingdom" as a field for investment. To accomplish this it was necessary to establish direct diplomatic relations so that the western nations could have a channel of communication with Chinese officialdom. The establishment of a diplomatic and consular service in China resulted in a constant pressure on the government and the people to undertake or permit the development of new activities of a commercial and financial as well as of a religious or philanthropic nature.

The struggle for a recognition of equality of relationship, and the consequent establishment of diplomatic relations was carried to a successful conclusion by means of the three so-called Opium wars. The first was brought to an end by the Nanking treaty of 1842 between England and China. The commercial footing of foreigners was then recognized and several ports opened to foreign trade. The right to maintain diplomatic establishments in Peking was not gained until the Anglo-French forces occupied that city in 1860 during the third war mentioned.

The years from 1860 to the Sino-Japanese war of 1894-95 were marked by the struggle on the part of the Powers to hold what had been gained by force; by the opening of new ports to trade and a great expansion of commercial activity; by the continued extension of the missionary propaganda and the establishment of mission schools and hospitals, and by the slow education of the Chinese to the point of acceptance and adoption of western mechanical devices such as the steam engine, with the consequent development of a system of railway transportation, the telegraph, and some of the machines of production.

During the first period (up to 1844) of limited foreign intercourse with China, that country found little difficulty in regulating the trade by means of the existing administrative system. By putting it under the supervision of one official he could be held responsible for all matters concerning foreigners and foreign interests. With the British trade, by far the most important, in the hands of the East India Company, which was interested solely in the maintenance of peaceful commercial relations, it was not difficult, by a threat of stopping the trade, to enforce the regulations confining it to Canton, and putting it in the hands of the monopoly of Chinese merchants known as the Co-hong. It was also found that by holding the foreign superintendent of trade responsible for the personal conduct of the foreigners, it was comparatively easy to keep them within the limits prescribed by the laws of the Empire. During this period there was no question of the amenability of the Europeans to Chinese law. All dealings were with the merchants, not as nationals of States equal to the Chinese Empire, but as individuals allowed to carry on their trade as a mark of the favor of the Emperor, and not as any matter of right. This status was constantly kept before them, and, during the period of the East India Company's control, was accepted by the merchants rather than risk the loss of the trade. As long as China was the dictator of the terms of intercourse and trade, and could keep it confined to one place far removed from the capital; so long as there was no desire to establish interstate relations with China; and while it was not necessary, in order to satisfy foreign demands, to have a uniform administration of the laws throughout the Empire, it was practicable to entrust the entire oversight of the trade to a commercial agent like the Hoppo[16] and hold him responsible for all matters connected

[16] The Hoppo "the administrator of the Canton Customs, is

with the foreigners.   But when the monopoly of the China trade was withdrawn from the British East India Company, thus opening it to unrestricted competition on the part of British subjects as well as other foreigners,[17] and when a representative of the British Government was appointed to deal with the Chinese government officials, the weakness of the Chinese administrative system was exposed.

Immediately upon the arrival of Lord Napier, in 1833, as the first Superintendent of trade appointed by the British Government, the Chinese feeling of superiority which made relations on a basis of equality impossible, was manifested. . . . "He was met at the outset by a refusal to treat with him as the envoy of a friendly power, enjoying a position of equality with China; he was refused an interview with the Viceroy, who required him to formulate his demands through the committee of Chinese merchants through whom the trade monopoly was worked; his letters were not received, and he was required to present his written communications in the form of a humble petition; and coercion was applied to the English merchants and their trade to force him to leave Canton."[18] Since Lord Napier and all succeeding British representatives, whether appointed as Superintendents of trade, as Consular representatives, or as Plenipotentiaries, were instructed to

a direct representative of the Emperor and entirely outside the provincial hierarchy, though, to give him due standing and authority, he takes official rank with, but after the Viceroy." Morse, "International Relations," p. 15.

[17] The American, French, Portuguese and other non-British traders had developed a considerable trade, and their trade was not in the hands of monopolistic companies. No consular officers were maintained to conduct official intercourse with the Chinese government, and the trade was dealt with largely through the British Superintendent, who was purely a commercial agent.

[18] Morse, "Trade and Administration," p. 18.

treat only with the representatives of the Chinese Government, and not to conduct their business through the Hong merchants; and since the very conception of intercourse with foreign nations on a footing of equality was unknown to the Chinese, it is evident that a situation was created which could result only in conflict.

The struggle for a recognition of the equality of the Western nations with "the Middle Kingdom" was brought to open conflict by the questions arising out of the opium trade. The first Edict against the importation of opium into China was issued in 1800, but until twenty years later practically no attention was paid to it by either Chinese or foreigners. The trade was carried on openly at Canton, the only difference being that after the prohibition the opium could not be brought to the factories, and it was liable to an irregular tax, on the principle of making it pay all that the traffic would bear. But, finally, the trade became so open that the Viceroy was forced to take some action limiting it. Receiving ships were then stationed by the foreign traders outside of Chinese jurisdiction, and the trade was still carried on at Canton. As the restrictions became more rigid there, the traders began to make voyages up the coast, selling their opium for cash and using the money to buy return cargoes at Canton. Even during the most rigid enforcement of the prohibitory Edicts at Canton, where trade was supposed to be confined, it was possible to bring opium into the country through the other supposedly closed ports. This was due to the fact, already pointed out, that the uniform enforcement of an Imperial Edict in China was a rare occurrence, each order being executed only so far as it was to the interest of each governor or commissioner to carry it out. It is an interesting commentary on the Chinese administration that while commissioner Lin at Canton was earnestly endeavoring to carry out the orders of the Emperor prohibiting the opium trade, other high officials of the government were openly disregarding them.

This same lack of uniformity was apparent in the observance of the provisions of the treaties negotiated with China between 1842-1860. In Shanghai, opened to foreign trade by the treaty of Nanking (1842), providing a place of residence for foreigners and the opening of the trade was attended with no difficulty, while at Canton the old hostility was exhibited by officials and people alike; the same attempts being made to retain by delay and negotiation what had been given up as the result of the terms of peace. In every case, the feelings of the people were alleged as the reason why treaty provisions could not be carried out. The officials claimed that they might not be able to hold the people in check if the English insisted on their right of entry into the city of Canton, although the same right had been given and attended with no difficulty at Shanghai. The people north of Canton found it to their interest to enter upon peaceful trade relations with the foreigners, so that in their case the law harmonized with the interests and the wishes of the people; while at Canton it had been found profitable to hold the foreigners under strict control. Another striking evidence of this predominance of local interests over national policy was presented in the request of the Imperial officials for British aid against the Taiping rebels at Shanghai at the time when Great Britain was making active war on the Imperial Government at Peking.[19]

Before the Powers forced a recognition of their equality with China, it had been possible to limit the control of the Central Government to the appointment of the officials of the provincial administration, and the dictation of the general

[19] These are but a few of the instances that might be cited to show this lack of unity of feeling and of administration throughout the Empire from 1842 to 1860.

policy of the government, leaving large discretionary power
in the hands of its appointees as to the actual execution of
this policy.   But with the establishment of treaty relations
with outside States it was absolutely necessary for the Central
Government to assume a more direct responsibility in the
conduct of affairs.[20]   In the words of one writer: "When
pressure began to come from without; when it became necessary, in order to satisfy the demands of foreign nations, for
the government to *control* the provinces, and, in order to resist the aggressions of those same foreign nations to be able
to marshal and unite the forces of the Empire; the de-central-
zation, the lack of uniformity, the lack of a sense of mutual
interests and obligations, the habit of independence, and the
natural disinclination to subordinate local interests to the necessities of the nation proved sources of hopeless weakness."[21]
The Powers were not satisfied to see the execution of the
treaty stipulations left to the individual initiative of each
governor of the eighteen provinces, but demanded that they
be enforced uniformly throughout the whole Empire.   At the
same time that they insisted on the exact execution of the obligations imposed on the Imperial Government, they took advantage of this known lack of centralized authority to impose
new penalties on the Chinese whenever foreign interests were
injured as a result of the inability of the Central Government
to control the provincial administration.   Thus in self-defence

[20] After the treaty of 1842 the Emperor still transferred responsibility for the conduct of foreign relations to the proper
provincial officials.   Official intercourse was rather with the
province as a unit than with the Central Government of China.
It was only with the residence of the Ministers at Peking, where
they could exert direct pressure, that any attempt at a uniform
administration of treaty provisions was secured.

[21] Hornbeck, "Contemporary Politics in Far East," p. 36.

the Imperial Government was forced to a closer supervision of the administration of the provinces.

In criticising the execution of treaty provisions it must be remembered that the idea of reciprocal obligations between nations as embodied in treaties or the principles of an international law was entirely new to the Chinese Government equally with the people of the country. Before 1842 they had been accustomed to look upon all outside nations as "barbarians," and inferior to the "Middle Kingdom." Ambassadors came only as bearers of tribute, and to learn the will of the Emperor. The fact that they had been forced at the cannon's mouth to concede an outward equality did not mean that they really recognized it as existing; forcing them to assume obligations did not carry with it a recognition of the binding quality of those obligations if it was possible to evade them. It took the entire period from 1842 to 1901, with its four wars and the final suppression of the Boxer uprising, the element of force being constantly kept before the eyes of the Government and the people, and China's weakness being consistently brought to light, to bring home to the Chinese a realization of the binding force of an international agreement.

A foreigner, familiar with China, if asked what is the greatest deficiency in the Chinese government, would reply immediately, "the lack of a sense of honesty among the officials as a class." Yet, from the Chinese point of view, there was nothing dishonest in the system of "squeeze." It meant simply this. The Emperor notified each province of its proportion of the revenue needed for the Central Government. The Governor added to this fixed sum a sufficiently large commission to enable him to maintain his official household properly and to add a reasonable amount to his own meager salary. This increased sum was then apportioned to the various prefectures. The Prefect took the sum assigned to his *Depart-*

ment for collection and added his commission. He then distributed the total amount among the Hsien under his jurisdiction for actual collection. But the Hsien Magistrate was
also entitled to his commission to pay those to whom he delegated the task of collecting the taxes, and to bring his own
salary to the level necessary to maintain the dignity of his
office. Therefore only a small proportion of the revenue actually collected reached the Central Government. The same
process was applied to the collection of all port duties and im-
posts. This practice was well known to the people and since
it was an established custom no great objection was made.
As long as the Imperial Government received its quota it was
content to pay the officials small salaries and let them add to
their incomes in any way they could, provided they kept the
people under their jurisdiction contented. Such a system
worked well enough so long as the expenses of the Government were only the nominal ones of the Imperial Household
and the payment of small fees to the officials. But when large
foreign indemnities were added one after another and the
expense of foreign wars and the great Taiping rebellion had
to be met, the Emperor was forced to increase the amounts
demanded from the provinces. This increase meant that the
people had to find a way to provide more,—not that the officials gave up any of their "squeeze" to meet the additional
expense. At a time when the entire country had been devastated by marauding bands of rebels, even a slight increase
in taxes worked a great hardship. The discontent growing
from this condition could be utilized by the Government in
part to keep alive a hatred of foreigners who had made the
new burdens necessary. But when it was seen that the Government was able neither to protect the country from the aggressions of the West, nor to preserve order at home, this
restlessness and discontent reacted directly on the Manchu

Government. If the people had felt that the Imperial Court was retrenching in every way, and that the officials were doing everything in their power to help meet the new burdens, it would have helped enormously to keep them loyal supporters of the established regime.

The contrary, however, was known to be the case. It was a notorious fact that the actual power in Peking was in the hands of the eunuchs. The revenues that should have been used for the protection of the country and for repairing the ravages of the Taiping rebellion were being used to enrich a few servitors in the Palace who had gained the ear of the ruler. Not only were the Imperial revenues going that way, but every official, from the highest to the lowest, was forced to pay huge sums to these eunuchs in order to get any official preferment, the officials being expected to reimburse themselves at the expense of the people. The Manchus had recog-nized from the beginning of their rule in China Proper that a eunuch-ridden Court meant a government in a state of decay. One of the earliest of the dynastic House-laws provided that eunuchs should never be allowed to hold official position of any kind, or to advise on matters of State.²² The corruption of the Ming Court, due to the ascendency of the eunuchs, and the consequent decline of the power of the Ming *Dynasty* brought this fact vividly home to the founder of the Great Tsing *Dynasty*.²³ But while the evil effects of the eunuch system were clearly recognized, it was not long until the system itself had become thoroughly established in the Manchu Government. In a despotic form of government those closest to the person of the ruler inevitably exercise the greatest influence in the government of the realm. In an Asiatic country

---

²² Bland and Backhouse, "Annals and Memoirs of the Court of Peking," p. 232.
²³ *Ibid.,* especially ch. V and ch. IX.

it is almost invariably the attendents of the harem, constantly in communication with the Emperor, who are able to influence him in his determination of the policy of the government. But the exercise of such an unofficial influence, where the wielder of the real authority is not accountable for his actions to anyone except his master who has given him the power, is certain to lead to corruption and misgovernment.

A realization of the futility of expecting protection from foes, either without or within, from the decentralized and eunuch-controlled Manchu Government was forced on the educated Chinese by the outcome of the war with Japan in 1894-95. Money that had been collected ostensibly to strengthen the defences of the Empire, and which, if properly expended, would have enabled China to make at least a creditable showing against Japan, had been diverted to the building of a summer palace for the Empress-dowager, Tzu Hsi. Most of the funds went directly into the pocket of the chief-eunuch Li Lien-ying, through the medium of the contracting firm that built the palace. Even such a humiliating defeat as was inflicted on the Empire at that time did not arouse the people as much as the knowledge that the heavy taxes imposed on them, instead of being used at least in part for their welfare, were enriching the favorites of Tzu Hsi. Strange as it seems to the Western mind, a military defeat does not serve to lower the prestige of the country in the minds of the Chinese. They came out of the wars with England as firmly convinced as before of China's superiority to all other nations of the world. This was due to the fact that in the Chinese civilization the profession of arms has always, until recently, occupied the lowest place in the estimation of the people. But the defeats inflicted by foreign Powers on the "Celestial Empire" did serve to bring home vividly to the

Chinese the inherent weaknesses of their system of government.

Briefly, then, by 1898 the Chinese had been shown conelusively the inability of their government to keep the foreigners out of the country or to protect Chinese interests when they were in conflict with the interests of European Powers, or even of Japan. The Powers had entrenched themselves in China on a basis of equality, and in so doing had imposed on the country a heavy burden of debt for indemnity and war expenses. Because of this foreign contact, the Central Government had been forced to exert a greater control over the provincial governments in order to secure the uniformity of administration made necessary by the provisions of the treaties entered into with the Powers. Because of the new finanelal obligations of the State, the Central Government had been forced to increase taxes. This increase of taxes carried with it an increase, not a diminution, of the "squeeze" of the officials. The corruption of the Court was notorious. The people were fast getting ready for revolt because of their economic grievances, and because of the weakening of the grip of the government. On the other hand, together with the obligations imposed on the government, England, France and the United States had been instrumental in carrying western ideas and methods to China and in a small measure introducing them to a few of the more open-minded of the Chinese, particularly in the South. So that it was partly under the influence of Occidental ideas that the first attempts at reform began. This influence made itself felt in the entire field of political change, whether constitutional or merely reformative, beginning with the first period of reform under the Emperor Kuang Hsu.

CHAPTER II

The Emperor of China at the time when the foreign impact first became definitely felt was Tao Kuang, who ruled from 1821 until 1850. Tao Kuang was a man of good intentions but lacked the understanding and vision necessary to deal with the host of new problems presented with the attempt of the foreign governments to secure intercourse with China on a basis of equality. Had the treaties of 1842-44 been carried out fully and their operation extended gradually there would not have occurred the later struggles that perplexed the reign of his successors. But Tao Kuang, safe in the North from immediate contact with the foreign problem, felt that it was wise to allow his officials to accede to the demands made and then to defeat the foreigner in the application of the terms of settlement.

Tao Kuang dying in 1850, one of his seven sons succeeded him, taking the reign title Hsien Feng. During the ten years comprising the period of his rule, affairs in China went steadily from bad to worse. Rebellion and brigandage became the rule rather than the exception. The great Taiping rebellion seemed for a time to presage the end of Manchu rule in China, and, had the rebels secured the aid of foreigners, the last half century of Chinese history might have been differently written. Fortunately or unfortunately foreign advice and active support was given to the Imperial rather than to the rebel forces, and the Manchu authority was finally re-established. Before the Taipings had been brought under control, however, the central part of the Empire had been terribly devastated.

23

While this struggle was still going on rebellion broke out in southwestern China in the form of a Mohammedan uprising. Here again it needed time and all of the remaining Manchu strength to restore the authority of Peking. These great rebellions were accompanied by minor uprisings in other parts of the country, and, because of the turmoil and disturbance and the consequent relaxation of the hand of authority, bands of brigands infested all parts of China. This condition, in the past, had always accompanied and predicated the downfall of the Dynasty, but the end of the Manchu rule was to be postponed for another half-century largely because, out of these major and minor uprisings, came no constructive leadership capable of unifying the country against the Manchu rule.

In the midst of these internal troubles the problem of foreign intercourse again became immediate and perplexing. Trouble broke out at Canton in 1856 over a minor incident. This difficulty was later extended to cover the question of the application of the treaty of 1842, and the British and the French united to carry the struggle to the North. The expedition was so far successful as to enable the plenipotentiaries accompanying the armed force to negotiate a more favorable treaty than that which China had been forced to sign at Nanking in 1842. This treaty of 1858, in addition to reaffirming and extending the operation of the principles of that signed at Nanking, gave also the right of residence at Peking to foreign diplomatic agents. But again the Chinese attempted to retain by procrastination what had been unwillingly conceded to superior might, and another expedition to the North was necessary before the issue was finally settled. This time Peking itself was taken, Hsien Feng and the Court fleeing north to Jehol, leaving only Prince Kung, a brother of the Emperor, to negotiate with the British and French.

While in exile from the capital, Hsien Feng died. Just before his death a struggle had been going on between two factions at the Court for ultimate control of the child who was heir to the Throne. In the result a joint regency was effected of the wife and the favorite concubine of the Emperor, with Prince Kung acting as their chief adviser. Since Tzu Hsi, the mother of T'ung Chih (the reign title taken by the successor of Hsien Feng) was not the Empress-Consort, she had at first to share the power with the Emperor's widow, but she gradually made herself the dominant factor in the government, virtually ruling China from 1861 until her death in 1908, with the exception of the two years of the majority of T'ung Chih and the nine years' rule of his successor known as Kwang Hsu.

It was under the direction of this remarkable woman that the Taiping and Mohammedan rebellions were put down, the problems of foreign relations handled with a fair degree of success, and reform finally undertaken by the Manchus.

T'ung Chih died in 1875, two years after he had attained his majority. The short period of his reign did not shed any increased lustre on the Manchu rule. Of a licentious and depraved character, he came under the influence of his eunuchs who encouraged his tendencies toward extravagent and immoral living. "It became cause for scandal in the Palace itself that His Majesty would return from his orgies long after the hour fixed for the morning audience with his high officers of State. He was mixed up in many a drunken brawl and consorted with the lowest dregs of the Chinese city, so that it was no matter for surprise when he contracted the germs of disease which speedily led to his death."[1]

[1] Bland and Backhouse, "China Under the Empress-Dowager," p. 121. All references to "China under the Empress *Dowager*" are to the 1910 (Lippincott) unabridged edition.

Upon his death, of small-pox, Tzu Hsi again took matters into her own hands and dictated his successor. Through her influence the son of Prince Ch'un, seventh son of the Emperor Tao Kuang, was chosen as the new ruler, and the Empresses-dowager were again called to the regency. The new "Son of Heaven" took the reign title of Kwang Hsu, meaning "Glorious Succession."

On reaching his majority in 1889, Kwang Hsu nominally took over the reins of government and the Empress Dowager went into retirement. But she still continued to exercise a supervision over his acts, leaving the young Emperor more or less of a puppet. Naturally this was galling to a man who felt that he was not unfitted himself to control the policies of the government of which he was the titular head. There were many others in the realm who felt that it was deplorable for the government to be controlled by a woman, and the Emperor kept in tutelage. This feeling was stronger in the South than in the North, so that it was largely on the southerners that the Emperor relied for support when he came finally to make the attempt to assert himself. The desire to exercise the real power himself, later joined to a feeling of the need for change in the government, led to the attempts at reform in 1898.

That the necessity of reform did not influence his policy until shortly before the reform edicts began to be issued was recognized clearly by the leader of the movement, K'ang Yu-wei himself. "According to K'ang's account the relations between the Empress-Dowager and the Emperor have never been anything but strained. She has resented all attempts on his part to exercise real power, and he has felt deeply the position of inferiority and subjection in which she has until recently succeeded in keeping him. Until the Emperor became an ardent convert to the cause of reform this struggle seems to have been mainly one for power generally without any striking difference in the ends for which power was to be used, and high officials sought the favor of the Emperor or Empress according to their belief in the probability of the one or the other obtaining or keeping the upper hand, the opinions of these officials as to the necessity of reform or their contrary determination to keep to the old ways, not entering into the question. It was in short a conflict involving no difference of principle."[2]

The feeling of an urgent need for reform in the Chinese State seems to have come home to the Emperor Kwang Hsü after the humiliating defeat of China in the war with Japan. It is a generally accepted fact that the Emperor had been interested for several years in the ideas of the West. Western mechanical contrivances such as toy railways abounded in the Imperial pleasure grounds; it is reported that he had taken some lessons in English; and he had actually manifested his interest in western knowledge by sending for the back copies of the *Review of the Times,* a magazine published in Shanghai. Then to this was added the knowledge that Japan had triumphed over China largely because she had adopted western methods. The way was prepared for the Imperial mind to accept the ideas of the group of reformers dominated by K'ang Yu-wei.

K'ang Yu-wei, the leader of the reform party in 1898, has been extolled as the far-sighted patriot and decried as the selfish seeker after office, the advocate of impossible reforms, who hoped to advance himself by arousing the spirit of change in the Emperor. In reality he was but the forerunner, the

[2] Memorandum of Conversation with K'ang Yu-wei on Voyage from Shanghai to Hongkong, Sept. 27-29, 1898. Correspondence Respecting Affairs of China (British), 1899. Enclosure 2 in No. 401.

John the Baptist, of those who desired to overthrow the old and substitute for it the new, economically and politically. Born in Kuangtung province, the home of most of the prominent reformers of this and the later period, K'ang had been given the usual classical education. When about twenty-nine years old he began an extensive tour of China. In the course of his travels he touched at Shanghai and Hongkong and was much impressed by the cleanliness and good order of the foreign settlements. Upon his return to Canton he began to make as great a study of Western ideas as was possible with the limited number of translations of foreign books at his disposal. As a result of his study K'ang founded, in 1891, a school of new learning. The extent of his progress in foreign knowledge may be determined from the subjects taught in his school: The Confucian Classics; Buddhistic Literature; Chinese Philosophy and History; and Western Knowledge.[3]

In spite of his own limited knowledge of the civilization of the West K'ang Yu-wei soon gathered around him a group of followers, many of them scholars of good standing according to the old standards. The most prominent of these was Liang Ch'i Ch'ao, a man who has, since 1898, far surpassed his teacher in the struggle for a new order in China.

This was the beginning of the party advocating reform under the Manchus, as opposed to the societies conducting an anti-dynastic agitation. From 1891 until he gained the ear of the Emperor in 1898, K'ang Yu-wei spread his ideas by means of leaflets and tracts, occasionally sending in memorials to the Throne. In 1893 he started a Reform Society in Peking, intending to establish branches throughout the Empire. But before long the society had become sufficiently well known to

[3] "K'ang Yu-wei, His Life, Ideas, and Character." Professor M. E. Tsur. (Reprinted from the *National Review* (China), 1915.

reach the knowledge of the court, and it was ordered dissolved by an Imperial Edict. This preliminary work of agitation and diffusion of knowledge was continued and bore
fruit long after the immediate reform programme had been
rendered impossible of achievement by the coup d'etat of 1898.

Before proceeding to the discussion of the reform edicts it
is advisable to note briefly the extent to which foreign ideas
had entered China. We have seen that the coming of the
foreigners had brought a great many new problems to be
solved by the Imperial Government. Trade had increased
continually on a reciprocal basis. The Chinese had begun to
use foreign-made goods, and to see that the trade was a good
thing for them as well as for the trading nations. At first
they had not needed foreign products, opium being almost the
sole import of any great value. With the extension of the
desire for goods from abroad commercial relations were put
on a much firmer basis than when China had been an export-
ing nation, a selling and not a buying State. The daily contact of Occidentals and Chinese in the treaty ports had brought
with it a greater mutual tolerance of the one for the ideas and
peculiarities of the other. The feeling of superiority of the
Chinese was not greatly lessened, but a growth of respect for
some western institutions and industrial methods was manifested. This was shown in a measure in the attempts made
by a few of the prominent Viceroys to construct arsenals and
shipyards; by the encouragement offered in some places to the
building of factories and workshops; and by the increased interest in the development of the coal and iron deposits of the
country. Before the Japanese war an abortive attempt had
been made to build up a modern navy for China on a small
scale. After the war the reorganization of the army along
western lines received great attention, although the venality
of officials prevented much being accomplished.

While the trade contact was responsible in some measure for the interest manifested in the material side of European civilization, the missionaries had been at work steadily awakening the people to a realization of the value of western education. Although they were impeded in their work by its limitation to only a few points in the Empire, and by the hostility of many of the officials of the old type, they had made continuous progress, partly by the publication and distribution of tracts and pamphlets, partly, where that was possible, by the foundation of schools for the Chinese. Many of the leaders in the movement for constitutional government and governmental reform were educated either wholly or in part in the mission schools, or early came into contact with missionaries. In some cases, because of their imperfect assimilation of the new ideas, they did harm rather than good. But even so, they had a place in the movement towards a new China.

Before 1900 there had been little attempt to secure a western education in foreign lands. But as early as 1872 a group of 120 Chinese boys was sent to America to study. The incentive to take this step came from a graduate of Yale University, Dr. Yung Wing, who was able to show the able Viceroy, Tseng Kuo-fan, the value of such a proceeding. In 1873 another detachment was sent to England to study her navy. China's defeat by the Japanese, a people closely akin to the Chinese in many ways, gave to modern Japan a great interest for the Chinese people. If Japan, a nation whose civilization was based on that of China, had suddenly become so strong, there must be, they thought, a reason for it. Those who came into contact with the Japanese either at home or abroad ascribed the change to the adoption of western political methods. "Why then," they asked, "could not China become strong by adopting the same ideas"? There were, however, very few who had been able by 1898 to study the changed Japan.

While a beginning had been made, then, in the introduction of the Chinese to the civilization of the West through contact with the trading class, by the sending of students abroad, and, to a greater extent, through the activities of the missionaries, it had not extended far from the treaty ports. The Chinese people as a whole, and the officials as a class, were as conservative as ever, and as wedded to the old institutions. They were still opposed to foreign ideas because they were foreign, and because it was felt that things Chinese, by the very fact of being Chinese, were superior to anything that came from abroad. They had not yet been brought to a realization of the fact that the old institutions were no longer adapted to the new needs of the State. Many felt the necessity for administrative reform, but few perceived that the system itself was antiquated and no longer capable of meeting the needs of the Empire.

As has been stated, the alignment of officials either on the side of the Empress Dowager or with the Emperor Kwang Hsü was determined by the feeling of the official that either the one or the other would be victorious in the struggle for power. And it was only after the Emperor began his career as a reformer that the officials developed any feeling for change. To quote again the conversation with K'ang Yu-wei: "Whereas any given official might previously have felt assured that if he adhered to the Emperor's side and the Emperor ousted the Empress from power he would have the reward of comfortable continuance in office on the old lines, it was now evident that supporting the Emperor meant acquiescence, if not zealous coöperation, in changes that might seriously affect the whole position of the official class, curtailing their authority, and diminishing their pecuniary gains, besides exposing them to the risk of being removed to make place for younger men in fuller sympathy with the sovereign's ideas."[4]

At the beginning of 1898 affairs were much as they had been since Kwang Hsü had reached his majority. The relations of the Emperor with the Empress Dowager were seemingly friendly. "Kwang Hsü never failed to consult Her Majesty before the issue of any important Decree, and Tzu Hsi was usually most cordial in her manner towards him. . . . Whenever the Empress came to Peking, he (Kwang Hsü) obeyed strictly the etiquette which required him reverently to kneel at the Palace gates to welcome her." But "when visiting her at the Summer Palace, he was not permitted to announce his arrival in person, but was obliged to kneel at the inner gate and there await the summons of admission from the Chief Eunuch. . . . At each of these visits he was compelled, like any of the Palace officials, to pay his way by large fees to the eunuchs in attendance on Her Majesty, and as a matter of fact these myrmidons treated him with considerably less respect than they showed to many high Manchu dignitaries. Within the Palace precincts the Son of Heaven was indeed regarded as of little account."[5] In these and many other little ways the Emperor was constantly reminded that he was only the ruler in name, and was so regarded by many of his officials.

The atmosphere of Peking, and especially of the Imperial City, was however, most favorable to the growth of cliques and parties. This condition befriended Kwang Hsü as it caused those not in the favor of the Old Buddha to look to him for preference. Since the beginning of his reign there

[4] Correspondence Respecting Affairs in China (British), 1899. Inclosure No. 2 in 401.

[5] Bland and Backhouse, "China under the Empress Dowager," p. 179.

had been growing up two parties in Peking, and from their leadership these parties had developed as representative of the North and the South. The leaders of the northern party were Hsü T'ung, one of the Chinese Bannermen, a devoted adherent of the Manchus, and tutor to the former Emperor T'ung Chih; and Li Hung-tsao, a native of the metropolitan province of Chihli. The southern party was led by Weng T'ung-ho, the tutor of His Majesty Kwang Hsü, and P'an Tsu-yin, both of them eminent scholars, as were also the leaders of the northern group. All of the literary graduates gradually ranged themselves on the one side or the other. Both Li and Weng were appointed to the Grand Council in 1894, and thereafter the Empress espoused the cause of the northerners while the Emperor looked to the southern party for support.

In less direct contact with the Manchus, the South had always been a source of trouble to the *D*ynasty. Any discrimination against the Chinese in favor of the alien Manchu was more immediately felt in the southern provinces than in the northern, and since the Empress *D*owager had always been of pronounced Manchu tendencies the Southerners naturally wished for an end to her control over the government. It was in the South, too, that foreign ideas had gained the greater hold, most of the reformers from this time on being men from the southern provinces and in many cases the reforms advocated being directed largely against the Manchu supremacy in the State.

On May 29, 1898, Prince Kung, one of the most capable of the Manchu statesmen, died. His death removed a great restraining influence from both parties in the Empire. "On the one hand the Manchu party lost in him its senior representative, an elder whose wise counsel had guided them, and a statesman whose influence had been steadily against their

tendencies toward an anti-Chinese and anti-foreign policy.
. . . On the other hand the Emperor had always deferred to
Prince Kung's advice, and it was not until after his death
that he embarked headlong on the reform schemes of K'ang
Yu-wei and his associates, many of which the Prince, though
no bigoted conservative, would certainly have condemned."[6]

Soon after the death of Prince Kung, Weng T'ung-ho
recommended K'ang Yu-wei to the Imperial favor.   Undoubtedly he took this step in the hope of strengthening himself and his party.   Prince Kung had been his best friend at
Court, and with his moderating influence removed it was
necessary to take steps to counteract the growing influence of
the pro-Manchu party, which was hostile to Weng.   The Emperor acted on the recommendation and K'ang Yu-wei was
summoned to audience on the 13th of June, 1898,[7] by an Imperial Edict.   He found Kwang Hsü favorably inclined to
reform and soon gained considerable influence over him.
K'ang's ideas had already been presented to His Majesty in
the form of a memorial.   As early as the third of January he
had been accorded an interview with the members of the
Tsungli Yamen, through the influence of Weng T'ung-ho, and
in that conference he offered for their consideration his proposals for reform, which were embodied in the memorial
subsequently presented at the request of the Emperor.

This memorial pointed out "that under the present system
there was no way of ascertaining the desires and opinions of
the people.   The present Ministers and Viceroys could act
only upon orders given them, and were unable to do any
original thinking.   It was necessary to select young, intelligent men, imbued with Western ideas, to assist in the regener-

[6] "China under the Empress Dowager," p. 184.
[7] *North China Herald*-Translation of Edict given Sept. 5, 1898.
China Year Book 1913 gives date as June 14.

ation of the Empire, to confer with the Emperor every day, discussing measures of reform, but first devoting their energies to a revision of the laws and the administration."[8] K'ang advocated the dispensing with old officials, and he suggested the creation of twelve new departments. In view of the fact that they hit directly at the official class, it is no wonder that the Tsungli Yamen reported unfavorably on these proposals when the Emperor asked for an opinion on them. It was only after his audience in June that K'ang Yu-wei had an opportunity to carry out some of his ideas.

In an edict issued a few days before the audience with K'ang Yu-wei, the Emperor set forth some of the reasons why reform was necessary for the good of the Chinese Empire. "In the present condition of Imperial Affairs, with an untrained army, with limited funds, with ignorant 'literati,' and with artisans untaught because they have no fit teachers, is there any difficulty in deciding, when China is compared with foreign nations, who is the strong and who is the weak? It is easy to distinguish between the rich and the poor. How can a man armed with a wooden stick smite his foe encased in a coat of mail? . . . We cannot in these modern days adhere to the ways of the five Kings (circa B.C. 2500); even they did not continue after the manner of their respective predecessors. It is like wearing thick clothes in summer and thin ones in winter."[9]

The "hundred days" of reform came as a great surprise to the Empire in spite of the known leaning of the Emperer toward reform. The decrees issued involved educational, industrial, agricultural, and army changes and reorganization, as well as some alterations in the administrative organization.

[8] Smith, "China in Convulsion," p. 132.
[9] Correspondence Respecting Affairs in China (British), 1899. No. 266.

The first of the Edicts[10] dealt with the need for change in the system of education in China. After urging the officials and literati to be diligent in their attempts to extend their knowledge, and not to be satisfied with a mere superficial learning, the Edict provided for the initial steps to be taken toward the establishment of a central University in Peking. Those eligible to enter this highest school in the Empire were: "Any of the compilers and graduates of the Hanlin College, the Secretaries of the Boards, the officers of the Palace Guards, expectant Intendants, Prefects, District Magistrates, and subordinate officials, sons and brothers of officials, the hereditary officials of the Eight Banners, and the sons of the military officials of the Empire."

By later[11] supplementary Edicts schools and colleges were to be established in the provincial capitals and all large cities throughout the country. These provincial schools were to act as feeders for the central University. *Dr.* W. A. P. Martin was appointed the head of the University faculty. It was made clear from the beginning that the primary purpose of the new schools was to be the dissemination of Western rather than of Confucian learning, although the latter, the old classical study, was not to be done away with. The faculty of the University was to consist largely of foreigners. The work of establishing the provincial schools was left to the Governors and other provincial officials, and they were asked to memorialize the Throne in regard to the progress made, presenting any suggestions for reform that they might desire to offer.[12]

[10] Issued June 11, 1898.

[11] Issued July 10, July 29, and August 4, 1898.

[12] The attitude of the officials toward the reform program may be inferred from the fact that the Emperor was forced to reprove two of the most progressive Viceroys (Liu K'un-yi and Fan Chung-lin) for dilatoriness.

Even more radical than the changes in the educational system were those made in the examination system. When it is remembered that by far the most influential class in the State was that of the scholars, and that it depended for its supremacy on the maintenance of the old method of study and of examination, it can be seen what powerful forces Kwang Hsü was arraying against himself and the party of reform.

On June 23d an Imperial decree abolished the literary essay as the standard for examination.[13] For the old literary effusions it was proposed to substitute practical essays on subjects connected with and drawn from the new learning. The edict stated: "We have been compelled to issue this decree because our examinations have degenerated to the lowest point, and we can see no way to remedy matters other than to change entirely the old methods of examination for a new course of competition."[14]

From this change it naturally followed that the old methods of instruction and of preparation for examination would be obsolete, and that the influence of the old time scholars would be reduced greatly, eventually if not immediately. The long-nailed, stoop-shouldered, shuffling-footed scholar of the old regime could have only a minor place in a world where the primary emphasis was placed on practical knowledge and efficiency. And it was on those two things that the attention of the Chinese would have to be focused if they were to attempt seriously to maintain themselves against the aggressiveness of

[13] Under the old system the candidate was required to write an essay on some subject taken from the classics. Practical administrative knowledge was never required for success in these examinations, although it was from the successful candidates that the officials of the Empire were invariably chosen.

[14] The Confucian Analects and the Classics were still to be studied in the schools, but studies of a practical nature were to be emphasized.

the younger nations of the West. This change in the examinations was but the logical forerunner of still more radical changes, all of which would menace the predominance of the literati. In the face of their self-evident interest, (for the literati and the officialdom were largely one), it is hardly to be wondered at that the Emperor complained of the laxity of the officials in giving effect to his edicts.

Together with the reform in education and in the system of examination came a plan for the systematic translation of the European books necessary to educate the older people in the new ideas, and for use in the schools. A translation bureau was to be established at Shanghai with Liang Ch'i Ch'ao[15] at the head. Its work was to be the "putting into Chinese Western works on science, arts, and literature, and text books for the schools and colleges."

The importance of such a step can be immediately seen. Before the new system of education could be put into operation it was necessary to have some sort of an approach to the new learning. Either the educated class in the future would have to rely on a foreign language for their knowledge, and instruction in the schools would have to be in a foreign language so far as modern science and learning were concerned, or the great field of Western investigation would have to be put into the Chinese language. The magnitude of this latter task was greatly increased because of the limited few who were competent to undertake such work, which, to be of any value, demanded a thorough training in foreign languages. Furthermore, it involved the creation of a vocabu-

[15] Liang Ch'i Ch'ao has since done a very valuable work along that line, although not working under the government, as planned in this edict. Among other works he has put into Chinese the lives of Cavour and of Bismarck. His translations are widely read by the students in China.

lary, such concepts as spirit, patriotism, etc., being entirely new to the Chinese language.[16]

Foreigners, especially the missionaries, had been working along this very line in their attempts to reach the Chinese, but their work had been limited largely to the translation of religious literature, the field of science being untouched. Liang Ch'i Ch'ao was then, and is today, one of the foremost of Chinese scholars. But he had only a limited knowledge of any language except his own and Japanese, and was hardly competent to go to the originals for the Western texts. Working with foreigners who had a knowledge of Chinese his scholarly ability might have surmounted the limitations of his own knowledge and training. But coöperation with foreigners in the task does not seem then to have been contemplated.[17] The great importance of this mandate lies in its emphasizing one of the greatest tasks incident to educational reform.[18]

The reformers of this period recognized that one great difficulty in their way was the unwillingness of officials to carry out the provisions of the edicts. It was also clear that misunderstandings would arise because of the ignorance of the people as to the importance of the steps being taken, and as to the reasons for any change being inaugurated. To avoid this two steps were taken. Official gazettes were to be published and distributed all over the Empire. The Shanghai publication, *Chinese Progress,* which had been edited by

[16] In making public addresses in Chinese, it is common for the speaker to give an English word, and then take three or four minutes explaining in Chinese its meaning.

[17] That is, no coöperation in China, although the Ministers to European Courts were ordered to carry on this work of translation in the countries where they were residing.

[18] This work of translation has become increasingly important in the past fifteen years. Further reference to it will have to be made later.

Liang Ch'i Ch'ao was made the leading organ of this nature. It was hoped that these publications would establish a direct relationship between the Central Government and the people. Formerly newspapers had been confined largely to the treaty-ports and were more in the nature of propagandist pamphlets than general news sheets. They had been used largely for anti-government agitation, being frequently under the ban of the authorities. The proposed gazettes were to be official newspapers, subsidized by the government and privileged to call attention to all kinds of abuses and evils.

The other attempt to bring about a closer understanding between the provinces and the Central Government was through an enlargement of the right of petition. Formerly only the highest officials and the censors were allowed directly to memorialize the Throne. The edict issued on September 12th, after rebuking officials severely for refusing to transmit memorials which had come in, extended the right of petition "to practically every soul in the Empire." "Next day, the thirteenth of September, another decree repeated the terms of the above in clearer detail, and laid down precisely the procedure each class was to observe, in making itself heard. The severest penalties were threatened should there be any interference with the free exercise of this privilege by the high officers of government, who were commanded to report by telegram the steps they were taking to fulfil the Imperial wishes."[19]   Honestly carried into effect, this change would have brought the Central Government into actual touch with the problems and abuses of the provincial administration, and enabled it to make the changes necessary to rectify these abuses and purify the administration. It would also have brought new life to the only body in the Empire whose function was

[19] (British) Correspondence Relative to China, 1899, No. 371.

criticism—the censorate. Under the system existing in 1898 the Emperor was forced to rely for information on the high officials, themselves the very men most interested in keeping from him a knowledge of abuses. The censors, too, had become open to bribery, and were kept, by fear of punishment, from too great criticism of the acts of the high officers of the government.

Other decrees, following one another in rapid succession, dealt with the need of agricultural, industrial, and military reform. A bureau of agriculture, arts and commerce was established. Agricultural education was to be undertaken and all new ideas calculated to improve land cultivation were to be investigated and made use of where they proved to be of value. Progress in invention was to be encouraged by the giving of exclusive rights to the inventor for a number of years,— really a provision for the granting of patent rights. "Rewards were also to be given to those who, with their own resources, establish colleges, open up mines, or set up arsenals for the manufacture of rifles and cannon."[20] As to army reform "two decrees, published on June 27th and July 5th, have reference to reform in the Chinese army, but they throw no light on the nature of them, and merely refer certain suggestions to various departments for examination."[21] In order to further the reconstruction of China's fleet the establishment of naval colleges was ordered.

Mention should also be made of the announced intention of the Emperor to hold military reviews both in Peking and Tientsin. In connection with the latter review it was planned to go by rail to Tientsin, the Imperial party including the Empress Dowager.[22] This would have been the first time

---

[20] (British) Correspondence Relative to China, 1899, No. 297.
[21] Correspondence Relative to China (British), 1899, No. 297.
[22] China under the Empress Dowager, pp. 196-7.

either the Emperor or Empress had travelled by rail, their experience with foreign locomotion being limited to the toy railroads that had been installed in the pleasure grounds of the Palace. This suggestion came as a great shock to the Manchu officials who felt that it would be a terrible thing for Their Majesties to demean themselves by breaking so far away from tradition. Tzu Hsi however was delighted at the prospect of such a novel experience. Later developments caused the abandonment of the plan.

When, in the course of his career as a reformer, the Emperor struck directly at the official class by the abolition of useless offices he sounded the death knell of the whole movement. Many who had been content to stand by without opposition so long as they were not directly affected and who were even believers, in theory, in the need for reform were immediately antagonized when they saw a possible attack on their pocketbooks. An edict of August 30 abolished six offices—i.e., the Imperial Supervisorate of Instruction, the Office of Transmission, the Grand Court of Revision, the Court of Imperial Entertainments, the Court of the Imperial Stud, and the Court of State Ceremonial. These offices had provided lucrative employment for Manchu idlers for many generations. "This decree was loudly denounced as contrary to the traditions of the Manchu *Dynasty*, and from all sides came urgent appeals to the Old Buddha to protect the privileges of the ruling class, and to order its cancellation."[23] The reform was called a direct blow at the Manchus, the first step in a movement calculated to overthrow the *Dynasty*. Further, "the decree specified the Governorships of Kuangtung, Hupei, and Yunnan, as well as the *Director-Generalship* of the Yellow River, as posts which could well be transferred to other

[23] "China under the Empress Dowager," p. 197.

officers, reducing many overgrown salaries and perquisites. The Tribute Rice Transport by the Grand Canal (one of the most wasteful extravagances even in China) was also abolished, and other offices pertaining to the Salt Revenue were cut off with a stroke of a pen."[24]

It is always much easier to create new positions without opposition than it is to abolish those which have been in existence even for a short time, so that it can readily be imagined how great an outcry arose among all the officials, since no one knew where such changes would stop. Many less important sinecures had been filled with the proteges of the high officials who were expected to provide for the members of their own families. They were also looked to as the source of official preferment by many of their fellow-provincials who had been successful in the examinations and were on the list of "expectant" officials.

Officialdom was affected in yet another way by this attempt to better the administration. With very few exceptions, every officer in the Empire had been forced to buy his place at a figure proportioned to its importance, so that he stood to lose materially by its abolition.

This fear on the part of the officials was intensified by the dismissal from office, two days after the issue of these decrees, of all of the high officials of the Board of Rites[25] for suppressing a memorial because of its radical suggestions.[26]

[24] "China in Convulsion," p. 144.
[25] Hsu Ying-k'uei and Huai T'a-pu, the two Presidents of the Board, and also the two Senior and two Junior Vice-presidents.
[26] This memorial, submitted by a third class secretary of the Board of Rites, is said to have advocated: "the abolition of the queue and the changing of the Chinese national dress to that of Western lands; the embracing the Christian religion as that of the State, with a national Parliament in prospect; and a journey by the Emperor and Empress Dowager to the Mikado, that they

The Empress Dowager had been sitting quietly by during this period waiting for the opposition to the reformers to become sufficiently pronounced to warrant her resuming the direction of the affairs of State. It was not until she learned that the reforms were to be safeguarded by rendering her incapable of interference that Tzu Hsi took drastic steps against the party of the Emperor. The details of the plot against her life are now a matter of history: How Yuan Shih-kai was entrusted with the task of securing control of the foreign drilled army of Chihli, and the destruction of the faithful adherent of the Empress, Jung Lu, then Viceroy of Chihli Province. It is equally well known how Yuan went to his blood-brother, Jung Lu, and disclosed the plot[27] instead of killing him, thus enabling Jung Lu to carry out what has become known as the *coup d'état* of 1898, by which the Empress assumed control and Kwang Hsü became a virtual prisoner until his death in 1908.[28]

After the restoration, edicts began to appear in rapid succession cancelling all of the reform measures enacted during the "hundred days," and providing for the punishment of K'ang Yu-wei and his followers. K'ang himself escaped to Tientsin and from there to Shanghai where he was enabled to elude the Imperial authorities by the aid of British officials. Many of his adherents made good their escape, principally to

might see for themselves the pitiful condition of China as compared with Japan." "China in Convulsion," p. 145. (See also British Correspondence Relative to China, 1898, No. 371.)

[27] For Yuan's version of the affair see his account in the *Times* reprinted and commented on in Kent's "Passing of the Manchus," pp. 17-22.

[28] As a matter of form a mandate was issued in the name of the Emperor calling the Empress Dowager into consultation on affairs of State. Thus the Emperor was forced to authorize his own virtual deposition.

Japan, and from foreign shores entered upon a new propaganda of reform ideas.

The very nature of the changes proposed in 1898 revealed a lack of an appreciation on the part of the reformers of the fundamental nature of the weakness of the Chinese administrative system. The reforms inaugurated would have been of undoubted value, and they marked an advance in the breaking away from the past. But even if Kwang Hsü had retained the power to put them into effect, many of the changes would have remained only on paper. The old theory that the relation of the Central Government to the Provinces was merely supervisory was not disturbed in the least by these decrees. The general policy of reform along certain lines was adopted by the Imperial Government, but it was left to the provincial authorities to put this programme into execution, and it has been pointed out already that the officials would act only when it was to their interest to do so, or when strong pressure was brought to bear on them forcing them to act against their inclinations.

The most essential step in carrying out any reforms of permanent value in China is the establishment of a direct relationship between the Central Government and the people. The mere power of appointment and dismissal, together with a general supervision and direction, is not sufficient to ensure a uniform administration. The reforms of 1898 provided for the introduction of new ideas, and, to a certain extent, enlarged the scope of parts of the existing machinery of government, such as the right of memorializing the Throne, but did not alter the structure or the form of the government. Neither did the history of the years following 1898 show that the reform movement of that year was the result of any "national and intellectual movement that permeated the provinces and moved the mind of the nation." It was simply the work of a group of thinkers who had come in touch, in a limited way, with the civilization of the West, and who were able to take advantage of the factional struggles in Peking to gain a hearing for themselves and their ideas. The movement failed because the reforms attempted came into conflict with the self-interest of the ruling class, including those who would have been glad to see China strengthened by changes that did not, at the same time, harm their own interests.

It is true that if the Emperor had been strong enough to maintain himself as the real ruler of the country against the opposition of the Empress Dowager he might have been able to play the benevolent despot, forcing officialdom and the nation to see with him, and aid him to carry out in good faith the regeneration of the State. But he seems to have become interested first in the idea of change because he perceived the evils of the system as shown in the government of the Empress. Until he was carried along by the influence of K'ang Yu-wei, his conviction of the need for reform was based on the feeling that he was being defrauded of the power that should have been his, and his action was dictated by a desire to gain that power. The "outs" are always better able to see a weakness than those in the supremacy. Kwang Hsü would have been no great exception probably if he had been the de facto as well as the de jure ruler of the Empire.

The chief importance of this movement in 1898 lay in the fact that it was the first definite attempt to adjust the administration of China to the new conditions that had arisen. It has been dealt with at greater length than its ultimate importance would warrant because from its failure came a new direction to the movement toward political reform. On the one hand this failure gave an impetus to the work of those men who felt that change could only come, and progress be made, with the overthrow of the Manchu Dynasty. While on the other hand the direction of the movement, together with the failure of the Boxer uprising, aroused a feeling among the Manchus and the high Chinese officials that only by admitting the necessity of change and assuming the control and leadership of a conservative party of reform could they hope to preserve their ascendency in the State.

To the failure of the K'ang Yu-wei movement and the consequent domination of the ultra-conservatives and reactionaries, both Manchu and Chinese, can be ascribed the growth of the Boxer movement, especially in its anti-foreign phase, which culminated in the uprising of 1900. The failure of that attempt to drive the foreigner and his demoralizing influence from the "Middle Kingdom" opened the door for the more gradual progression toward reform which marked the period from 1901 to 1910.

CHAPTER III

The failure of the Boxer movement has a direct bearing on the inauguration of reform by the Empress Dowager in 1901 so that a few words may be advisable in explanation of that strange and yet natural attempt to drive the foreigners from the "Middle Kingdom." In 1894, when war broke out between Japan and China, the latter, in her great potential strength, was feared by the Powers of Europe. They might push their demands, and force redress for the injuries of their citizens, but they took aggressive action always with the fear of going too far and awakening the "Sleeping Dragon." Japan, on the other hand, was not considered formidable. She shook off foreign interference more quickly and easily than China has, but she did it by accepting the West and adopting and adapting to her own needs its ideas and institutions. When war came between the two countries it appeared to be a contest between unequals—between a giant and a dwarf. When, in the struggle, the dwarf was easily victorious, it caused the Western governments to go to the other extreme in their thoughts of China. No longer was she feared as the "Dragon" whom all dreaded to see awake! The decay of the Empire was seen in the ease with which Japan had imposed her will on China. Consequently the Powers became more aggressive and imperialistic in their policy and the "concession grabbing" period in Chinese history was inaugurated. Germany, Russia, France and England all staked out their spheres of interest and secured leased territorial footholds in the Empire. The actual partition of the country was freely predicted. When the Powers stopped for breath before taking the final plunge, the Emperor embarked upon his ill-fated reform adventure in an attempt to check the process of internal disintegration.   Had the cause of reform triumphed the western governments still had a sufficiently wholesome fear of China and her recuperative powers to stand aside.   When reform failed the last hope of China seemed gone.

The people of the country, however, felt that China might yet be saved.   Their unrest and dissatisfaction, which well might have been directed against the Manchus at that time, because of this foreign aggression, was diverted from their rulers and directed against the foreigners.   Anti-foreign societies known as Boxers (Societies of Harmonious Fists) sprang up all over the North and Central parts of China. Their one great aim was to drive the foreigner into the sea, after which China could enjoy again the old peace and quiet. The relation of the Government to the movement in its inception has never been fully established.   After its growth Tzu Hsi seems to have thrown her weight definitely with the Boxers.   The legations in Peking finally were beseiged, but later were relieved by the allied force of Europeans, Americans and Japanese thrown into the country.   The Court, for a second time, fled from the capital and negotiated a peace settlement that meant the end of the anti-foreign phase of recent Chinese history.

The Boxer uprising and its failure logically should have hastened the movement toward the partition of China among the Powers.   That it did not is due largely to the position taken by the government of the United States in 1899, when, in an attempt to protect potential American commercial interests in China, by preserving the country from a division as colonial territory among the European nations, the policy of the "Open *Door*" was enunciated by John Hay.   This policy directed to the preservation of the territorial integrity of China, and thus the preservation of an equality of commercial opportunity for all nations, was reaffirmed during the negotiations leading to the protocol of 1901 reëstablishing peace between the Chinese Empire and the other States of the world.[1] The overthrow of Boxerism marks the end of the period of active hostility to change in China. It was recognized that either progress along modern lines would have to be made or China would lose her place as an independent member of the family of nations.

After the failure of the Boxer movement the Empress Dowager herself recognized the inevitability of some sort of reform in the Chinese Empire. There were three ways in which changes might be made: an honest reform of the government by the Manchu Dynasty itself, thereby strengthening its hold on the Empire, and enabling it to regain the position which had been lost during the nineteenth century by inefficient and corrupt administration; on the other hand, if the Manchus persistently refused to set the house in order, the ever-increasing anti-Manchu agitation in the South and overseas would attain its object of a reform which would eliminate the Ta Ts'ing Dynasty altogether. The third alternative, feared by Manchu and Chinese alike, was a forcible reform through foreign domination of China.

[1] The Russian activity in Manchuria was primarily responsible for the United States asking the Powers a second time to put themselves on record as favoring the maintenance of China in her territorial completeness, in spite of her attempt to maintain herself entirely apart from contact with the world. England and Japan, because of their peculiar interest in the developments in the Far East, threw their weight behind the proposals of the American government, thus forcing the other Powers, including Russia, to give a reluctant reaffirmation of their adherence to the general principle of the "Open Door" for commerce in China.

Tzu Hsi accepted the situation and, even before the return of the Court to Peking, had announced her decision. The decree in which, in the name of the Emperor, she proclaimed the need of reform, is a remarkable document. The Empress *Dowager* was under the necessity of "saving her face" by making it clear that, carried out under her direction, the reform ideas were something radically different from and superior to those which she had opposed in 1898. It was also essential that the opponents of the early reform movement should be reassured, and at the same time she must convince the reformers themselves of her sincerity. This first reform edict of the Empress *Dowager* was issued from Hsianfu on January 28, 1901.

It is unnecessary to reproduce the entire edict, but certain portions bearing directly on government change are well-worth quotation. The text runs:

"Throughout the entire universe there exist certain fixed principles which govern the conduct of men, but nowhere do we find any finally fixed form of government. It is written in the Book of Changes that when any given condition of affairs has run its natural course, and has been succeeded by another there is no saying how long this new State may last; also in the Dialogues of Confucius it is written that there is no difficulty in tracing the changes and reforms which each Dynasty has made in regard to the methods of its predecessors. . . . Looking at the matter broadly, we may observe that any system which has lasted too long is in danger of becoming stereotyped, and things which are obsolete should be modified. The essential need which confronts us is at all costs to strengthen Our Empire, and to improve the condition of Our subjects. . . . At this moment when peace negotiations[2] are proceeding, it is a matter of urgent necessity that steps be taken to reorganize our system of government so that hereafter Our Celestial Empire may recover its ancient place of wealth and power. The Empress Dowager has now decided that we should correct our shortcomings by adopting the

[2] With the Powers after the Boxer uprising.

best methods and systems which obtain in foreign countries, basing our future conduct on a wise recognition of past errors.[3] ... The chief defect in our system of administration is undoubtedly too close an adherence to obsolete methods, a too slavish devotion to the written word; the result is a surfeit of commonplace and inefficient officials, and a deplorable lack of men of real talent. The average commonplace man makes a god of the written word, whilst every bureaucrat in the land regards it as a talisman wherewith to fill his purse so that we have huge mountains of correspondence eternally growing up between one government office and another, the value of which is absolutely nil so far as any good to the country is concerned. On the other hand men of real ability lose heart and give up the public service in disgust, prevented from coming to the front by the mass of inefficiency that blocks the way. Our whole system of government has come to grief through corruption, and the first steps of progress in our Empire are clogged by the fatal word 'precedent.'

"Up to the present the study of European methods has gone no further than a superficial knowledge of the languages, literature and mechanical arts of the West, but it must be evident that these things are not the essentials upon which European civilization has been founded. The essential spirit of that civilization is to be looked for in the fact that real sympathy and understanding exists between rulers and people, that officials are required to be truthful in word and courageous in action. The teachings handed down to us by our sacred Ancestors are really the same as those upon which the wealth and power of European countries have been based, but China has hitherto failed to realize this, and has been content to acquire the rudiments of European languages or technicalities while changing nothing of her ancient habits of inefficiency and deep-rooted corruption. Ignoring our real needs we have so far taken from Europe nothing but externals; how can we possibly hope to advance on such lines? Any reforms to be effective and permanent must be made with a real desire for efficiency and honesty.

"We therefore hereby decree and command that the officials

[3] Here follows a paragraph repudiating connection with the K'ang Yu-wei reforms, stating that they were dangerous and treasonable. "Their main object is not reform but a revolution against the Manchu Dynasty."

concerned shall now make close inquiry and comparison as to the various systems of government in force in European countries with special reference to those which obtain in China today, not only as regards the constitution of the Court and Central Government, but also concerning those things which make for the prosperity of our subjects, such as the system of examination and education, the administration of the army and the regulation of finance. They will be required to report as to what changes are advisable and what institutions should be abolished; what methods we should adopt from abroad and what existing Chinese institutions should be retained. The things we chiefly need are a constant supply of men of talent, a sound basis of national finance, and an efficient army. Reports on these matters must be forwarded within two months, and upon them we shall humbly address Her Majesty,[4] and ask for Her decision before we take any definite action."[5]

While foreigners looked skeptically on, the work of the Dowager Empress was begun. That the reactionary, autocratic "Old Buddha," who had brought to naught the previous movement partially to modernize the Empire, and who had connived at the abortive attempt in 1900 to drive all foreigners into the sea, should seriously intend to lead in the introduction of Western institutions into China seemed incredible. And, granting her sincerity, could even the dominating and masterful Tzu Hsi overcome the passive resistance of her Court and the official class?

The years from 1901 to 1905 witnessed the acceptance by the country of many of the changes advocated by the reformers in 1898. The old examination system was abolished; the educational system was brought into harmony with Western ideas, largely under the guidance of two men, Yuan Shih-k'ai and the well-known Viceroy Chang Chih-tung;[6] and steps

[4] This edict purported to be from the hand of the Emperor, although written by the Empress herself.
[5] "China under the Empress Dowager," pp. 419-424.
[6] Author of the widely read book, "China's Only Hope."

were taken looking toward the consolidation of governmental posts, with the practical effect of doing away with a good many sinecures.

In 1905 a Special Commission was sent abroad to study foreign constitutional systems. From the return of this Commission in 1906 dates the beginning of the period of constitutional reform under the Manchus, as distinguished from the reform movements of previous years. The feeling had gradually been growing that there must be some germ of strength in Occidental governments that was unknown to the Chinese. To locate and introduce that source, it was thought, was all that was needed to enable China to regain her position of superiority in the world. The ten years from 1895 to 1905 had prepared the people of the Empire to accept conservatively radical innovations in their government. The foreign impact had served in the place of what Mill lays down as one of the essential functions of a good government—educating the people for a better form of government. In China this meant, first of all, breaking down the conservatism of the official class and extending the view of the class known as the literati. This had been brought about to a limited extent by a combination of several factors.

One of the most promising fields for the investment of foreign capital in China was early seen to be in the development of railways and allied means of communication. It took a long time to overcome the prejudices of the Chinese against such an innovation as the steam engine. After the war with Japan, however, the government felt itself unable to resist the demands that were being pressed continually for concessions to build railways, develop mines, etc. Consequently the period from 1895 to 1905 saw projects under way which bade fair to connect up the whole country in a system of railways.

The Chinese attitude gradually changed from that of hostility[7] to the building of railways to a recognition of the dangers involved in the political influences which, through such concessions, were gradually marking off China into spheres of interest.   This change of attitude did not check development but rather tended to promote it by causing the Chinese themselves to go into the work.

These railways, together with the postal and telegraph systems that had been developed under foreign supervision, brought Peking into direct and immediate touch with the provincial governments, and made it possible for the central government to exercise a greater degree of control over its agents in the provinces.   The very fact that the initiative had been taken by the Imperial authority instead of coming from the provinces individually and that the work was thus under its immediate control gave a direct impetus to the movement toward centralization of the government.   With easy and rapid communication, problems arising in the provinces came to be referred to Peking for settlement to a much greater extent than had been possible in the past, so that not so great a necessity remained for the former practical autonomy of the provinces.   Naturally the gentry in the provinces fought against being brought under the control of what was to them almost a foreign authority, and their opposition was far from negligible.   But certainly, up to the beginning of the attempt at constitutional reform in 1905, the growth of the new systems of communication had made practical the endeavor of the Imperial Government to centralize the administration at Peking.

Perhaps the greatest incentive to constitutional change in China came from Japan.   That country owed all of her early

[7] The Woosung Railway, opened June 30, 1876, was 're-deemed' by the Chinese, and in 1877 the rails were torn up and shipped to Formosa.

civilization to China. Confucianism had as much weight in Japan as in China. Buddhism had come to the Islands by way of China. The Japanese literature was Chinese in origin as was their written language. Their art was developed under Chinese tutelage. The Chinese people in thought and feeling, consequently, refused to admit their neighbors to a position of equality. But of recent years a change had come in the relations between the two countries. Japan was getting her inspiration from foreign sources, and under this inspiration was continually growing stronger while China had become the prey of foreign nations. The Japanese had grown so strong that they had been able to secure release from the humiliating system of exterritoriality, at the same time gaining control of their customs service. China herself had felt the humiliation of defeat by Japan, who had then asserted her right to a voice in Chinese affairs and had ranged herself with the despoilers of the "Middle Kingdom." The great and powerful England had come to Japan to ask her friendship and alliance.[8] And, finally, Japan had become strong enough to wage a successful war against the colossus of the East, Russia. When the Chinese asked himself what the reason for this change in the respective positions of Japan and China could be, he found the answer ready-made,—Constitutional Government. Japan's growth in strength and power dated from 1867 when she had accepted the inevitable and begun to study and adopt Western institutions. This study had resulted in the promulgation of a constitution. In that constitution was to be found the source of power. Had not all the Powers of the West, with the exception of Russia, con-

[8] While England did not take the initiative in opening negotiations for an understanding with Japan, the Chinese justifiably felt that the conclusion of the Anglo-Japanese agreement of 1902, and alliance of 1905 were visible signs that Japan had been raised to an equality with the Powers of the West.

stitutions? This sort of reasoning led to the conclusion that if only China was governed under a constitution she too might be able to grow strong and regain her ancient position as dictator of the terms of intercourse with the "outer barbarians."

The nature of constitutional development under the Manchu *Dynasty* shows clearly the influence of the study the Commission made of the Constitution of Japan. In that country it was found that constitutionalism and Imperial authority were far from antagonistic. Fundamentally the power of the Emperor and of the great Lords had not been weakened. A study of the political institutions of Japan might well have convinced the Empress *Dowager* of the innocuous nature of foreign innovations in the government of that country. And the advantages were readily apparent that would accrue to her and to the *Dynasty* through a reform which would show the people that she had their welfare at heart, and at the same time would not limit her own power. So it was not long after the return of the Special Commission until the Manchu *Dynasty* had definitely committed itself to a programme of constitutional change.

The members of the Special Commission sent abroad to study governmental systems submitted their reports in 1906. An Imperial edict ordered that these reports should be considered by Tsai Feng, the Prince of Ch'un, with the Ministers of the Grand Council, the Ministers of the Council of State, the Grand Secretaries, and Yuan Shih-kai, the Superintendent of Trade for the North; and that after such joint consideration they should "request an Imperial decree authorizing the proper form of procedure." The programme of reforms laid down in the decree issued[9] as a result of the joint memorial was very far reaching in its provisions, and laid an enormous task on the government if honestly carried into effect. The

[9] September 1, 1906.

weakness of China was stated to be due to the lack of confidence between the highest and the lowest—"between the Throne and the Ministers and the Masses." The strength of foreign nations was found to be in the constitutions granted to the masses, and in universal suffrage. Applying this principle, the Empress laid down the fundamentals which must guide the Throne in introducing this universal panacea into China.

"As for ourselves, it is necessary at present to make a careful investigation into the matter, and prepare ourselves to imitate this government by constitution, *in which the supreme control must be in the hands of the Throne, while the interests of the masses shall be given to the elect, advanced to such position by the suffrage of the masses.*"[10]

The Empress Dowager knew instinctively where the difference lay between representative government and constitutional autocracy. As Mill so well says: "the meaning of representative government is, that the whole people, or some portion of them, exercise through deputies periodically elected by themselves the ultimate controlling power, which, in every constitution, must reside somewhere. This ultimate power they must possess in all its completeness. They must be masters, whenever they please, of all of the operations of government."[11]

It was no part of Tzu Hsi's programme of constitutional reform that the ultimate power should pass from the Throne to the people. So she stated as the first principle of China's constutionalism that the supreme control lay in the hands of the ruler. From this it followed that the representatives of the

---

[10] China Year Book, 1912, p. 353. The italics are the author's. See also Am. For. Relations, 1906, p. 349-50. Inclosure 1 in No. 386, for a similar translation.

[11] "Representative Government," Ch. V. Everyman Ed., p. 228.

"masses" were merely to be periodically called into consultation, their advice being accepted or rejected at the will of the Throne. In their attempt to introduce constitutional forms and at the same time preserve autocratic power the rulers of the Empire had a guide close at hand, as has already been pointed out. The Japanese constitution reserves the ultimate control to the Emperor and his advisers, leaving only the right of criticism and of petition to the Assembly or *Diet*. The tendency, of course, has been for the *Diet* gradually to extend its sphere of action, and one of the interesting features of Japanese political development has been the struggle to bring the Ministers of the Crown under the control of the Assembly. But the fact still remains that the final control lies with the Crown. The essence of Japanese constitutional government is autocracy, and it was that principle which Tzu Hsi tried to transplant to China in her endeavor to strengthen the hold of the Manchu *Dynasty* on the Empire. To anyone familiar with the history of constitutional development in Japan, the similarity of the Manchu movement in China will be increasingly apparent as the different steps leading up to the establishment of the Constitution and the summoning of the first Parliament are considered.

In a constitution, then, the Empress *Dowager* expected to find the means of strengthening the Empire, and at the same time of preserving the supremacy of the Manchu. She was wise enough to perceive, however, that the transition from the old form to the new could not be made in a day; that before the Chinese could hope to derive any benefit from the introduction of constitutional government they must be educated and prepared for it. There was the further necessity for her to let it be definitely understood that her programme involved gradual rather than precipitate reform in order to conciliate the conservatives and secure their support.

"Any impetuosity shown in introducing these reforms," said Her Majesty,[12] "will at the end be so much labor lost. How can we then face our subjects in such circumstances, and how regain their confidence and faith in us? It is incumbent upon us as a beginning, therefore, to reform the official system; next to revise carefully the laws in their most minute details; promote and encourage universal education; regulate the finances and sources of revenue of the Empire; reorganize the army; and establish a strong gendarmerie throughout the Empire. The gentry and people will then understand the kind of government needed for the country, and be prepared to start the foundations of a Constitutional Government, whilst the officials, high and low, in Peking and elsewhere, will use their best endeavors to bring our desires to a triumphant completion. In a few years time, when it is found that there is a rough outline of what is needed, the time will come for appointing a day for the inauguration de facto of a Constitutional Government." The Edict concludes with the usual exhortation to high officials "to issue proclamations to their people, to show an enthusiastic desire for education, to be loyal and patriotic, to sacrifice for the good of all, and to refrain from destroying a grand structure through petty strife and private quarrels. Let all observe law and order, and prepare themselves to enjoy the solid advantages of a Constitutional Government."[13]

The first of the reforms preparatory to the establishment of a constitution was the reorganization of the administrative system. An Imperial edict issued on November 6, 1906[14] set forth the changes that were to be made, following the suggestions of the Royal Commission that had been appointed to

[12] Edict of Sept. 1, 1906.
[13] China Year Book, 1912, p. 353. Ch. XXI.
[14] *Ibid.,* p. 354.

consider administrative reform. In effect the changes made amounted either to a mere alteration in the name of a department or Board, or to the consolidation of Boards under the old or a new name. Thus "the Hsunchingpu (Board of Public Safety) is changed to the Minchengpu (Board of the Interior)"; and "the Board of War (Pingpu) is to be changed to the Army Board (Luchunpu), and the Council of Army Reorganization and the Court of the Imperial Stud are to be amalgamated with it."[15]

Before this time each Board had two Presidents and four Vice-Presidents, divided equally, in theory, between Manchu and Chinese. This edict provided, however, that no distinction should be made in the future between the two peoples,[16] and that each Board, with the exception of the Waiwupu,[17] should have only one President and two Vice-Presidents. Ostensibly aimed at promoting a closer feeling of union between the two races by removing the distinctions between them, this provision had the opposite effect, for it resulted in the appointment of Manchus to the greater number of important offices,[18] where formerly the Court had been under the necessity of balancing a Manchu appointment with a Chinese. The first direct reference to a National Assembly (Tzechengyuan) was also made, this edict stating that it was to be created as an additional department.

The zeal for constitutional reform, or the introduction of representative government, did not abate during 1907. But in spite of all the exhortations of the Throne to the officials

[15] For a description of the reorganized Boards of Ministries see China Year Book, 1912, Ch. XIV. The Government.

[16] See also edict August 10, 1907 and Sept. 27, 1907, giving instructions for abolition of privileges of Manchu Bannermen.

[17] Board of Foreign Affairs, known before 1900 as the Tsungli Yamen.

[18] China Mission Year Book, 1910, Ch. Reforms and Changes.

urging the education of the people and the introduction of local self-government, there was little real progress. It is true that the "Office for the Investigation of Administrative Methods" which had been established with Prince Ch'ing at its head, was specialized and made an "Office to arrange for Constitutional Government." Furthermore, in response to a memorial from Prince Ch'ing and H. E. Sun Chia-Nai, regulations for the reorganization of the Provincial Governments and of the Manchurian Administration were drawn up and promulgated, but these naturally had very little immediate effect. It is not necessary to dwell at any great length on many of these memorials and edicts.

Nevertheless a few steps in advance were taken and must be noted. Hitherto while there had been recognition of the need for a National Council or Assembly no move had been made to establish such a body. By an Imperial decree of September 20, 1907, the declaration was made that "as the principle of constitutional government requires that political questions be decided by public opinion, and as the Upper and Lower Houses of a Parliament are the source of political acts, it is extremely urgent that a National Assembly (Tzechengyuan) be created to serve as the foundation of a Parliament, inasmuch as the latter cannot be established at present. Accordingly We hereby appoint Pu Lun and Sun Chia-nai to be Presidents of the said Council, who, in conjunction with the Grand Council, shall carefully draw up detailed regulations therefore for promulgation."

The making of regulations is both a pastime and a profession of the Chinese official class, so that very often drawing them up becomes an end in itself, instead of merely the means to an end. Frequently, with the promulgation of regulations the reform is considered to be accomplished. Thus a month after the above provision was made for establishing the Assembly it was considered to have been duly instituted.[19]   The National Assembly having been provided for, the Empress next proceeded to outline another step in her constitutional programme.

One of the great benefits that foreign countries were supposed to derive from their constitutional governments was a closer sympathy between the governed and their rulers.   In order to realize this advantage there must be some way for the Central Government to ascertain and direct public opinion. The administrative officers could not be expected to point out the evils in their own administration of the laws, or to suggest changes by which their authority might be limited.   There were, it is true, the censors, of whom mention has been made. The Censorate consisted of about fifty-six men,[20] but they were scattered throughout the Empire, usually two to a province, and they lacked the intimate touch with local conditions and needs necessary to make them effective spokesmen for the people of China.   Furthermore, their representative capacity was limited by the method of their appointment and by the nature of the duties laid upon them.   They were not expected to represent the people, but were rather agents of the Imperial Government sent out to report, not on the needs of the people, but on the acts of the various officials: whether they were faithful to the *D*ynasty, and how well they were carrying out the wishes of the Emperor.   Sometimes their criticisms were expressions of public opinion, as in the case of the memorials sent in urging the necessity of providing an heir for the Emperor T'ung Chih, to carry on the worship at

[19] "We some time ago issued an edict establishing a National Assembly in the Capital to serve as the foundation of the future Parliament" states a decree issued a month after the one quoted above.

[20] "China in Law and Commerce," p. 156.

his tomb. But as a rule they gave voice to the views of the literati and the official class rather than the sentiment of the masses.

While the National Assembly was intended to advise the central government concerning the needs and desires of the people, the freedom of action left to the governors of the provinces made it advisable to establish similar informative Councils at the seats of provincial government. These provincial assemblies were in the nature of training schools for service in the National Assembly.

Although the elective principle was introduced, membership in the assemblies was in fact by appointment. The Governors and Viceroys were "carefully to select upright and experienced officials and gentry to begin the work, and to order qualified people to elect worthy and able men to be the members of the said assemblies, and vigilantly to guard against the entrance of persons of an insubordinate disposition or of disorderly conduct, of selfish pursuit, or of wilfulness."[21]

The function of the assembly was purely advisory. The members were authorized to discuss local affairs and make recommendations to the Viceroy or Governor, but they could not enforce their will in opposition to that of the administration. The Throne reserved to itself the right of final decision on all matters of importance. Provision for a degree of cooperation between Peking and the Provinces was made through the National Assembly being empowered to communicate directly with the provincial assemblies and vice versa, in addition to the right of address through official channels.

This edict was followed by one issued just before the close of the year[22] reiterating the need of constant preparation be-

---

[21] Edict of Oct. 19, 1907, China Year Book, 1912, pp. 355-56.
[22] December 25, 1907, China Year Book, 1912; December 24, 1907, American Foreign Relations, 1908.

fore the Constitution could be promulgated. The need for orderly progression was emphasized and the people were urged to leave the decision of public matters to the duly constituted assemblies, which would discuss all popular grievances. When the provincial assembly reached an important conclusion its decision was to be forwarded to the National Assembly for further consideration. The communication was to be made through the highest provincial officer. The edict announced that regulations governing the press and public meetings were being drawn up in order to check the tendency manifested toward unlicensed and revolutionary criticism of the government and the *Dynasty*.[23]

It can of course be seen, from the nature of these later proposals and changes, that the Empress was facing a growing feeling of unrest in the provinces. Hard times resulting from poor harvests brought forth the usual results,—brigandage and an outspoken criticism of a government which could not bring peace and plenty to the people. It must be remembered that the Emperor and his people stood in the relationship of a father to his children. So long as there was food in the larder and clothes on the backs, the people would find little reason for censuring the government. But during these years conditions were changing from bad to worse and immediately the Manchus were blamed. General criticism might easily become so widespread as to lead to revolution. For this reason Tzu Hsi called attention to the fact that steps were being taken to relieve the condition of the people by giving them a constitutional government; that agencies had been created

[23] This edict was generally considered to have been called forth by the popular meetings which had been held in the provinces protesting against certain policies of the Imperial government in connection with railway loans, policing of the West River, etc. See Am. For. Rel., 1908, p. 176-7. Inc. in No. 804 and No. 804.

through which abuses could be pointed out and criticisms made; and finally that it was essential to the maintenance of peace and order that the people should not harass the officials but should make known their wants through the agencies provided and wait patiently for a change for the better.

The steps taken by the beginning of 1908 may be summarized as: (1) the acceptance in principle of the idea of Constitutional Government; (2) the establishment of a commission to investigate procedure; and (3) the issuance of instructions for the institution of a National and of provincial Assemblies. It should be noted however that these instructions were vague in nature and were so enacted as to free the Throne of responsibility for their observance. No time was set within which the assemblies were to be constituted, and there was danger that they would exist only on paper.

CHAPTER IV

In China more than in most other countries internal progress has been both hastened and retarded by forces apparently unconnected with those definitely at work to bring about institutional changes. From the standpoint of international affairs, even after the second enunciation of the policy of the "open door" in 1901, Chinese integrity was menaced by the maintenance of Russian power in the North which might at any favorable moment be directed against the Empire. The Russian menace was removed by the success of Japan in 1905, and it was some time before Japan's policy unfolded itself so fully as to cause her to be regarded as threatening China. In addition to the struggle in the North between Japan and Russia, however, the foreign contact was being felt by China in the economic field. Railway concessions were granted and the Empire bade fair to be bound together in that way. But during the first few years of the century the old policy of the Powers of using railway concessions to develop spheres of interest was continued and it again appeared as though the integrity of the Empire was menaced by this comparatively new process of so-called peaceful penetration. In the years preceding the revolution of 1911, however, came the beginning of the movement toward international coöperation instead of competition in railway development in China. But before this the building of railways by foreigners and their operation under foreign supervision began to be looked upon with suspicion by the Chinese people. This suspicion was not unjustified, especially during the six or seven years after 1900. One result of this suspicion was the attempt of the Chinese themselves to build railways. Another was an increased hostility to the Central Government, and this strengthened the lack of belief in its reform programme. Again, the building of roads under the old sphere of interest idea led the Manchu government to embark on the policy of centralization of construction and operation which brought it into direct conflict with provincial interests and which precipitated the outbreak of 1911.

The ability of the Powers to dictate to China, after the Boxer uprising had been put down by foreign arms, led them to insist on modernizing the governmental and also the economic system. From the latter point of view the Powers desired to see the abolition of the internal customs barriers and wanted a thorough investigation and reform of the currency system. Up to the outbreak of the revolution nothing had been done, but the Ministers at Peking continually agitated the question of these reforms. Governmentally the Powers desired to see an extension of the control of the Central government over the provinces in order that treaty provisions might be uniformly carried out, and so that they could hold the Imperial government responsible for the protection of foreign interests throughout the Empire. For these reasons they were interested observers of the movement toward constitutional government and served as a continual stimulus to the reform zeal of the Manchus.

The events of the years after 1894 served in another way to complicate the task of the Central government. The war with Japan left China with an indemnity to pay as, to a far greater extent, did the Boxer uprising. Necessary military reorganization, currency reform if undertaken, and the abolition of the internal customs all presented new and serious financial problems to the government. Taxes were fixed by custom rather than by the changing needs of the State, and to gain the sums needed by increased taxes meant the arousing of certain antagonism at the time when the Manchus needed to conciliate instead of stirring up ill-feeling. To borrow meant the pledging of revenue services or the granting of concessions and could only give temporary relief. In both cases the people were certain to be aroused against a government which was apparently giving over the country to the foreigner.

During the first half of the decade of Manchu reform the government itself did not see clearly what was happening. Consequently the Manchus were not so interested in reforms that would really strengthen China as they became in the last two years of the period. As has been pointed out already not much was really accomplished in the way of reform, except on paper before 1908. The edicts issued were vague in their pronouncements and the activity of Peking was mainly hortatory.

A much greater definiteness characterized the important enactments of 1908 than had been shown in any of the edicts of previous years. The movement began to assume a more concrete form. The action taken during 1908 followed three distinct lines: 1) regulations governing the provincial assemblies were sanctioned by the Throne, the assemblies to be summoned within a year; 2) the fundamental principles of the Constitution were promulgated; and 3) a definite programme of constitutional change, leading up to the calling of the National Parliament within nine years, was issued under the Imperial sanction.

The provincial Assemblies were provided for as part of the national constitutional machinery, and not merely as local self-government bodies, so that an examination of their organization, powers, and limitations is essentially a part of a study of constitutional development.[1]

[1] "The method of operation of the Parliament and the pro-

The difference between the existing provincial system of the Chinese Empire and local government in foreign countries like England or Germany seems to have been clearly recognized by the "Office" to which had been given the task of drawing up regulations governing the provincial Assemblies. The regulations were embodied in a memorial submitted to the Throne, and sanctioned by an Imperial Rescript of July 22, 1908. The memorialists stated that "owing to the size of the Chinese Empire local administration centers in the Viceroy and Governor, thus marking a differentiation from the foreign type of government. The provincial authorities are under the direct control of the Throne, another point of difference. The provincial assemblies, while concerned with local government and designed to voice popular opinion, cannot be held .to diminish the supreme authority of the Central Government. It must not be forgotten that all deliberative bodies are restricted in their functions to debate. They have absolutely no executive powers."[2] The next few sentences indicate the countries from a study of whose institutions had been drawn the principles of constitutional government applicable in China. "In foreign constitutional governments the powers of popular deliberative bodies are similarly restricted. In Germany the promotion and removal of officials is expressly reserved as a prerogative of the Throne, likewise in Japan."[3]

We have seen that the Empress *Dowager* based her whole programme on the principle that constitutionalism did not imply a lessening of the Imperial power. It followed, then, that the functions of the assemblies would be so limited as not

vincial deliberative assemblies will be identical" wrote the memorialists whose regulations for the provincial Assemblies received the Imperial sanction.

[2] Translation, Inclosure in No. 989, Am. For. Relations, 1908.
[3] *Ibid.*

to infringe on Royal prerogatives. The provincial deliberative assemblies, according to section 1 of the regulations, were to "act as places where the public opinion of the respective provinces may be ascertained; they shall also deliberate as to what would seem to be beneficial for the Province and shall advise their superiors of their opinions. The above shall be their principal function."[4]

The assemblies were not expected to act as critics of the government nor to hold it to accountability for its acts. It would seem that a large scope for discussion and action by the assemblies was allowed since they might: 1) determine the policy of the province; 2) make preliminary estimates of the income and expenditure of the province; 3) settle the amount of the above; 4) determine the taxes to be levied and the funds to be borrowed; 5) decide as to innovations in the provinces (additional taxes, etc.); 6) decide as to changes in the administration of the provincial government; 7) elect delegates to the constitutional assembly; 8) answer questions put by the constitutional assembly; 9) answer questions put by the Viceroy or Governor; 10) supervise the local self-government societies; and 11) receive and consider the proposals of the local self-government societies and the people.[5]

But in their discussions on the first seven topics enumerated they were limited to a consideration of specific propositions brought before them by the Viceroy or Governor. No debates were allowed on the budget, the assembly only making estimates and settling the amounts. If the recommendations of the assembly were considered unwise by the authorities they were to be reconsidered. If they did not choose to revise or withdraw their proposals after reconsideration, the

[4] Trans. Incl. in No. 989, Am. For. Relations, 1908, p. 183.
[5] *Ibid.*, p. 186. Art. VI, Powers and Duties of the Assembly sec. 21.

provincial officials were empowered to lay the matter before the assembly in Peking, whose decision was final. Owing to the limitations imposed on the National Assembly, reference to Peking amounted simply to bringing the difference
of opinion before the Imperial administration. While the
Viceroy or Governor had the right to question the assembly on
any matter, the converse did not hold true. The assembly
could request information from the administration but a detailed answer could be avoided on the ground that a certain
amount of secrecy was necessary.[6]

The indirect method[7] of selecting members of the assemblies was chosen as more applicable to a country in which representative government was a novelty. The right to vote for
electors was extended to all males twenty-five years of age
who possessed any one of five sets of qualifications. These
were: 1) Having been successfully engaged for three years or
more in teaching or in some other occupation conducive to the
public good; 2) having graduated from a middle school, or
school of corresponding grade, in China or abroad, and pos-
sessing proof of the same; 3) having the former literary degree of a senior licentiate (kung-sheng) or a higher one; 4)
having held any substantive official post of the seventh civil
or fifth military rank or higher, and not having been degraded

[6] *Ibid.*, Arts. 22-30, sec. 26.

[7] "The method of election is a double or indirect one, the members of the Council (Assembly) being elected by electoral colleges, one college in each Fu. The members of the electoral colleges are elected by the voters of all the hsien in one Fu. Each
hsien elects so many voters to the electoral college, each voter
casting a single vote irrespective of the number of members to
be elected from the particular hsien. In the second election each
Fu electoral college elects so many members of the Council, each
voter in the electoral college casting only one vote." Prof. L. R.
O. Bevan, China Mission Year Book, 1911. Ch. III. The New
Chinese Constitution.

on impeachment; 5) having any business capitalized for $5,000 or possessing real estate to that value.[8]

The reasons for not granting universal suffrage were stated by the memorialists to be that "at the present time when a beginning is being made in the establishment of elective offices, the universal franchise cannot be granted. If a property qualification alone were demanded it would tend to inculcate money greed among the people and lead them to honor the rich. So various qualifications have been selected and the range has been widened to include other things besides material wealth. There have been added qualifications of reputation, learning and official office, all of which are adjudged of equal importance with wealth, and any one of which will entitle a man to vote. And thus the admission of unqualified men to vote will be avoided and no partiality will be shown."[9]

Each regular session of the assembly was to last about forty days, but provision was made for continuity through

[8] Am. For. Relations, 1908, p. 184, Art. III, sec. 3. Sec. 4 provides that men who were not natives of the province but had lived there ten years and had money invested there to the amount of $10,000 might vote. Further, any native of a province or any non-native over 30 years of age, who had lived ten years in the province, might be elected to the Assembly.

[9] Sec. 6—disqualifications were 1) any turbulent or lawbreaking person; 2) any person who has suffered imprisonment or any more serious penalty of the law; 3) any person who has been engaged in a disreputable business; 4) any person who has been put under suspicion in a business matter and not been exonerated; 5) any opium user; 6) any insane person; 7) any who himself or a member of whose family is engaged in a disreputable pursuit; 8) any illiterate person. Sec. 7—Occupational disqualifications—1) tenure of public office in province or acting as private secretary to any official; 2) enrollment as a soldier, or in first or second reserves; 3) holding a commission as a police officer; 4) religious occupation as Taoist or Buddhist priest or teacher in any other creed; 5) being enrolled as a student in any school.

the establishment of a permanent committee which should carry on the work of the assembly while it was not in session. Furthermore when necessary, special sessions could be called by the Viceroy or Governor.

The power of adjourning the assembly for cause was vested in the head of the provincial administration, as was also the right to dissolve it with the sanction of the central authorities. The acts for which an assembly might be dissolved were four in number: The expression of sentiments reflecting unfavorably on the Throne; any act calculated to disturb the peaceful rule of the country; refusal to adjourn when ordered to by the Viceroy or Governor, or *refusal to yield after having been adjourned several times;* and, finally, the refusal of a considerable number of the members of the assembly to attend its meetings, after having been summoned several times.[10]

It is hardly necessary to point out that in no way had the hold of the official class on the administration been directly relaxed by the creation of these assemblies. They did offer a point of departure for resistance to disliked governmental policies, it is true, and they were so used subsequently. But their chief value to the cause of reform in China lay in their ability to bring the government into touch, to a certain extent, with local sentiment. Public opinion is far from being despised in China, the great necessity being to devise a way to give it true national expression. The provincial assemblies, in spite of their limited sphere of action, were able to bring a surprising pressure to bear against unpopular government measures from the very fact that they did give a voice to the popular opinions.[11]

[10] Art. VII and Art. VIII. The italics are the author's.

[11] Furthermore, they were stronger relatively than the national assembly from the beginning because of the traditional administrative decentralization of the country which resulted practically in provincial autonomy.

In this connection it is interesting to note that the greatest efforts of the assemblies were bent towards checking the increasing assumption of authority by the Central Government over the provincial administration; in other words, as we shall see later, the creation of these assemblies checked the Imperial policy of centralization.

Turning our attention again to Peking, an edict was issued on August 27, accepting the "Principles of the Constitution" as presented in a memorial from the officials to whom had been given the task of framing the constitution. In the memorial was embodied a discussion of the different ways in which constitutions are gained—some being granted from above, and some coming from the pressure brought to bear on the Government by the people. "It should be noted," the memorialists wrote, "that the nations of the East and the West all have established constitutional governments. Some have done so by pressure from below and some under influenees from above. All have constitutions and Parliaments. Those which have established their constitutions under pressure from below have commenced with strife between sovereign and people, and have ended the work by mutual concessions between sovereign and people. Those that have established their constitutions under influences from above have first determined the ultimate authority of the Court, and thereafter there has been granted to the people the advantage of inquiring about the affairs of government. . . . In most of the nations in which the constitution has been 'granted from above the origin of all powers is in the Court. The Parliament must grow out of the Constitution, not the constitution out of the Parliament. *The government of China is to be constitutional by Imperial decree. This is an unchangeable principle.* Therefore in regard to establishing a parliament, the general principles of the constitution will be settled as a preliminary. When they are announced the Parliament may be assembled. *The principles of the constitution are the great laws which may not be discussed.* Once fixed they may not be lightly altered. . . . *The constitution is designed to conserve the power of the sovereign and protect the officials and the people.*"[12]

The general purport of the "principles" is so clearly laid down in the above passage that it is only necessary to examine the method by which the powers of the sovereign were to be conserved, and parliamentary institutions operated without impairing them.

From the first section of the "principles" which provided that "the Ta Ts'ing Dynasty shall rule over the Ta Ts'ing Empire for ever and ever, and be honored through all ages" to the last clause of section fourteen "Parliament cannot interfere" the supreme power of the Emperor was jealously provided for and safeguarded. All legislative, executive, and judicial power was to remain concentrated in his hands. The Emperor alone could appoint and dismiss officials, and fix their salaries. As commander-in-chief of the army and navy he was to have the power to make laws and regulations for both forces. In addition to the general legislative authority, the Emperor was given the right to issue ordinances within the limit of the law. All control over foreign relations was vested in the Crown, as was the right to declare war and make peace. Naturally the affairs of the Imperial Household and the Imperial Ceremonies including the expenses of the Court were withdrawn from outside interference. Unwilling to leave anything to chance the framers of the constitution put in two emergency clauses: one giving the Emperor the authority, if circumstances required it, to issue edicts restricting

[12] Am. For. Relations, 1908, Incl. 1 in No. 1005, p. 192. The italics are the author's.

the liberty of his subjects; and the other providing that "in time of emergency, when Parliament is not in session, the Emperor may issue edicts for the purpose of carrying on the government, and for raising the necessary funds—these measures however must be submitted to Parliament when it next assembles."[13]

All regulation of the time of meeting or adjournment of Parliament was taken from its hands and maintained as one of the prerogatives of the Crown. While the Assembly was created ostensibly to aid in the government of the Empire the sphere of parliamentary activity was so hedged about with limitations as to render it impotent as a controlling or directing organ. The fact that it did exercise an influence on the administration was due not to its granted but to its usurped powers, and to the political condition of the Empire at the time it was first summoned.

Parliament was given power to propose legislation for the consideration of the government; it might adopt measures of government; and it might impeach Ministers for illegal acts, but no action it took had any weight or validity save that derived from the Imperial sanction. All matters affecting a single province were removed definitely from its consideration. It was granted the privilege of *assisting* in the compilation of the budget of the Empire, but nowhere was the Assembly given any control over it. Indeed such control was expressly denied, since the Constitution provided that "regular expenditure, authorized by the Emperor, and expenditure already fixed by law shall not be abolished or reduced except in consultation with the government."[14]

[13] "Principles of the Constitution," Powers of the Sovereign, 14 sections. Am. For. Relations, 1908. Incl. 1 in No. 1005, pp. 194-6. See also China Year Book, 1912, for synopsis.

[14] Sec. 3, 12 clauses. Am. For. Relations, 1908, Incl. 1 in No. 1005, p. 195. Also China Year Book, 1912, Ch. XXI.

In order to give effect to their decisions, after agreement had been reached in both houses of Parliament, the conclusions formulated had to be embodied in a memorial to the Throne, transmitted through the President of the Upper House. The presiding officer was not elected by the House but was appointed by the Emperor. He was given control over deliberations in the Parliament, with the right to order anyone committing a breach of parliamentary rules to desist from speaking, or to retire from the House. In addition to this right, the President was empowered to strike off the roll of the House any member found to be unqualified or unfit for membership.[15] Thus the Parliament was not even allowed to pass on the qualifications of its own members, and their freedom of expression was restricted by the condition that they must not use disrespectful language concerning the Court or abuse other persons.

In addition to the above provisions of the Constitution, a section was included laying down the duties and privileges of subjects of the Empire. The usual provision was made for freedom of speech and meeting, subject to law; for the right of legal trial in properly constituted courts; and for freedom of property and residences from interference without due legal reason. Their duties were to pay duly imposed taxes, to perform military service, and to generally obey the laws.[16]

The limitations imposed on both the provincial assemblies and the National Parliament certainly justified the conclusion reached by Mr. W. W. Rockhill[17] that the object of the Im-

[15] The principles governing elections were laid down in the "Principles of the Constitution." They were general in nature, principally providing for supervision and due care in elections. *Ibid.*

[16] Sec. 2, The Duties and Privileges of Subjects, 9 clauses. Am. For. Relations, 1908. Incl. 1 in No. 1005, p. 195.

[17] American Minister at the Court of Peking.

perial Government was "no other than a perpetuation of the existing system under a thin veil of constitutional guarantees." But as a matter of fact the institution of organs representative in their nature was a step so far in advance of anything previously attempted that due credit must be given the hitherto reactionary Empress Dowager and Court for having any connection with such reforms. Furthermore such is the force of what may be called public opinion in China that it would have been almost fatal to the Dynasty continually to disregard the recommendations of a legally constituted Parliament, especially in matters vitally affecting the interests of the nation. That one is justified in assuming that Parliament would have been able to exercise a considerable and ever increasing influence is evident from the pronounced activity of the National Assembly in the last days of the Manchu rule,[18] and from the influence exerted from the first by the provincial assemblies.

Simultaneously with the promulgation of the "Principles of the Constitution," a programme of constitutional preparation, covering a period of nine years, was adopted. Each year was to witness certain changes, such as the introduction of local self-government, law reform, census taking, police reorganization, the extension of the educational system so as gradually to reduce illiteracy, the introduction of a budget and auditing system, and the issue of constitutional laws, Imperial House Laws and Parliamentary Laws. The whole programme culminated in the establishment of a Parliament and the organization of a Privy Council and a Cabinet in the ninth year.

The idea of extended preparations before the summoning of a Parliament was undoubtedly borrowed from the Japanese who had gone through a somewhat similar process before the

[18] The work of the National Assembly is discussed in the following chapter.

granting of their constitution. What the Manchu *Dynasty* needed more than anything was a breathing space,—a time in which to take stock of themselves, their weakness and their strength as rulers of the Empire. This nine year period would give just the opportunity so badly needed. Further, it was felt that the reforms outlined would serve to convince not only the Chinese but foreigners as well, of the zeal of the government for reform and change. If these nine years had been conceded to the Manchus, the *Dynasty* might have been able to control the situation so as to introduce political institutions of a constitutional nature much better fitted to China and the state of western political education of the Chinese people than anything the Republic has been able thus far to develop. But the very elaboration of the programme, bringing home to the radicals in the Empire the slowness of the movement, served to defeat its purpose, for it immediately called forth an agitation for a material reduction of the time alloted to preparation. The times were out of joint for the Manchus; things were moving too rapidly to suit them, and after 1908 they were forced to bend every effort to stem the rising tide of radicalism, anti-dynastic in its nature.

The reform movement was controlled and directed by Her Majesty, the Empress *Dowager*, until the very hour of her death. When it was clear that the Emperor Kwang Hsü would not survive the year (1908) steps were immediately taken to name his successor. The Empress was not content even then to allow the reins to slip from her own hands, and she practically forced the appointment of the infant son of Prince Ch'un as the heir to the Throne. At the time when this was done the Empress herself undoubtedly expected to survive Kwang Hsü, continuing to govern as the virtual regent. However, she caused Prince Ch'un to be named the nominal Regent.

The ill-fated Emperor Kwang Hsü passed away October 14, 1908, and within twenty-four hours the death of the "Old Buddha" herself was reported. With her death one of the most masterful personalities of Chinese history quitted the world, leaving an infant on the *D*ragon Throne. The reign title of Hsuan T'ung was assumed.

The new Regent, Prince Ch'un, was a brother of the late Emperor. He had held many high government offices under Tzu Hsi, and had been connected directly with the work of constitutional reform. Naturally now that the control was in his hands all were interested in ascertaining his attitude toward the changes that were under way.

The year 1909 was marked by the issuance of edicts pledging the new administration to the continuance of the reforms outlined by Her Majesty the *D*owager Empress in the nine year programme.[20] Thus the work of establishing local self-government was pushed, the officials being urged to exercise the greatest diligence in putting into effect the wishes of the government.[21] One of the greatest dangers was that the officials would take action only on paper. This was clearly recognized and deprecated. "It is, however, to be feared, that committing a long standing error, some of them (i.e. the provincial officials) may seek to discharge their responsibilities by presenting a mere memorial, without taking any definite action. They should bear in mind that these measures are of the highest importance, and are to be carried out in com-

[20] In an edict of November 25, 1909, are the following words: "We will reverently obey the edict issued on the first day of the eighth moon last year (August 27, 1908)." This edict contained the "Principles of the Constitution" and the "Nine year programme." See also, edict of March 6, 1909.

[21] Edict of January 18, 1909—Financial reorganization was discussed in an edict of January 11, 1909.

pliance with the plans of the late Emperor, as well as to satisfy the aspirations of the people."[22]

The most important event of 1909 was the meeting of the provincial assemblies for the first time[23] in accordance with the decree promulgating their regulations, and setting the time for their initial convocation.[24]   From the beginning they became a factor to be reckoned with in provincial government.[25] No detailed account of their labors was published, but it may be said that these assemblies more than fulfilled expectations. On the whole, they conducted their deliberations with dignity, sincerity, and with due regard to the limits imposed on their powers by the Throne.   There were cases of friction between the assemblies and officials, when the former did not scruple to denounce what they considered the wrongful practises of the latter.[26]   In addition to their activity in the affairs of the province, the assemblies led in the agitation for the early convocation of Parliament, bringing all the force of provincial opinion to bear on the Central Government, and giving real weight to the agitation of the National Assembly.

The National Assembly met for the first time October 3,

[22] Edict of November 25, 1909.   China Year Book, 1912, Ch. XXI, p. 367.

[23] Oct. 14, 1909.

[24] Edict of July 22, 1908.

[25] The expectations of the Throne with regard to the provincial assemblies was as follows: "The respective Viceroys and Governors are desired to gather and accept without predeliction or prejudice the suggestions of the Assemblies, and put them into operation after due deliberation, so that a unity of mind may be established, and good government attained in course of time. After the opening of the Assemblies the Viceroys and Governors are further commanded to superintend their deliberations in accordance with the regulations and to see that the measures decided upon neither exceed the proper bounds of authority, nor contravene the laws of the land."   Edict, Oct. 13.

[26] China Year Book, 1912.

1910, under regulations that had been sanctioned by an Imperial Edict of October 26, 1909. These rules were revised in a few particulars in 1911.[27] They were in ten chapters. The principles governing the Assembly were first laid down. The President was to be chosen from among the Princes, *Dukes*, or Ministers of State "of recognized merit," and he was to direct all the affairs of the Assembly. In addition to the President, there was to be a Vice-President, an official above the third rank. Both of these men were to be appointed by the Throne. Two principles governed the choice of members of the Assembly,—i.e. Imperial selection and election. Out of the total membership of two hundred the Emperor had the right to choose one hundred, the other half being elected by the provincial assemblies from their own membership. The Imperial appointees were to come from seven different classes, including representatives of the Manchu, Chinese, Mongolian and Tibetan nobility, as well as representatives of the official and literary classes, and the class of large tax-payers.[28]

---

[27] Since the revised rules were substantially the same as the regulations of 1909 the former alone are discussed here. The translation used is that given in the China Year Book for 1912, pp. 377-396.

[28] In deciding upon the representatives from these different classes a method of elimination was adopted. A list of all eligible candidates in the first three groups was compiled and submitted to the Throne for a selection of the proper number. Choice was made from the other four groups by a combination of election and Imperial selection. First of all an election was held, under proper supervision, by all of those who were listed as members of a particular group. This election provided a list of two or three times the number of representatives the group was entitled to have in the Assembly. Then the Emperor selected from this number those who were actually to serve.

The hundred representatives from the provincial assemblies were apportioned among the different provinces, according to their size and estimated population. Thus the Chihli assembly had the right to select nine, the Kuangtung assembly six, et cetera. The assembly was to choose twice the number of representatives it was entitled to have, submitting its choice to the Superintendent of Elections,—the Viceroy or Governor of the Province. He then selected the proper number from the head of the list and confirmed them as the members of the National assembly from his province. Since the members of the provincial assemblies were all chosen indirectly by a carefully restricted suffrage, it can be seen that little was left to the popular choice in the selection of even the half of the membership of the National Assembly representative of provincial and local interests.

The functions of the Assembly were to be substantially the same as those laid down for the future Parliament in the "Principles of the Constitution." It was to consider the national budget; national revenue and expenditure; revenue collection and public loans; legislation; compilation of new laws and revision of old ones, with the exception that matters affecting the constitution were excluded from its consideration; and matters specially referred to the Assembly by the Throne. However, proposals under any one of the first four classified heads had to be made by the Cabinet or the ministries and submitted to the Throne before being considered by the Assembly. So that in fact it was only empowered to discuss matters submitted to it by the Emperor.

Chapter IV of the revised regulations dealt with the relations between the Assembly and the executive. The Ministers were to be represented in the Assembly either in person or by deputy, and had the right to present their views on its floor. In its turn the Assembly might question the Ministers, the

President or Vice-President serving as the medium of communication. But the Ministers of State were not required to answer these questions, although they did have to give reasons for a refusal to reply. In case of disagreement between the executive and the Assembly the final decision rested with the Emperor. The National Assembly had the right to impeach Ministers of State in a memorial to the Throne, the memorial to be drawn up by the President and Vice-President only after a two-thirds majority of the members present at the meeting voted for such an impeachment. Here again the final decision rested with the Emperor.

While the Assembly had the right to call upon the provincial assemblies for information concerning the public welfare, all other direct communication with the provinces was denied it. Differences of opinion between the provincial assemblies and the Governors, as has already been noted, were to be submitted to the National Assembly for discussion, after which the final decision would be made by the Throne. "But this rule shall not apply to questions affecting the executive government. All such shall be sent forward to the Cabinet for its consideration." The people were to have the right of petitioning the National Assembly, providing that the person so addressing it was guaranteed by a member from his own province. The petition could only be considered by the Assembly if it accorded with the law, and was free from disrespectful language, and providing it concerned a matter with which the Assembly was competent to deal.

An Assembly so constituted by Imperial appointment and indirect election might well have been expected to remain subservient to the Emperor and the Court. But quite the contrary was true. From the time of its convocation the National Assembly led in the agitation for an early summoning of Parliament and a shortening of the time of preparation.

The result of the movement was the issuance of an Imperial decree on November 4, 1910[29] promising the Parliament for the fifth year of Hsuan T'ung (1913) instead of four years later. At the same time a modified programme of constitutional preparations was promised. However the Throne did not give the assemblies the credit for having brought about the change. The edict says, "there is no need for the high Ministers and the people to beg and pray. We Ourselves have arrived at this conclusion." And again, "the shortening of the time limit is the result of taking the ópinions of memorials from the Viceroys and Governors, and of the most careful counsel of the Princes and Ministers who have requested Our decision."[30]

While this edict did not satisfy the wishes of the National Assembly for the immediate establishment of a Parliament, other matters began to assume a greater importance. From the first the Assembly and the Council of State came into confliet. Once it was over a loan contracted by the Governor of Hunan province without consulting the provincial assembly. Again, the Assembly attacked the Ministers because it had not been consulted concerning some Salt Gabelle matters. Several times the Assembly was on the point of impeaching the Grand Council in a memorial to the Throne, but gave it up because of concessions on the point at issue. Finally it did call the attention of the Emperor to the fact that the Council was an irresponsible body and should be placed under the control of the Assembly, demanding the creation of a responsible Cabinet, and memorializing to that effect. As a result an edict was issued[31] ordering the promulgation of the revised

[29] China Year Book, 1912, pp. 372-3.
[30] *Ibid.*
[31] December 25, 1910.

programme of constitutional preparation,[32] and also ordering the Commission of Constitutional Reform to frame the official constitution of the Cabinet and submit it to the Throne. This practically conceded the point raised by the Assembly, so it withdrew the memorial attacking the Grand Council.

According to the promise given the National Assembly, an edict, creating a Cabinet and containing the regulations under which it should be organized and carry on its duties was promulgated on May 8, 1911. By this edict the old advisory bodies were abolished, the Cabinet taking their place. Far from meeting the demand for a responsible ministry, the constitution and regulations of the Cabinet showed clearly an attempt on the part of the government to persuade the Assembly to accept the shell for the kernel of the nut.[33] The new Cabinet was simply the old Grand Council under a new name. The Ministers were the old heads of the Boards. All members of the Cabinet were to be appointed by the Emperor and were responsible to him alone. Nowhere was there the slightest suggestion that the Assembly would exercise any control over the Cabinet. The membership was to consist of a Prime Minister, a Minister of Foreign Affairs, of Civil Affairs, of Finance, Education, Agriculture, Industry and Commerce, Justice, Posts and Communications, and finally, the Minister of Dependencies. The members of the Cabinet were to have access to the Throne, but always in company with the Prime Minister, who might be received at any time and alone. Only the Ministers of War and of the Navy had the right to present memorials directly to the Throne, without using the intermediation of the Prime Minister.

[32] For the revised programme see China Year Book, 1912, p. 376.

[33] For translation of "Constitution of the Cabinet" and regulations, see China Year Book, 1912, pp. 222-226.

The functions of the Cabinet were precisely those of the old Grand Council: to deliberate and advise on affairs of State; to supervise the work of the different departments; and to "formulate the national policy, in obedience to Imperial commands, and maintain the executive unification." The Cabinet had the right to discuss: 1) law bills, Imperial Rescripts, and the official system; 2) budget balance; 3) expenses not detailed in the budget; 4) treaties and important diplomatic affairs; 5) movements of officials above those appointed by memorials; 6) conflict of powers of the different departments; 7) matters submitted for discussion by special edicts, or petitions of the people transmitted by Parliament; 8) important administrative questions of the different depart- ments; 9) matters which should be discussed by the Cabinet according to laws and regulations; 10) matters which, in the opinion of the Prime Minister or the Ministers of the different departments ought to be discussed by the Cabinet. All questions were to be decided by majority vote.

The decisions reached by the Cabinet were not to have the force of law, except after the Imperial sanction, which could be given or withheld at will. In other words the members of the Cabinet had only the right to memorialize the Throne for its decision in a matter, and to submit advice on questions when the Emperor wished their opinion. They received their appointments from, and were responsible only to, the Emperor.

The same edict of May 8 created a Privy Council, which was to consist of "personal advisers to the Emperor." This Council was given no administrative power, but might memorialize the Throne on matters of ceremonial, investigation and interpretation of constitutional laws, treaties and diplomatic negotiations, and the revision of its own regulations.

In addition, special matters might be referred to it by the Throne.[34]

The progress of constitutional development during the last months of 1911 was strongly influenced by the revolution in the Yangtze valley. For this reason it should be discussed in connection with the revolution rather than as a part of the normal course of constitutional development under the Manchus.

The revolution which broke out at Wuchang in October 1911, created an abnormal condition. It is impossible to do more than guess as to what would have been accomplished by way of establishing a limited constitutional monarchy if the Manchus had been allowed to carry out their programme under normal conditions. Certainly the National Assembly and the assemblies in the provinces showed from the very beginning a decidedly progressive and at the same time obstreperous spirit. The members of the National Assembly, many of them Nobles, and all of them from the higher classes of society, were practically unanimous in their decision that the essence as well as the form of constitutionalism must be introduced. Their ability to take matters into their own hands, to assume an initiative and a power of direction in the reform movement was indicated clearly during the first session. They did not accomplish all that they wished to, but they did force concessions from the Throne and the Ministers sufficient to show them their power. It is safe to assume that they would have been able, gradually, to gain the position in the governmental system that Parliament holds in the English system, relegating the Emperor to the position of a figure-head. Every concession granted by the Crown to the Assembly would have become, by usage, an inviolable right in a country where pre-

[34] China Year Book, 1912, p. 226.

cedent is all important. Of course there is the possibility that as the Assembly grew in power and importance it would have tended to lose in progressiveness, but, together with the gradual assumption of control by the Assembly would certainly have gone a growth of political consciousness on the part of the people of China, perhaps even greater than has resulted from the introduction of republican institutions. So that, as the gentry and upper classes established themselves, through the Parliament, in place of the Imperial family as the supreme governing power, they would have been subjected to as strong a pressure from below as they themselves had exerted formerly on the Crown. At any rate, if the constitutional programme of the Manchus had been carried out, China would have been given at least as stable and enlightened a government as that of the Republic of the last eight years.

A comparison of constitutional development in Japan and in China during the last days of the Manchu *Dynasty* is often made, invariably lauding the success of the Japanese and disparaging the work attempted in China. As a matter of fact the conditions were so different as to make a comparison valueless. Japan was a small and compact nation, whose rulers and nobility were of the same stock as the common people. Compared with China the government of Japan was highly centralized. The feudal condition of Japan made it possible to set up a constitutional government which left the actual governing power in the hands of the small group of nobles, who had exercised the actual governing power prior to the Restoration, and who were experienced administrators. The *Diet*, nominally elective, was in reality controlled by the nobility and not by the people. In case of a conflict between the Ministers and the *Diet*, it was only necessary to call upon the sacred name of the Emperor to secure the acquiescence of the people in the wishes of the government. In Japan the people were willing to accept an autocratic constitutionalism because it meant simply the continuance of the old government.

Contrast with this the conditions faced by the Manchus in China! They wished to gain the consent of the people to a system intended to consolidate the supremacy of an alien race. They were bent on centralization of the government, a policy which found great opposition in the hitherto practically autonomous provinces. The work of reform had been undertaken to placate a hostile people, and to counteract an anti-dynastic agitation throughout the country. There was no such respect for the word of the Emperor in China as in Japan. And finally there was no group of capable administrators with sufficient strength to dominate the administration. China had no "Elder Statesmen" to lend equilibrium to the government!

There is a better reason to compare the progress made by the Manchus with the constitutional progress under the Republic than to contrast it with the Japanese Restoration, and the introduction of constitutional government into that country. It is unquestionable that the Manchus attempted to impose the form of a constitutional government on China which did not realize the spirit of such a system. But from the first meeting of the assemblies it was evident that the control of the situation had passed from the Throne to the representative body. While neither the National Assembly nor the provincial assemblies were representative of the mass of the people, they represented, what is more important in a country like China, different interests in the State. It was a class representation undoubtedly but the Chinese people have always been governed by a distinct official heirarchy and are not fitted at the present time for anything else.[35] The classes repre-

[35] It must be remembered, of course, that admission to the official class was open to all who could qualify in the examinations, but this does not mean that the government was any the less class government.

sented in the assemblies were the Manchu and Chinese nobility, both representative of the same class of interests; the bureaucracy, through the members who were selected from the officials of the ministries; the literati, one of the most influential of all classes in China; those interested in the government because they supported it by the payment of taxes; and, finally, the provincial interests were given the largest representation. The fact of the appointment of the membership of the National Assembly does not take away from its representative character.

As has been stated, all of the signs pointed to an eventual control of the government by the Parliament, and not by the Emperor. This change would have come about step by step instead of all at once as has been the case since republican institutions have been introduced. It would have left a definite symbol of power in the person of the Emperor, to which the people could have rendered homage, instead of giving them only the abstract conception of the State to hold their loyalty. One-man-power is something understandable to the Chinese mind. Representative government as a limitation of that power is also understandable, but government by an Assembly without one "Son of Heaven" to personify the power of government is not so easily comprehended.

The main thing emphasized by the constitutional monarchists from the very beginning was the need of preparation in order to fit the Chinese people to share in the government. This was partly due to their imitation of the Japanese method of introducing a constitutional regime; it is to be explained in part, perhaps, by a desire to placate the people by words instead of acts; but it was certainly owing, to a large extent, to a realization of the real need for such preparation and training. That representative or constitutional government is nothing more than a phrase to many of the Chinese has been demonstrated beyond question since the establishment of the Republic. The Republic itself has done a great deal to justify the Manchu desire to "make haste slowly."

What China needed was what John Stuart Mill has called a "government of leading strings." This is what constitutional government under the Manchus would have given. But such a government is desirable only if it prepares the nation for higher forms of political institutions. In other words, the supreme duty of a "government of leading strings" is the political education of the people so that they may be progressively better fitted for self-government. This educative function was emphasized by the Manchus in their insistence on the need for a period of preparation before true constitutional government was introduced. It was a debatable question, certainly, how far the Manchu rulers of China, if left to themselves, could be trusted to carry out their own programme in good faith. But the constant criticism and interference of the National Assembly was calculated to help the Imperial government to be true to its promises, and warrants the belief that the ideal of political education would not have been negleeted.

Further speculation as to the possibility of ultimately achieving true constitutional government under the Manchu *Dynasty* is useless. A new phase of constitutional development appeared as a result of the series of events which culminated in the establishment of a Republic at Nanking in 1912.

CHAPTER V

The revolution which accomplished the overthrow of the Manchu *Dynasty*, and the establishment of a Republic in China, broke out at Wuchang on October 10, 1911. From a mere mutiny of the Wuchang garrison the movement rapidly spread up and down the Yangtze until it had become a formidible opposition to the Manchu rule. The foreign educated Chinese and the European and American residents in China alike hailed it as the first step in the regeneration of the nation. At last the sleeping *Dragon* had shaken off its lethargy! The Chinese people had arisen in their might and declared their intention of replacing the autocracy of the Manchu with the democracy of the West. Very few stopped to question the basis for the claim that the revolt was an expression of the desire of the people for a free government. Foreigners saw the revolution as an accomplished fact and were satisfied. The Manchus had never welcomed foreign trade or foreign innovations of any kind, and it was believed that the new government, founded on foreign ideas, would be instrumental in promoting a more friendly intercourse between the East and the West. The establishment of a Republic in China seemed to mark the end of the idea that "East is East and West is West, and never the twain shall meet."

This feeling of the Europeans and Americans was played upon by the revolutionary leaders to secure the support of the Powers for the revolution. Great stress was laid on the fact that foreign interests must be protected, and were protected by the republican forces. The appeal addressed to the Powers by *Dr.* Wu Ting-fang in a communcation to the foreign press

94

is well worth quoting. "The foreign Powers individually and collectively have stood hammering at the door of China for centuries pleading for the diffusion of knowledge, a reformation of national services, the adoption of Western sciences and industrial processes, the jettisoning of the crude, out-of-date and ignoble concepts which have multiplied to keep the nation without the pale of the great family constituting the civilized world. They have failed. . . . "The Manchu Dynasty has triumphantly carried on its reactionary policy despite the strongest pressure exerted from within and without, until the oppressed people could endure the disgrace and contumely of it no longer. They rose, and with what result the history of the past few weeks has shown. . . . "The Manchu *Dynasty* has been tried by a patient and peaceful people for centuries and has been found more than wanting. It has sacrificed the reverence, forfeited the regard, and lost the confidence freely reposed in it by all Chinese. The popular wish is that the Dynasty must go."

Concerning the policy of the revolutionists Dr. Wu wrote: "We have, in short taken every possible step to protect vested interests, safeguard international obligations, secure continuance of commerce, and shield educational and religious institutions; and what is even more important, striven continually to maintain law and order, sustain peace, and promote a constructive policy upon sound and enduring grounds. . . . "We must not be judged by the past; we are trying to bring China into her own; to elevate her to the standard that the people of the Occident have ever been urging her to attain, and the stumbling block today, as it has been during the past centuries, is the Manchu *Dynasty*. Our foreign friends must from a sheer sense of fairness concede that we have the right to win the laurels of freedom by fair fight in the field, and to avoid the rest we again appeal to them to use their influence to secure in the Manchu mind recognition of the utter hopelessness of the continuance of the *Dynasty*."[1]

Such an appeal was well calculated to secure the support of foreigners for the revolution. The prejudices of the past, self-interest, love of humanity and the spirit of fair play were all invoked in turn. Nothing was said of the part the *Chinese* had played in opposing the introduction of western industrial methods, of western education, of railroads and the telegraph. No mention was made of the part played by the people in the anti-foreign riots and especially in the Boxer uprising. And in fact foreigners were glad to accept the Republican protestations of friendship at their face value; to forget the past, or blame it on the Manchus; and to hail the foundation of the Republic as the dawn of a new era in the history of the Orient.

When defenders of the Republic were asked how an Oriental despotism could be suddenly and permanently transmuted into a modern democratic State, they pointed to the local self-government which the Chinese had enjoyed for generations; the common management of the affairs of the village under the leadership of the head man chosen by the people and under their control. The ability of the people to manage their own local affairs, it was said, showed that they could be entrusted with the larger affairs of the nation.

But this local democratic government had engendered a spirit of locality in the Chinese people which must be considered in estimating their ability to assume control of the general government of the Empire. They had, and still have, no conception of national as opposed to local interests. If Russia seized territory in the North the people of Kuangtung or Yunnan provinces felt no especial concern. Let the North protect itself, was the feeling. If the Yellow River over-

[1] China Year Book, 1912. The Revolution, pp. XVII-XX.

flowed its banks, Shansi Province took the necessary steps to protect itself without regard to the situation in Honan or Shantung Provinces, perhaps even at their expense.

This spirit of locality had been strengthened by the nature of the central authority to which the Chinese had become accustomed. The Manchu government had been interested in the provincial administration only so far as the revenues had been affected, or anti-dynastic agitation had arisen. It was only in the last years of Manchu rule that an attempt had been made to unify and centralize the administration.

John Stuart Mill, perhaps the ablest expounder of the principles of representative government, lays it down as a general rule that a people who have a strongly developed spirit of locality are not ready for the introduction of representative government. "One of the strongest hindrances to improvement," he says, "up to a rather advanced stage, is an inveterate spirit of locality. Portions of mankind, in many other respects capable of, and prepared for, freedom, may be unqualified for amalgamating into even the smallest nation. . . . They may, like the citizens of an ancient community, or those of an Asiatic village, have had considerable practice in exercising their faculties on village or town interests, and have even realized a tolerably effective popular government on that restricted scale, and may yet have but slender sympathies with anything beyond, and no habit or capacity of dealing with interests common to many such communities."[2]

It is partly because such a spirit of locality had grown up among the Chinese people, that it has proven, so far, impossible for them to apply their local democratic institutions to the national government, or to substitute a representative republican government for the old Imperial rule.

[2] "Representative Government," Everyman Edition, p. 222.

In order to appreciate the Chinese attitude to the revolution and the Republic we must briefly review the conception of government common to all but the educated few. The government has always been something apart from the life of the people, something with which they have no direct concern and in which they have no great interest. Because of this it has always been easy for an alien rule like that of the Manchus to maintain itself in China. The only direct connection between the rulers and the ruled came in connection with the payment of taxes. However, in return for the taxes which they paid to the government, the Chinese people demanded that they should be given protection for life and property. If you like, their attitude was that of the property owner who pays a detective to guard his possessions. He is willing to pay so long as he gets the return asked.

The visible sign of decay of every dynasty in the history of China has been its weakening of control internally, with a consequent prevalence of brigandage and piracy. In a country where a large number of people live always near the starvation line the government must exercise a strong authority in order to protect those who have property from those who have none. If conditions get too bad the government is doomed. Usually the *D*ynasty has been able to maintain itself until a leader has arisen strong enough to rally the disaffected to his banner, thus centralizing opposition. The exhaustion of the "mandate of heaven" has come usually simultaneously with the appearance of such a leader, and he has been able to establish his family as the ruling House.

For about seventy-five years the overthrow of the Manchu *D*ynasty had been confidently predicted. One uprising followed another throughout the Empire. Brigandage and piracy were the accepted order of things. But until 1911 the *D*ynasty had always been able to recover itself sufficiently to retain its hold on the Throne.   This had been due, not so much to its strength as to the inability of the opposition to concentrate and obtain competent leadership.   The leader of the Taiping revolt bade fair to overthrow the Manchus, except for two things.   He was able to destroy the power of the government but lacked the constructive ability necessary to reörganize the country under his own control.   The second reason for the maintenance of the Manchus in control was the aid extended to them by foreigners.   The great Mahommedan rebellion, which arose almost simultaneously with that of the Taipings was also put down largely because of its lack of organization and leadership.   Aside from these two great rebellions there were innumerable smaller uprisings throughout the country.   Wherever there was a lack of equilibrium between the food production and the increase of population a revolt against the government was certain to occur.   After foreign aggression in China became pronounced this local dissatisfaction could be diverted for a time into anti-foreign channels.   But foreign aggression together with the lack of power to preserve order in the country soon revealed the weakness of the Manchu *Dynasty.*

After 1900 the efforts of the Manchus to maintain themselves in power took a new form.   Hitherto they had opposed the introduction of foreign ideas into the country, feeling that their very life depended upon the continuance of the old order.   Finally, however, they tried to use foreign ideas and institutions to strengthen their position.   If foreign education was to be introduced let it be under the direction of the Central Government!   If railroads were necessary they should be constructed under agreements concluded with the Peking government, and not through provincial initiative.[3]

[3] This conclusion was reached particularly during the period after 1905.

This movement toward a centralization of the government at the expense of the old provincial autonomy however aroused immediate opposition in the provinces. It was provincial opposition that forced the cancellation of the American loan agreement to construct the Hankow-Canton line. When an agreement with the Four Power group to construct the same road was concluded in the spring of 1911, provincial opposition again developed. The gentry of the provinces concerned claimed the right to build the road themselves, and began an agitation for the cancellation of the agreement. It was the whole policy of the government that was objected to, rather than this single agreement. So firm was the attitude of the provinces that the government was forced to adopt a conciliatory policy. The blame for the trouble was laid on the Minister of Communications,[4] under whose direction the policy of railroad centralization had been developed. Here again the weakness of the Manchu rule was revealed. Their policy of centralization had come too late, and had furnished one more weapon for the opposition to the Dynasty.

As Manchu weakness became increasingly clear to the country, revolutionary secret societies, which never entirely disappear from China, sprang into new life. Probably the most influential of these organizations at the time of the revolution was that known as the Tung Meng Hui.[5] This society had been formed shortly after the failure of the 1898 reform movement and in its aims was avowedly anti-dynastic. The

[4] Sheng Hsuan-hui, (he is better known perhaps by his title Sheng Kung-pao). The agitation against him personally and his policy of centralization resulted in a victory for the provinces when he was removed by Imperial Edict, issued at the request of the National Assembly.

[5] For description of the Tung Meng Hui see sec. "Political Societies and Parties." China Year Book, 1913, pp. 663-666. Also Hornbeck, Ch. V, Pol. Parties.

Tung Meng Hui resulted from the union of several independent revolutionary organizations which had been formed in Japan by Chinese students. Its recognized leader was Sun Wen, or, as he is better known, *Dr. Sun Yat-sen*.[6]

For ten years preceding the revolution Dr. Sun had spent his time in travel in Europe and America wherever there were Chinese, carrying the doctrines of the revolution and securing financial support for the movement to overthrow the Manchus. The great strength of the Tung Meng Hui lay in its overseas membership rather than in its adherents in China, but its propaganda had also enlisted the support of many in China proper, especially in the Southern provinces.

The history of the revolution of 1911 shows, however, that it was not the result of a carefully planned movement, but was rather a spontaneous and contagious uprising at isolated points, which was later partially unified and coördinated. The Wuchang outbreak was preceded by a rebellion of serious proportions in Szechuan province[7] with which the government proved unable to cope successfully. As the news of the successes at Wuchang and Hankow spread up and down the Yangtze one section after another repudiated the Manchu authority, but always under local leaders, and without accepting any central control. The leader of the revolting troops at Wuchang, Li Yuan-hung, had never been identified with any revolutionary organization before he was compelled to assume the direction of affairs. The Republican Committee at Shanghai, which

[6] The name Sun Yat-sen has been used throughout because of its greater familiarity to foreign readers.

[7] Caused by the conflict over the assumption of control over railroad construction in the province by the Central Government. The trouble arose over the refusal of the Government to pay more of the obligations of the provincial Board than those incurred for materials actually purchased and work actually done. This lost the Gentry much of their "squeeze" on the undertaking.

finally claimed the right to represent the revolution in negotiations with the Manchu government, was organized almost
a month after the outbreak of hostilities.   Nevertheless, all
had a common determination that the Manchu rule must go—
and this hatred of the reigning dynasty provided the bond
of union which held the revolutionary leaders together so
long as the common foe existed.

It is outside the scope of a discussion of constitutional development to give a detailed account of the revolutionary
movement, except in its bearing on the establishment of a
constitutional regime in China.   While the Manchu authority
was being overthrown in the Yangtze valley, in Peking the
National Assembly was continuing to force concessions from
the Imperial government so limiting the power of the Throne
as to give the Assembly practical control.   The effect of the
revolution was very marked in the influence it exerted upon
this struggle between the Throne and the National Assembly.

The National Assembly reconvened on October 22, ten days
after the outbreak of hostilities at Wuchang.   Its first act was
to secure the dismissal of Sheng Kungpao, the Minister of
Communications, whose policy of railroad centralization had
aroused such opposition in the provinces as to lead directly to
the revolt of the Szechuanese.[8]   Then it turned its attention
to constitutional questions.

During the latter part of its first session the members of
the Assembly had demanded the establishment of a responsible Cabinet, and had secured the promise of the Emperor to
organize it.   We have seen that this promise was carried out
by a mere change of name, the Grand Council being trans-
formed into a Cabinet, with a responsibility only to the Throne.
Prince Ch'ing, an old and reactionary member of the Imperial

[8] China Year Book, 1912, pp. xx.

family, was made 'the Premier and most of the Cabinet posts were held by Manchu Nobles.[9]   Such a body was far from satisfactory to the Assembly, both in its composition and because it was responsible only to the Emperor.

Emboldened by its success in forcing the dismissal of Sheng Hsuan-hui, and by the compliant attitude of the government, due to conditions in the South, the Assembly immediately made three demands on the Throne.   They were: 1) that a constitution should be framed only after consultation with the Assembly; 2) the exclusion from the Cabinet of members of the Imperial family, and the immediate appointment of a capable and virtuous person to organize a responsible Cabinet; and 3) an immediate amnesty to all political offenders, including those who had been proscribed in 1898.[10] Added weight was given these demands by the refusal of the troops stationed at Lanchou, on the Peking-Mukden railroad, to entrain for the South until the demands had been acceded to.   The action of the troops was supported by their commanding officer.

There was nothing for the Regent to do but yield.   All the demands of the Assembly were conceded in a series of edicts issued on October 30.[11]   The first of these acknowledged the negligence of the Throne, assuming, according to the Chinese custom, the responsibility of the Emperor for the unsettled and weakened condition of the country.   "In Szechuan trouble first occurred, the Wuchang rebellion followed; now alarming reports come from Shensi and Honan.   In Canton (city) and Kiangsi (province) riots appear.   The whole Empire is seething, the minds of the people are perturbed and the spirits of our nine late Emperors are not able properly to enjoy the

[9] See China Mission Year Book, 1912, p. 41.
[10] China Year Book, 1912, pp. xx.
[11] *Ibid.*, pp. xx-xxiii.

sacrifices made to them, while it is feared that the people will suffer grievously.

"All these things are my own fault. Hereby I announce to the world that I swear to reform and with Our soldiers and people to carry out the constitution faithfully, modifying legislation, developing the interests of the people and abolishing their hardships, all in accordance with the interests and wishes of the people. . . . Being a very small person standing at the head of my subjects, I see that my heritage is nearly falling to the ground. I regret my fault and repent greatly. I can only trust that my subjects will support the soldiers in order to support me, to comfort the millions of my people, to hold firmly the eternity of the *D*ynasty, and to convert danger into tranquility. The patriotism of the Empire's subjects will be appreciated and trusted forever."[12]

After this most humble "apologia" the direct demands of the Assembly were discussed. In each of the three cases it was stated that the Assembly was only asking for the faithful observance of principles already well established. For this reason it was possible to give in and yet "save the face" of the Emperor. As to the adoption of the constitution the edict said: "Now as memorialized by the said Yuan (Assembly), constitutional law is a law to be faithfully respected by both sovereign and people, it should be advisable to permit the officials and people to give their advice at the outset before its final adoption. Again it says that their deliberation and advice should be after the conclusion of the framing and before the Imperial sanction. *This will not in the least affect the principle of Imperial sanction as ordered by the former Emperor.*[13] Pu Lun[14] and others are hereby commanded to

[12] China Year Book, 1912, pp. xxi.
[13] The italics are the author's.
[14] A Prince of the Imperial family.

obey the main principle which was Imperially sanctioned, by framing the clauses of the constitutional law speedily, and then handing them to the Tszechengyuan for careful deliberation and discussion, and to wait upon Us to give Imperial sanction before promulgation."[15]

It is apparent that this was far from the idea of the Empress-Dowager. She thought of the constitution as a document promulgated by the Throne and depending for its validity only on the Imperial sanction. In the "Principles of the Constitution," it will be remembered, discussion of the constitution both before and after its promulgation, was a privilege expressly withheld from the Assembly. This was a very different principle from the one now established. The Empress Dowager emphasized the absolute supremacy of the Throne while the Regent was compelled to acknowledge that the Assembly had an equal right with the Throne to a voice in the determination of the principles of the constitution.

The question of the Cabinet was just as fully conceded. The members of the Assembly objected to the personnel of the Cabinet, as well as to the fact that they were not able to assume any control over it under the "regulations" which had been sanctioned by Imperial edict.

The edict of October 30 marks the end of the attempt to maintain old institutions under a new name. "Relatives of Nobles," it runs, "in holding political supremacy, are contrary to the general usage obtaining in all other constitutional countries. The Law of Our Dynasty forbids them to interfere with political affairs. Our ancestral rules are very explicitly worded, they fit well with the spirit of a constitutional nation. After the reign of T'ung Chi(h), national calamity not having ended, prince councillors were first created to support and assist (the government), and the practice has been handed

[15] China Year Book, 1912, p. xxi.

down to the present. During this year, princes, dukes and others have been again appointed Ministers of State upon the formation of the Cabinet. *This was a matter of temporary policy*,[16] and the Throne had not done it intentionally. Now, as memorialized by the said Yuan, a Cabinet of members of the Imperial family cannot exist concurrently with a constitutional form of government. It requests the cancellation of the temporary rules for the Cabinet, the genuine establishment of a complete system for a Cabinet, and the discontinuation of the employing of relatives or Nobles as Ministers of State, etc. These suggestions are made with a view to enhancing the nobleness of the Imperial House, and solidifying the foundation of the Empire, and are much appreciated and approved by Us. As soon as affairs get a little settled, and competent officials are obtainable, We shall order them to form a complete Cabinet, and not again to appoint relatives or Nobles to be Ministers of State, and at the same time, to have the temporary rules for the Cabinet cancelled, in order to conform with the principles of constitutional government and to establish national foundations."[17]

The proclamation of mercy for political offenders was embodied in the fourth of this series of edicts issued on October 30, 1911.

The National Assembly was not slow to take advantage of these concessions. Within three days a new set of principles to be embodied in the constitution had been drawn up and adopted. These principles were immediately submitted to the Throne and received the Imperial sanction on November 3.

While providing for the continued reign of the Manchu Dynasty it was made evident that the Imperial family was no longer to rule. Instead of the constitution being granted by

[16] The italics are the author's.
[17] China Year Book, 1912, p. XXII.

the Emperor, it was to be drawn up and adopted by the Assembly and promulgated by Imperial mandate. Even the right to withhold his assent to the provisions of the Constitution was taken from the Emperor.

Instead of the Parliament being merely an advisory body, the new "principles" gave it a supervisory power over the entire administration. "Parliament shall elect and the Emperor shall appoint the Premier, who will recommend the other members of the Cabinet, these also being appointed by the Emperor. The Imperial Princes shall be ineligible as Premier, Cabinet Ministers or administrative heads of provinces." Then followed the provision for a Cabinet responsible to Parliament: "If the Premier, on being impeached by Parliament, does not dissolve Parliament he must resign, but one Cabinet shall not be allowed to dissolve Parliament more than once."

While the command of the army and navy was vested in the Emperor, "when that power is used with regard to internal affairs he must observe special conditions to be imposed by Parliament." The legislative power was transferred to the Parliament as was the treaty making power. The privilege of discussing the budget, which had been given the Assembly by the "constitutional principles" sanctioned by the Empress-Dowager, was changed into an absolute control over the national finances. And, finally, the Parliament alone was authorized to amend the constitution.[18]

No greater confession of weakness could have been made by the Manchus than their acceptance of this work of the Assembly by which the centre of control was shifted from the Crown to the Parliament. Instead of strengthening their hold on the country and enabling them to retain their old

[18] For a summary of the new "principles" see China Year Book, 1912, pp. XXIII-XXIV.

position of supremacy in the State, the representative institutions which the Manchus had called into being had brought about a complete limitation of their authority. The National Assembly, carefully selected so that it would act at the dictation of the Government, had shown a spirit of insubordination from the time of its convocation in the fall of 1910. It had not been content with the minor position assigned to it, and had bent every effort to secure a recognition of the responsibility of the Government to the duly selected representatives of the nation. It is remarkable that such a spirit should have been manifested by an Assembly consisting of representatives of the Nobility and the official classes, as well as the stubbornly conservative literati, and the gentry of the provinces. It might be said that the liberal element injected from the provincial assemblies was responsible for the attitude of the National Assembly, but this does not account for the practical unanimity of all classes of representatives in their opposition to the government. It would have been interesting to watch the development of a constitutional monarchy out of an Oriental despotism, but the demand of the Southern revolutionists for the abdication of the Emperor ended the possibility of such an evolution. No matter how limited the power of the Throne, the Manchus were no longer acceptable to the country, especially the South.

While the National Assembly was busy wresting concessions from the Throne, the revolutionary movement had been spreading rapidly. The actual military successes of the one side or the other do not furnish any indication of what was happening. The strength of the revolution was measured not by defeats inflicted on the Imperialists, but by defections from the Imperial ranks. Soldiers mutinied and joined the revolutionary forces; districts and whole provinces, one after the other, declared their independence of the Central Government.

The cry of "down with the Manchus" was fast becoming universal. The moderation of the attitude of the government toward the Assembly, and the successes achieved by that body seemed to have no effect in the South. The feeling was that voiced by *Dr.* Wu T'ing-fang, that the Manchus had forfeited the respect of the country, and that they could not be trusted, no matter how conciliatory their attitude. Nothing short of abdication would satisfy the people.

The Regent, however, was not prepared to succumb without a struggle. It was felt in the North that only one man could cope with the situation. This man was Yuan Shih-kai, who had been in retirement since the accession of Hsuan T'ung. The last expressed wish of the late Emperor, Kwang Hsü, is said to have been that Yuan Shih-kai should be killed.[19] He had always been blamed by the Emperor, and rightly, for the overthrow of the reform movement in 1898. The Regent had not dared to carry out his promise to Kwang Hsü to kill Yuan, but he had immediately sent him to the country to "recover" from his activities in the service of the State. The condition of the Empire now made Prince Ch'un, the Regent, feel that the safety of the State demanded the "recovery" of Yuan Shih-kai and his return to active political life. Since the death of the Empress *Dowager* there had been no outstanding personality in the Manchu administration. Men of the strength and ability of the old Viceroys, Tsung Kuo-fan, Tso Tsung-t'ang, Li Hung-chang, and Chang Chih-tung were sorely needed. The only one left was Yuan Shih-kai, and he had been in retirement since January, 1909. With him had gone many of his able lieutenants, foreign educated men of the type of T'ang Shao-yi.[20]

[19] "China under the Empress Dowager," p. 286.
[20] Later Yuan's representative in negotiating with the South, and first Premier of the Republic after the election of Yuan as President.

In response to the generally expressed desire, the Regent issued an edict recalling Yuan to service on October 14, 1911. He was appointed Viceroy of the Hukuang provinces, and given supreme command of the Imperial forces in Hupeh and Hunan, with full power of granting pardons. Yuan Shih-kai, however, did not manifest any great desire to return to office. While he did not refuse to obey the command of the Emperor, he made it perfectly plain that he would come back only on his own terms. His stipulation being for practically a free hand in dealing with the South, his terms were accepted in an edict of October 27, which conferred on him substantially a military dictatorship.[21] He was placed in command of all the Imperial forces, both the army and the navy, and immediately assumed direction of the military operations in the Yangtze valley. On November 8, he was elected Premier by the National Assembly, and returned to Peking to take charge of the almost hopeless affairs of the Dynasty.

As a result of Imperial successes at Hanyang, the head of the Wuchang revolutionary organization, Li Yuan-hung, opened negotiations with Yuan Shih-kai in the last days of November. These negotiations were almost immediately transferred, first to Shanghai and then to Nanking. Out of the resulting conferences between the representatives of Yuan Shih-kai and of the Provisional Republican Government came the settlement by which the Manchu Emperor abdicated and the Republic established itself as the recognized government of China.

Since Li Yuan-hung and the other leaders of the revolution acknowledged the right of the Shanghai Revolutionary Council to speak for them, it is advisable to discuss that organization briefly. It was not until November 3 that Shanghai took

[21] Edicts of October 14 and October 27, 1911. China Year Book, 1912. "The Revolution," p. xxviii.

its stand on the side of the Revolution. On that date control of the city passed into the hands of an organization calling itself "The Military Government of the Chinese People," or as it later styled itself, "The Republican Government of China." Several meetings of the inhabitants of Shanghai were held and Chen Chi-mei was chosen as the military governor of the city. Dr. Wu T'ing-fang acted as the Minister of Foreign Affairs of the Shanghai government. November 13 Chen Chi-mei issued a letter to the newly established Military-Governors of the provinces under the control of the revolution asking them to see that representatives of the provinces were chosen to act as a National Council for the Revolution. The Council met first at Hanyang and later at Nanking where it secured recognition as the Republican Assembly.[22]

It was with the self-styled "Military Government of the Chinese People" that Yuan Shih-kai finally opened discussions. The first move toward peace came from General Li Yuan-hung at Wuchang, and while he did not insist on the negotiations being conducted under his own supervision, he did insist that conferences be held by duly accredited agents of the Revolution with the representatives of the Imperial government. Yuan Shih-kai, anxious to secure a settlement as soon as possible, appointed his old henchman, T'ang Shao-yi, as his representative, with full powers to act for the Imperial government.[23] Dr. Wu T'ing-fang was appointed as the chief representative of the Revolution.

[22] "This Council was composed of delegates from most of the provinces (fourteen in fact), some duly authorized by the respective Provincial Assemblies, and others self-appointed or nominated by some local official of the faction in control of the affairs of the province." China Year Book, 1913, p. 466.

[23] The text of T'ang's credentials read as follows: "I, Yuan Shih-kai, in compliance with the said edict (empowering him to reach a settlement with the South) appoint your Excellency

At the first meeting of the conferees, December 18, 1911, the revolutionary demands were presented to T'ang and transmitted by him to Peking. They were that the Manchu Dynasty abdicate and a Republic be established as the government of China; and they promised liberal treatment for the Imperial family.[24] While negotiations were at a standstill pending the reply of the Emperor, Dr. Sun Yat-sen arrived in Shanghai from Europe where he had been at the outbreak of the revolution. He immediately made himself an important factor in the future negotiations. He arrived on the twenty-fifth of December, and readily consented to become a candidate for the presidency of the Provisional Republican Government which had been formed at Nanking by the representatives of the provinces who had assembled in response to the call of the Military Governor of Shanghai. The Nanking Council elected Dr. Sun President on the twenty-eighth of December.

On the day that Dr. Sun was elected the reply of the Emperor to the demand for abdication was received. Instead of giving a definite yes or no, the edict suggested that the whole question be referred to a legally constituted National Assembly, the Throne agreeing to accept the decision of such a body as final.[25] This concession was a great step towards a basis of settlement, since always before the idea of abdication had been totally repudiated by the Manchu government. The revolutionaries agreed to the proposal, but laid down such conditions as would have made impossible any solution other than abdication. T'ang Shao-yi accepted their terms, but his

(T'ang Shao-yi) as my delegate with full powers, and request you to proceed there (to Shanghai) immediately in accordance with the edict." China Year Book, 1913, p. 467.

[24] *Ibid.*, p. 466.
[25] Edict 28 Dec. Trans., *Ibid.*, p. 467.

action was repudiated by Yuan Shih-kai, and T'ang resigned from his post as Imperial delegate, although he continued to act as the intermediary between Yuan and the Republican leaders.

Yuan Shih-kai's position was a very delicate one throughout the period of these negotiations. He was the head of the Imperial government, with full power to take any steps necessary to bring about a settlement between the North and the South, but he did not have the money or the supplies to force a fight to the finish. The best he could hope for was to secure the retention of the Emperor, stripped of practically all power, as the nominal head of the State. The first conferences showed clearly that the Manchus must go,—that the Republicans would not permit them to retain even the semblance of power. Yuan's task eventually came to this, then: he must use the threat of continued fighting to secure the best terms possible for the Imperial family, and he had to keep the strength of the revolution constantly before the Manchus in order to bring them to the point of abdication when favorable terms had been secured. It was well known that the revolutionary party was even more urgently in need of funds than the Imperialists, so that the desire for peace was as great at Nanking as at Peking. By skilfully playing on the fears and weaknesses first of the one and then of the other side, Yuan Shih-kai was able to secure a settlement which was comparatively satisfactory to both, and which left him as the strongest single factor in the State.

About the middle of January Dr. Sun Yat-Sen, seemingly on his own initiative, telegraphed Yuan offering him the presidency of the Republic after the abdication of the Manchu Dynasty, which was then a foregone conclusion.[26] This was

[26] China Year Book, 1913, pp. 474-76.

on the condition that Yuan would become a Republican and promise to uphold the government established by the Revolution. The acceptance of this proposition in the final settlement might be called the first compromise of the Chinese Republican Constitutionalism. The South did not like Yuan Shih-kai, and, as it later developed, did not trust him. But his position in the North was unassailable, his control of the Imperial army giving him the balance of power in the struggle between the revolutionaries and the Manchus.

The Emperor met this offer by conferring on Yuan the honor of the second order of Nobility, with but one exception, the highest rank possible of attainment for a Chinese. While he had not accepted Dr. Sun's proposal, at least openly, neither did he accept the Manchu distinction. Four times it was offered and four times he declined it![27] There was then no doubt of the final outcome. On January 28 a telegraphic memorial was received in Peking signed by the Hukuang Viceroy and all the Imperial Commanders urging abdication as the only possible solution.[28]

On February 3 the end was heralded in a secret edict which ran as follows: "As we have received the telegraphic memorials from Tsun Chun-hsuan, Yuan Shu-hsun, and Minister to Russia Lu Cheng-hsiang, and others, and Tuan Chi-jui and the other Military Commanders, requesting us speedily to adopt the Republican form of government to avoid further bloodshed, and in view of the perilous situation of the country and the industrial depression from which the people have suffered, We cannot bear to see the millions in misery for the glory of one Family. But the questions of the matters relating to Our Ancestral Temples and the Imperial Masolea are im-

---

[27] Account in the *London Times*. Reproduced, China Year Book, 1913, pp. 477-480.

[28] China Year Book, 1913, pp. 477-480.

portant, and the courteous treatment of the Imperial House and the Imperial kinsmen, the treatment of Manchus, Mongolians, Mohammedans, and Tibetans should be prearranged. We, therefore, give whole powers to Yuan Shih-kai to make the arrangements carefully, and speedily to consult with the People's Army beforehand in regard to the articles of treatment, and to report the whole to Us."[29]

The terms of abdication having been agreed upon, a series of three abdication edicts[30] was issued on February 12, 1912, providing for the transfer of sovereignty from the Emperor to the people, through the establishment of the republican form of government. By so doing the Imperial Family "would gratify on the one hand the desires of the whole nation who, tired of anarchy, are desirous of peace, and on the other hand would follow in the footsteps of the Ancient Sages, who regarded the Throne as the sacred trust of the Nation." No mention was made, in the Abdication Edicts, of the Republican Government at Nanking, headed by Dr. Sun Yat-sen. The responsibility for the organization of China as a Republic was transferred to Yuan Shih-kai as the representative of the Emperor. The edict stated: "Yuan Shih-kai was elected by the Tzucheng-yuan to be the Premier. During this period of the transfer of the government from the old to the new, there should be some means of uniting the South and the North. Let Yuan Shih-kai organize with full powers a provisional republican government and confer with the Republican Army as to methods of union, thus assuring peace to the people and tranquillity to the Empire, and forming the one Great Republic of China by the union as heretofore of the five peoples,

[29] *Ibid.*, p. 481.
[30] *Ibid.*, pp. 481-484.

namely, Manchus, Chinese, Mongols, Mohammedans, and Tibetans together with their territory in its integrity."[31]

The manner in which the Manchu *Dynasty* gave way to the Republic may not seem important so long as the Republic was established. But it is worth noting that the Emperor did not abdicate in favor of the already existing Republican government. He simply gave way to Yuan Shih-kai, who was to establish a Provisional Republican Government himself and then negotiate a settlement with the Army of the Republic in the South. Thus Yuan was continued in control of the situation. It was just as essential to a settlement that an agreement be reached with him as it had been to force the abdication of the Emperor. Furthermore it would seem to the people as though the Republic had been established by the action of the Throne, rather than by the strength of the revolution, if it was organized under the delegated authority of the Emperor. That this was not desirable was recognized by the Nanking government. *Dr.* Sun, in acknowledging the message from Yuan Shih-kai announcing the abdication, said that "the Republican Government cannot be organized by any authority conferred by the Ch'ing Emperor. The exercise of such pretentious power must surely lead to serious trouble." Yuan, however, assured Dr. Sun that he did not intend to take advantage of the wording of the edicts, and the republicans accepted his assurances. Whether he took advantage of his peculiar position or not, unquestionably Yuan Shih-kai was greatly strengthened in the eyes of his countrymen because of the power bestowed upon him by edict, although the Imperial authority had ceased to exist.

The understanding had been that upon the abdication of the Emperor Sun Yat-sen would resign from the presidency in

[31] China Year Book, 1913, p. 482.

favor of Yuan, providing he had first given his unconditional promise of support to the Republic. This Yuan did in announcing the abdication. His statement follows: "A Republic is the best form of government. The whole world admits this. That in one leap we have passed from autocracy to republicanism is really the outcome of the many years of strenuous efforts exerted by you all, and is the greatest blessing to the people. The Ta Ch'ing Emperor has proclaimed his abdication by edict countersigned by myself. The day of the promulgation of this edict shall be the end of Imperial rule and the inauguration of the Republic. Henceforth we shall exert our utmost strength to move forward in progress until we reach perfection. Henceforth, for ever, we shall not allow a monarchical government in our country."[32]

On February 14 *Dr.* Sun submitted his resignation as the provisional President of the Chinese Republic, at the same time presenting the name of Yuan Shih-kai for the consideration of the Assembly. "Today I present to you my resignation and request you to elect a good and talented man as the new President. The election of President is a right of our citizens, and it is not for me to interfere in any way. But according to the telegram which our delegate *Dr.* Wu was directed to send to Peking, I was to undertake to resign in favor of Mr. Yuan when the Emperor abdicated and Mr. Yuan had declared his political views in favor of the Republic. I have already submitted this to your honorable Assembly and obtained your approval. The abdication of the Ch'ing Emperor and the union of the North and South are largely due to the great exertions of Mr. Yuan. Moreover, he has declared his unconditional adhesion to the national cause. Should he be elected to serve the Republic he would

[32] China Year Book, 1913, pp. 485-6.

surely prove himself a most loyal servant of the State.   Besides, Mr. Yuan is a man of political experience, upon whose
constructive ability our united nation looks forward for the
consolidation of its interests.   Therefore, I venture to express
my personal opinion and to invite your honorable Assembly
carefully to consider the future welfare of the State, and not
to miss the opportunity of electing one who is worthy of your
election.   The happiness of our country depends on your
choice.   Farewell."[33]

[33] China Year Book, 1913, pp. 487-88.

CHAPTER VI

The abdication of the Emperor left Yuan Shih-kai in control in the North, with delegated authority to organize the government as a Republic. Sun Yat-sen's resignation and the election of Yuan to the presidency by the Nanking Council consolidated the two governments. Officialdom transferred its allegiance from the old regime to the new. The same local government agencies remained. But the new government was confronted with problems similar to those that have been faced by all authority established as a result of revolution. The revolution had caused the recruiting of large bodies of soldiers. These men were under arms largely because of the pay promised them and not because they wished to see a principle triumph or to bring about a new political order. Their allegiance was not to the Nanking Council or to the Peking government, but to the commander who fed and paid them. What he ordered they would execute if they were confident that their stipend would be forthcoming. In most cases the military leaders themselves were not unselfish servers of a cause. This was more true of the southern soldiery than of the Imperial troops.

At the time of the settlement between the North and the South, districts and even entire provinces were under the control of self-constituted authorities maintaining themselves by force of arms. So long as a commander led a considerable body of men he could exercise a great deal of influence, but let him disband his soldiers and his influence would be negligible. Thus Yuan Shih-kai faced a situation that demanded his immediate and earnest attention. The people expected the new regime to reëstablish peace and order. But many of the provinces were dominated by men over whom the President had only a nominal control, and who, in many cases commanded as large forces as he himself had under his immediate authority. The situation was further complicated by the fact that the pay of the soldiers in many cases was in arrears, and the men refused to disband until they had received a complete settlement. Their commanders had been paying them by requisitions on the people, and by the collection and disbursement of the governmental revenues. Lacking the power to enforce the demobilization of the troops, the Government could get rid of them only by buying off their leaders with substantial sums, and meeting the demand of the common soldiers for their back pay.

Yuan, then, had to consider the question of ways and means of getting this money at a time when the public purse was empty; when the normal sources of revenue could not be depended upon; when the interest on foreign obligations had not been paid for some time; and when the authority of the government was not widely recognized.

Neither had the abdication of the Manchus served to end the general unrest. The presence of armed bands living on the peaceful inhabitants promoted rather than discouraged a feeling of uncertainty. The establishment of a Republic in place of the Empire was not fully understood by the people. To whom did they owe obedience? Formerly they knew that the Emperor and his agents represented authority of no uncertain kind. The Republic, they were told, meant that the people controlled. Many understood from this that they could do as they pleased, and a feeling of freedom from all restraint inevitably resulted.

Furthermore, in many of the provinces the revolution had resulted in a temporary breakdown of the administrative machinery. The officials, where they were not merely self-appointed military chiefs, and where they acknowledged the authority of the government, were awaiting instructions from Peking to guide their action. The uncertainty of the people as to the meaning of the new order had thus communicated itself to the officials.

Republicanism had to justify itself by bringing in its train peace and prosperity as well as the principles of liberty, equality and fraternity. Yuan Shih-kai knew better than any one else, perhaps, what the first demands of the people were of their government—whether Manchu or Chinese, Monarchy or Republic. The machinery of administration must continue to function. His first act after the abdication, therefore, was to provide that there should be no suspension of the routine of government. A proclamation issued on February 13, 1912, emphasized this fact. It read: "Now that the republican form of government has been announced, Yuan Shih-kai has been entrusted with the duty of organizing the provisional government. His ability being limited and his responsibility being great, he is conscious of his incompetency. He is of the opinion that the governmental machinery cannot be suspended for even a single day, and in the course of the organi·zation of the provisional government, all of the political affairs of yore shall continue to be prosecuted as usual. In the present new regime there are hundreds of details to be attended to. Coöperation and mutual assistance are to be depended upon and the maintenance of peace and order and the preservation of the public welfare should be regarded as being of great importance. "Pending the promulgation of the new administrative system, all of the civil and military officials in the Metropolis as well as in the provinces should discharge their respective functions as heretofore, and should not shirk their usual responsibility. All of the affairs to be transacted by the various governmental offices, all of the responsibilities to be assumed, and all of the public funds and public property should be carried on or properly taken care of as before, and no negligence will be tolerated. . . . All of the military and police regulations of the old regime should be enforced as usual; thus may power be unified and order preserved. In the event of anyone making trouble under whatever pretext, to disturb the peace, he is to be dealt with according to law."[1]

The formality of giving Yuan the sanction of the Revolution as the first head of the Republican Government of a united China was accomplished on the fifteenth of February when he was unanimously elected by the Nanking Council. A few days later General Li Yuan-hung was chosen Vice-President. One of the conditions of Yuan Shih-kai's election was that the seat of government should be changed from Peking to Nanking. This transfer would mean a closer control over the government by the South than would be possible if Peking remained the capital city. Since the President was reluctant to leave the North, the stronghold of his power, a deputation was sent to Peking to show him the necessity for the change. A very opportune mutiny of the troops in Peking which was marked by extensive looting occurred at this time, however, and weight was given to Yuan's contention that it was unsafe for him to go South.[2] Consequently the Republican leaders

[1] China Year Book, 1913, pp. 486-87.
[2] Yuan was generally believed to have been chiefly responsible himself for this mutiny. The fact that it was so timed as to strengthen his argument against leaving the North, taken with his previous and subsequent excellent control of the Peking soldiery certainly lends color to the allegation.

were forced temporarily to absolve him from his promise, and his inauguration took place on March 10 in the old capital. The oath of office prescribed was as follows: "At the beginning of the establishment of the Republic there are many matters to be taken charge of. I, Yuan Shih-kai, sincerely wish to exert my utmost (strength) to promote the democratic spirit, to remove the dark blots of despotism, to obey strictly the constitution, and to abide by the wish of the people, so as to place the country in a safe, united, strong and firm position, and to effect the happiness and welfare of the five divisions of the Chinese race. All these wishes I will fulfill without fail. As soon as a President is elected by the National Assembly I shall at once vacate my present position. With all sincerity I take this oath before the people of China."

On the same day that Yuan Shih-kai was inaugurated as President of the Republic, the Provisional Constitution was adopted by the National Council at Nanking. The first section of the constitution vested the sovereignty in the whole body of the people, to be exercised through their representatives—the National Council, the Provisional President, the Cabinet, and the Judiciary. The territory of the Republic was defined (art. 3) so as to include the twenty-two provinces, Inner and Outer Mongolia, Tibet and Chinghai (Kokonor). The second section included a bill of rights of citizens of the Republic. Stipulations of freedom of speech, of the press, and of public meeting, together with provisions for the security of property and freedom of persons from punishment except in accordance with the law were incorporated in this section.

The legislative power of the government was given to the National Council until the convocation of the National Assembly. Then all powers vested in the Council were to be transferred to the Assembly. It was impossible immediately to work out regulations for the election of an Assembly, so that a continuance of the Nanking Council for the time being was necessary. This body, according to the Constitution, was composed of five members from each of the provinces and dependencies, with the exception of Chinghai which was allowed one representative. The method of election was to be determined by each province for itself. Consequently some of the members were chosen by the provincial assemblies, where such bodies were in existence; some were selected by the Military Governors of the provinces; and some were self-constituted representatives of their locality. Those disqualified for membership were: a) men who were under the age of twenty-five; b) men whose rights of citizenship had been removed or temporarily suspended; c) opium smokers; d) employees in the army or navy; e) holders of offices in the executive or judicial departments.[3]

The most notable feature of the Provisional Constitution was its concentration of power in the hands of the National Council at the expense of the executive branch of the government. The aim of the Nanking Council which framed the Constitution, was certainly to limit as extensively as possible the authority of Yuan Shih-kai. He represented the North and they the South. His election as President was a compromise pure and simple, made necessary by his control north of the Yangtze. The easiest solution was to confer on him the dignity of the presidency and then, by constitutional provisions, to strip that high office of all real weight in the Government. In other words the intention was to legislate Yuan Shih-kai out of his control of the situation.

[3] Regulations of Council, sec. 2. See China Year Book, 1913, p. 503.

This was accomplished, on paper, by vesting all legislative power in the Council; giving it a control over the finances of the State and a supervision over the administration; and by the creation of a Cabinet which, while appointed by the President, must be acceptable to the Council. In addition to the legislative authority and a control over the budget and State finances, including taxation, the Council had the constitutional right to impeach the President, if he were guilty of treason, and to impeach any member of the Cabinet "if he be held to have failed to perform his official duties or to have violated the law."[4] It was within the power of the Council to convoke, conduct and adjourn its own meetings, and to decide upon its own procedure.

By article 29, it was provided that "the Provisional President and Vice-President shall be elected by the National Council, by vote of two-thirds of the members present at a sitting of the Council consisting of over three-fourths of the total number of members." The President was given the general supervision over the administration, although the National Council was required to approve all regulations promulgated for the administrative and official system. As the head of the executive branch of the government the President was the "fountain of all executive powers," and all laws were to be promulgated by him as well as orders for the "execution of laws and of powers delegated to him by the law." The supreme command of the army and navy was vested in him, and he had the right to declare a state of siege in case of necessity, and to declare war, with the concurrence of the National Council.

As the representative of the State the President might conclude treaties, again, however, with the concurrence of the

[4] China Year Book, 1913, p. 490.

Council, and he received Ambassadors and Ministers of foreign countries. The power of appointment was conferred on him, with the limitation that he must have the concurrence of the Council in the appointment of the Cabinet, Ambassadors and Ministers. The general pardoning power was placed in the hands of the provisional President, with the restriction that he might not grant a general amnesty without authorization from the National Council. In case of impeachment of the President "he shall be tried by a special Court consisting of nine judges elected among the Justices of the Supreme Court of the realm."

The Cabinet consisted of the Premier and the heads of the government departments. By the law defining the duties and powers of the Cabinet it might consider: 1) law bills and ordinances; 2) budget bills, estimated and executed; 3) expenditure apart from the estimate; 4) organization of the army; 5) treaties; 6) declarations of war and treaties of peace; 7) appointments and removal of officers specially appointed by the President; 8) differences regarding the special powers of the Ministries; 9) matters which according to law should pass through a Cabinet meeting; 10) petitions of citizens which are transmitted by the National Council; 11) matters which the Premier or a Minister of State considers should pass through a Cabinet meeting. A majority vote was to decide all Cabinet discussions. Both the "regulations" and the provisional Constitution provided that all laws and ordinances, before promulgation by the President, must be countersigned either by all the Ministers of State, or by the Premier and the Minister whose department was especially affected by the measure. The Premier was given control over local administration, subject to any limitations imposed upon him by law. The close relationship which should exist between the Council and the Cabinet was recognized as the Council was given the right to make suggestions to the Government, and might question the Ministers, insisting on their appearing in person or by deputy to answer the interpellation. On the other hand, members of the Cabinet had the right to be present and to speak in the National Council.

Section six of the provisional Constitution established a judicial system for the country. All judges were to be appointed by the President and the Minister of Justice. They were to try civil and criminal cases, "but cases involving administrative affairs or arising from other particular causes shall be dealt with according to special laws.'"

This provisional Constitution was to remain in force until after a National Assembly, elected to replace the Council, should have promulgated the permanent Constitution of the Republic. The election regulations for the National Assembly were to be drawn up by the Council and the Assembly convened within ten months from the promulgation of the provisional Constitution on March 10.

It was by no means an easy task that developed on Yuan Shih-kai as President of the Republic. Both the old Imperial Government and the Nanking Revolutionary Government were without financial resources. The collection of taxes had been impossible in many of the provinces since the outbreak of the revolution. Where they had been collected the money had been applied largely to meet local needs. The policy of the Powers during the revolution had been not to lend financial support to either side, and for that reason they had discouraged their nationals from entering into loan agreements. The sympathy of the world had been, unquestionably, with the revolutionary leaders, but, on the other hand, there was a pronounced feeling among foreigners in China that a strong man was essential to the development of a stable government from the revolutionary chaos, and it was doubtful whether such a man would emerge from among the leaders of the republican movement. Yuan Shih-kai was considered the strongest personality in the country, and while he was at the head of the Imperial government, it was felt to be safest to defer judgment as to the future of the Imperial rule.

When, however, Yuan was given the Imperial Commission to establish a Republican government as the President of the Chinese Republic, thus concentrating in the one hands the prerogatives of the crown and the executive powers of the Republican President, the Powers were willing to resume negotiations for a loan to China. The negotiation of this loan, and the reëstablishment of the finances of the State on a sound basis was one of the first tasks to which the new government addressed itself.

At the same time, Yuan Shih-kai had to organize an administration (under the limitations of the provisional Constitution) which would be acceptable to the National Council, and could secure its coöperation in the necessary work of reorganization and reconstruction. This was no slight undertaking, since the Council at Nanking represented the South and was suspicious of every move made by a President whom considerations of expediency had forced it to elect. As the first step in the formation of a Cabinet, the President appointed T'ang Shao-yi as the Premier. T'ang immediately began the formation of a Cabinet, but since his first proposals were not well received at Nanking he left for the South to undertake personal negotiations with the Council. After several days of negotiation Mr. T'ang, supported by Dr. Sun Yat-sen, was able to reach an agreement with the Council, his nominees for Cabinet positions being accepted. The greatest contest came over the appointment of the Ministers of War and of Finance. The southern party insisted that these posts be held by Southerners, while the North, equally aware of their importance, refused to concede them to the South. A compromise was finally reached, and the appointment of Tuan Chi-jui, Presi-dent Yuan's nominee for Minister of War, was confirmed, on the understanding that the post of Resident-General of Nan-king, with control of the armies in the South, should be held by Huang Hsing, a well known revolutionary leader. Hsiung Hsi-ling, the final choice for Minister of Finance, was a Hu-nan man, and had been very active in support of the revolu-tion in his native province. He was not a member of the southern radical party, however, and was not the first choice of the southern delegates,[5] so his selection was essentially a compromise.

The Cabinet as finally constituted was representative of neither the North nor the South. Yuan Shih-kai's aim in choosing this first Cabinet, as well as later ones, was to se-cure the best men possible, irrespective of party, for the heads of departments. It was necessary for his own security that the Minister of War should be in close sympathy with him, since "whoever controls the army controls China." And in view of later developments, his wisdom in insisting on the appointment of Tuan Chi-ju instead of Huang Hsing cannot be questioned. The other Cabinet portfolios were held by men who were either members of the Tung Meng-hui (the radical southern party), or who claimed no party affiliations which would unfit them for coöperation with the National Council.

During his visit to Nanking the Premier, T'ang Shao-yi, became a member of the Tung Meng-hui. As a Cantonese he had more interests in common with that party than with any other. Although he had been the representative of the North in the negotiations preliminary to the abdication of the Man-

[5] Their first choice was Chen Chin-tao.

chus, and had long been a follower of Yuan Shih-kai, T'ang had shown an interest in the revolutionary movement even while acting as the Imperial representative at Shanghai and Nanking. A Cantonese, dealing with the Cantonese leaders of the republican movement, *Dr.* Sun Yat-sen and *Dr.* Wu T'ing-fang, he was more inclined to compromise with them than to act as the out and out advocate of the Manchu Dynasty, or even the conservatively progressive party of the North. It may be that in affiliating himself with the Tung Meng-hui he sought to secure a greater influence in the government than he could hope for as the recognized henchman of the President. Whatever his reasons, T'ang's adherence to the radical southern party, of which he rapidly became the leader, made coöperation between the President and his Prime Minister difficult, and finally led to their estrangement.

Before passing on to the problems confronting the new regime it is worth our while to note the composition of the National Council when it assembled in Peking for its first session under the provisional Constitution. It will be remembered that the original intention of the Nanking republicans had been to make Nanking the capital city. But since it was impossible to get Yuan Shih-kai out of the northern capital it was necessary for the Council to move from Nanking to Peking. It was hardly possible to conduct the affairs of government with the President and Cabinet several hundred miles away from the legislative organ. On April 29, then, the National Council was formally opened by the President, in Peking. At that time there were three principal parties in the Council, no one group strong enough by itself to control. The Tung Meng Hui (the Alliance Party) and the Kung Ho-t'ang or Conservative party were nearly equal in voting strength, so that the balance of power lay with the third party

mentioned, the Tung-yi-kung-ho-tang (the Coalition party).[6]
This coalition party was more closely allied to the Tung Meng
Hui than to the Conservatives, but exercised entire freedom
of action, sometimes voting with the one and sometimes the
other.[7] Because of this division in the Council it was possible
for its deliberations to be brought to an end by the lack of a
quorum whenever the members of any one of the parties chose
to absent themselves from the meetings.

Naturally the chief interest of the early part of 1912 centered on the attempts the government was making to secure
funds for the reorganization of the country. The provisional
Constitution provided that the Council should control all of
the financial affairs of the State, including measures for negotiating loans.[8] Before the Council had assembled in Peking,
however, the first steps had been taken to negotiate a loan
with the Four Power Group.[9] The government desired to secure monthly advances to meet its immediate needs, estimating
that 10,000,000 taels would be required at once, and monthly
advances of Tls. 6,400,000 would be necessary during the reconstruction period. On February 28 the Hongkong and
Shanghai Bank, acting for the Four Power syndicate, made
an advance of Tls. 2,000,000, and on March 7 a further advance of Tls. 1,100,000 was made to the government. In
consideration of these advances Yuan Shih-kai agreed: "That
the Banks hold a firm option for the provision of further

[6] China Year Book, 1913, pp. 504-505, shows the party division of the members of the Council.
[7] Some of the members of the Tung-yi-kung-ho-tang were also
members of the Tung Meng Hui, and vice versa. For the organization of the parties see China Year Book, 1913, pp. 662-670.
[8] Provisional Constitution, Art. 19, clauses 2-3-4.
[9] The original members of the International Loan Group were
representatives of Great Britain, France, Germany, and the
United States.

monthly requirements of the Chinese Government for the months of March, April, May, June, and possibly July and August, which the Four Groups have already been requested to finance, against the delivery of additional sterling Treasury Bills on terms to be arranged. (4) That in consideration of the assistance rendered by the Groups to China in the present emergency, and of their services in supporting her credit on the foreign markets, the Chinese Government assures to the Groups (provided their terms are equally advantageous with those otherwise obtainable) the firm option of undertaking the comprehensive loan for general reorganization purposes already proposed to them, to be floated as soon as possible, and to be applied in the first instance to the redemption of the sterling Treasury Bills aforesaid."[10]

In spite of this undertaking, a loan agreement with an Anglo-Belgian syndicate was signed by the President on March 15, six days after he had written the above to the representatives of the Four Power Group. When this became known, the Four Power Group immediately suspended negotiations with the Chinese Government, charging it with acting in bad faith.

Immediately after the conclusion of this so-called Belgian loan agreement, T'ang Shao-yi, who had been conducting all loan negotiations, left for Nanking. While there he was able to secure the consent of the Council to the Belgian loan, taking occasion at the same time to address it on the subject of the dangers of a foreign financial monopoly in China. In this way he sought to arouse a hostility to the Four Power Group which could be used to secure a moderation of the terms on which it was willing to undertake the financing of the Government.

[10] China Year Book, 1913, pp. 349-50.

When he returned to Peking a month later he found that in order to get the large sum necessary for immediate expenses he would have to resume negotiations with the Groups. Since they would consider further advances only if the Belgian agreement was cancelled, the Premier definitely undertook to cancel it, except in so far as the advances already made were concerned. With this understanding negotiations were resumed on May 3. The rock on which they finally split was the question of foreign supervision of the moneys advanced, and of the securities given.

Because of the demand of the foreign bankers for supervisory rights, the National Council took occasion to criticise the entire loan policy of the Government. This critical attitude was natural since the Council was determined to assert its supremacy and could not do so if such important negotiations as those with the Four Power Group (extended by May to include Japan and Russia, and from that time known as the Six Power Group)[11] were conducted independent of its supervision. The criticism of the Council came at a time when the breach between the Premier and the President was constantly widening. As Premier, T'ang Shao-yi felt that he should have a greater control over the policy of the Government than Yuan Shih-kai was willing to give him. Yuan had the old Manchu idea of a Cabinet which should carry out the policy dictated by the head of the Executive, in this case the President. T'ang on the other hand, was determined that the Cabinet should be the real executive, assuming the responsi-

[11] Neither Japan nor Russia were lending nations nor were they in a position then to absorb their shares of the loans, but for political and international reasons it was considered advisable to admit them to the consortium.

bility for the administration.[12]   As a member of the party which had as its chief aim the limitation of the power of the President, and with his desire to assert himself, it was impossible for him to act long in coöperation with the President.

On June 15 T'ang Shao-yi suddenly left Peking for Tientsin, absolutely refusing to continue in office.   The reasons he gave for his action were: 1) the President's refusal to carry out his (the Premier's) undertaking to appoint Mr. Wang Chih-hsiang as Tutuh of Chihli province; and 2) a disagreement with the President in regard to the action of General Chang Hsun in continuing to occupy a position upon the Tientsin-Pukow Railway.[13]

That T'ang was determined to force recognition of the principle of party government was evidenced by the action of the other Tung Meng Hui members of the Cabinet.   They resigned with the Premier and in spite of Yuan Shih-kai's plea for harmony refused to reconsider their resignations.   The attitude of the Tung Meng Hui was that the Cabinet Ministers must either be members of one party or of none.   In spite of the action of the Tung Meng Hui Ministers, however, the President insisted that the time had not yet come for the introduction of Cabinet or party government.

The first requisite of party government is the presence in the Assembly of one party which has an absolute majority,

[12] The provisional Constitution provided that every act of the President must receive the sanction of a member of the Cabinet. That is, every measure must be countersigned by a Cabinet Minister.   Thus it was intended by the framers of the Constitution that the real executive power should be vested in the Cabinet, the President being simply a figurehead.

[13] General Chang Hsun was the Imperialist Commander at Nanking, and after his defeat and retreat he occupied various positions upon the Tientsin-Pukow line, where he retained and even augmented his forces.   The Premier demanded the disbandment of these troops, to which the President refused to agree.

and of an opposition so organized as to be capable of assuming control of the government when the existing majority is overthrown.   In July 1912, when a one party Cabinet was demanded, there were three groups in the Council none of them with a controlling vote.   Each of the parties was made up of several smaller groups united only by the exigencies of the moment.   A Tung Meng Hui Cabinet could endure only so long as it was supported by a majority of the votes of the third party which held the balance of power between it and the Kung Ho Tang.   The same would have been true of a Kung Ho Tang Cabinet.   It would have been equally impossible to construct a Ministry from the membership of this third party (the Tung Yi Kung Ho Tang).   Until there was a regrouping of the membership of the Council under the standards of two parties, one of which controlled the Assembly, President Yuan was quite right in insisting on a Cabinet of the ablest men in the country rather than one representative of party.

Determined not to recognize the principle of party government, Yuan Shih-kai attempted to form another coalition Cabinet.   His choice for Premier was Lu Cheng-hsiang, a non-party man who had been filling the position of Minister for Foreign Affairs.   Mr. Lu's nomination was confirmed by the Council without much hesitation.   The other Ministries to be filled were Finance, Justice, Education, Agriculture and Forestry, Commerce and Industry, and Communications.   To fill these vacancies the President nominated two members of the Tung Meng Hui, two Kung Ho Tang men, and two non-party men.   All of the nominees were rejected by the Council after a heated debate in which the Premier took part.   The Tung Heng Hui members voted against them because of their insistence on a party Cabinet, and the Tung Yi Kung Ho

Tang members for the opposite reason, i.e., because they were given no representation.

This action of the Council in obstructing the work of forming a Cabinet caused a considerable agitation against the Council itself, especially on the part of the Military. The apparent deadlock that had been reached was broken, however, when the Council accepted all but one of the next set of nominees sent to them by the President. The one rejected was a member of the Tung Meng Hui, the only one nominated for a Cabinet position. Two of the others were members of the Kung Ho T'ang.

From the time of this first Cabinet crisis the partizan activity of the Tung Meng Hui tended to discredit it more and more in the eyes of the country, which wanted above all things peace and harmony. After the Council had finally agreed upon a Cabinet from which members of the Tung Meng Hui were excluded, that party began to look to the future, and to lay its plans ultimately to control the government. With this in view steps were taken to amalgamate with several of the smaller factions. A union of four other groups with the Tung Meng Hui was finally effected (August 13), the name chosen by the new party being the Kuo Ming Tang. The objects of the Kuo Ming Tang were stated to be: "1) to protect and uphold a strong and united Government, and to organize a system of centralization so that all constructive measures will be systematized and coördinated. 2) To promote and support local government, and to develop in our people such powers of self-government as are necessary for a Republic, so as to be able to mend the deficiencies of the Central Government. 3) To carry out effectively all measures to unite the different races in China, and to practice real equality and civilization so that our people will soon be united and strong. 4) To adopt the principles of social service, to prepare the way for the introduction of socialism in order to facilitate and better the standard of living, and to employ the powers and strength of the Government quickly and evenly to develop the resources of our country. 5) To cultivate friendly feelings with foreign nations, and to use our wisdom in, and show our due respect for, our diplomacy with them, so as to be able to hold the balance of power and to devote a good part of attention to our self-improvement."[14]

This programme, although very vague in most particulars, embodied many good principles, notably the determination to effect the centralization of the government. But the basic doctrine of the Kuo Ming Tang was not stated in their programme—i.e., the determination to subordinate everything to the attainment of a controlling power over the government. Their tactics were obstructive rather than constructive, and did more to prepare the way for the attempted overthrow of the Republic than to secure the acceptance of the principle of party government.

The antagonism between the Government and the Council during July and August was increased by the seizure and execution of two prominent revolutionaries. They were accused of participation in a plot against the government, the accusation being made by the Vice-President, Li Yuan-hung, then acting Viceroy of Hupeh province. Great criticism was aroused over the way in which the seizure and execution took place. Both men were seized at night and shot in the morning after a hurried trial by a Military Court. When the Council demanded proofs of their guilt and questioned the right of the Government to act in such an arbitrary manner, the President refused any explanation on the ground that it was inexpedient to present the proofs of their guilt at that time, although later

[14] China Year Book, 1913, p. 670. For the best discussion of political parties in China see Hornbeck, Ch. V, Political Parties.

it was stated that General Li had made ten specific charges against the accused. The President's attitude was not considered satisfactory and the Council threatened to impeach the government. The effectiveness of the impeachment power given the National Council, however, was greatly lessened because, on the threat of impeachment proceedings, the supporters of the government always absented themselves from the Assembly, thereby preventing further action because of the lack of a quorum.[15]

Just when affairs were reaching a crisis, Dr. Sun Yat-sen visited the capital in response to an oft-extended invitation of President Yuan. His visit did much to clear up the situation, since he came out definitely in support of the President, criticising the actions of the party of which he was one of the leaders, the Kuo Ming Tang. Dr. Sun's visit was followed by the arrival of Huang Hsing and Mr. Chen Chi-mei, and the understanding apparently reached between Yuan Shih-kai and these leaders of the radical party paved the way for a better coöperation between the Government and the Council.

During the time of the Cabinet crisis due to the resignation of T'ang Shao-yi negotiations had been conducted intermittently with the Six Power Group. Several advances were made to the Government during May and June, but the conclusion of the comprehensive loan seemed to be blocked by the disagreement over supervision. In his endeavor to get money, and at the same time to satisfy the demand that no supervisory rights should be granted foreigners, the Minister of Finance was finally forced to conclude a loan outside the Groups. This loan, known as the Crisp loan, was for ten million pounds. But the Groups were too powerful, and they were successful, because of the support of the six governments concerned, in

[15] An attempt had been made to impeach the Premier, Lu Cheng-hsiang, on July 29, but it had failed for lack of a quorum.

forcing the cancellation of the Crisp Loan Agreement, and eventually Mr. Crisp agreed to the cancellation of the flotation of the second half of the loan, in return for a compensation of £150,000. Unable to secure money outside of the Six Power Group in large amounts, the Chinese Government was finally forced to agree to the terms of those Bankers. These were announced to be: 1) That the purposes for which the funds were required should be stated by the Chinese Government to the approved Groups; 2) That China should adopt a system of audit which would ensure the effective expenditure of the loan funds for the purposes specified; 3) that the Salt taxes should be hypothecated for the service of this loan, and should be administered either by the existing Chinese Maritime Customs organization, or by a separate service, similar to the Customs, under foreign direction, thus safeguarding the proper administration of the security, despite the possible continuance or recurrence of the unsettled conditions in China.[16]

On December 27 the proposed loan contract was submitted to the National Council and accepted by it. Before the actual signature of the contract, however, disagreement arose among the Groups as to the distribution of the posts that were created under the Agreement, such as the directorship of the Salt Gabelle, and the head of the Audit Bureau.[17] By the time this had been satisfactorily adjusted, and some smaller disagreements with the Chinese government smoothed over, it was April of 1913. On April 8, the New National Assembly met for the first time, and the Kuo Ming Tang members of the Assembly protested against the conclusion of the loan before it had been passed upon by the Assembly. The government, however, disregarded their protest on the ground that the

[16] China Year Book, 1913, p. 357.
[17] China Year Book, 1914, pp. 381-384 for discussion of this disagreement and the final settlement reached.

loan had been sanctioned by the old National Council. The Bankers making up the Group took the position that they were dealing only with the government, and could not recognize any parliamentary protest unless it was brought to their attention through the Chief Executive. The contract was finally signed on the 26th of April 1913.

There has been a good deal of controversy over the policy of the Powers concerned in supporting certain Groups of their nationals in their attempt to finance the Chinese Government. It has been alleged that, because of this government support. the Group imposed unduly harsh terms on the Chinese, and made unnecessary stipulations infringing on the sovereignty and limiting the independence of the Republic in her internal affairs. We are not concerned with the rights and wrongs of the question, but only with the influence of this loan on constitutional development in China. Unquestionably in the light of the experience of several South American Republics, it was far better for China that responsible concerns should undertake the financing of her government, and that the borrowing should be done by the central authority. Only through some such union as was effected by the Powers interested could the large sums so urgently needed by the Chinese Republic have been secured. If the Group had not insisted on a virtual financial monopoly in return for the flotation of the big Reorganization loan, the resources of the different provinces would have been hypothecated in order to secure funds for local needs,[18] and such a financial disorganization would have resulted that not only the central government but the provinces as well would have gone eventually into bankruptcy. As it has turned out, the reorganization of the Salt Gabelle under foreign supervision has taken care of the loans for which

[18] This was actually happening during the negotiations, provincial loans being made through concerns like the Krupps.

the Salt Revenues have been pledged, and in spite of the continned disturbances in China, has always provided a surplus which has been held in safety at the disposal of the government. This surplus has been not unwelcome certainly to the party gaining the upper hand after one of the periodical outbursts which have marked the recent history of China.

On the other hand it was only the conclusion of this loan that so strengthened the hand of the President that he was able to make himself virtually dictator, and finally to embark on the fatal attempt at restoration of the monarchy. His position was considered so strong by the foreign Powers that they were willing to conclude this loan agreement with him in spite of the announced opposition of the radical party which controlled the first Assembly elected under the laws promulgated by the National Council.

The National Assembly which met in April of 1913 was elected under the laws promulgated by the National Council in August of 1912. The provisional Constitution stipulated that a National Assembly should be summoned within ten months of the adoption of the Constitution, and the Assembly actually met within three months of the scheduled time. Since the provisional Constitution did not provide for the organization of the Assembly, only stipulating that there should be a duly elected Assembly to replace the Council, the latter body undertook the organization of the Assembly as well as passing the laws governing elections.

The "Rules for Organization" promulgated on August 10, 1912, provided that the National Assembly should consist of two Chambers, the Ts'an Yi Yuan (Senate) and the Cheng Yi Yuan (House of Representatives). The members of the Senate were to be chosen by indirect election as follows: 1) Ten representatives to be elected by the Provincial assembly of each province; 2) twenty-seven elected by the Electoral College of Mongolia; 3) ten representatives elected by the Electoral College of Tibet; 4) three elected by the Electoral College of Chinghai; 5) eight members selected by the Central Educational Society; 6) six representatives elected by the Electoral College of Chinese resident abroad.

The House of Representatives was to consist of members chosen directly by the people. Each 800,000 of the population was to have one representative, every province, however, having at least ten even where the provincial population fell below 8,000,000.[19] Mongolia, Tibet and Chinghai were entitled to the same number of representatives as Senators.

The term of office was placed at six years for Senators, one third of the body being elected every two years. Members of the House were to be elected for three years, the whole House being renewed at the same time. The powers and duties of the National Council were transferred to the National Assembly, each Chamber acting separately, the decision of the Assembly being by the concurrence of both Chambers.

Each Chamber, independent of the other, was given the right: 1) to institute a debate; 2) to question the government; 3) to demand investigation of charges of bribery or violation of the law made against officials; 4) to reply to inquiries from the government; 5) to receive petitions from the people; 6) to permit the arrest of its members; and 7) to adopt regulations and rules of procedure.

[19] For the first Assembly the distribution of representatives was:

Chihli 46	Honan 32	Fengtien 16	Shansi 28
Kirin 10	Shensi 21	Heilungkiang 10	Kansu 14
Kiangsu 40	Sinkiang 10	Anhui 27	Szechuan 35
Kiangsi 35	Kuangtung 30	Chekiang 38	Kuangsi 19
Fukien 24	Yunnan 22	Hupeh 26	
Hunan 27	Mongolia 27	Shantung 33	
Kuei Chow 13	Tibet 10	Chinghai 3	

The estimates and accounts of the Government were to be discussed in the House of Representatives before being presented to the Senate. In addition to the general powers given it, the National Assembly was charged with the task of drafting the permanent constitution for the Republic. The actual drafting was to be done by a committee composed of an equal number of members from each Chamber, and the constitution was to be passed upon and adopted by the Chambers in joint session. For such joint meetings a quorum of two-thirds of the total number of members of the Assembly was required before any business could be undertaken, and all decisions were to be by a three-fourths majority of the members present.

The Senate was to be representative of the provinces and the dependencies rather than directly of the people. The qualifications for election to the Senate and the House were the same, except that the age limit was placed at thirty years for Senators instead of twenty-five. Any Chinese male citizen thirty years of age was eligible to election as a Senator subject to the usual disqualifications: illiteracy, opium smoking, insolvency, and deprivation of civil rights. Service in the army or police, the holding of executive, judicial or administrative office, or service in a monastic order constituted a disqualification for serving either as an elector or as a member of the Assembly.[20]

The members of the Senate, as has been noted, were to be chosen by the provincial Assemblies in China proper, and by Electoral Colleges in the Dependencies, and where special classes were given representation as in the representation of the Chinese resident abroad. A candidate had to secure one third of the total number of votes cast in order to be elected.

[20] The disqualification attendent on office holding or membership in a monastic or religious order did not apply to Mongolia or Tibet.

If the first ballot did not result in an election of the entire number to be chosen, balloting was to continue until the full number had been selected. In addition to the selection of members of the Senate, the electors were required to choose an equal number of reserve candidates in order to fill any vacancies that might exist through resignation or otherwise. The provincial Assemblies might select half of the number of Senators for their province from their own membership.

Mongolia and Chinghai were divided into electoral districts, each entitled to choose a certain number of members of the Senate. The electors making up the Electoral Colleges were Nobles and Princes. Tibet was similarly divided into two districts, each entitled to return five members, the membership of the Electoral Colleges to be appointed by the Delai Lama and the Tashi Lama, acting in coöperation with the Chinese Resident in Tibet. The Central Educational Society, which was entitled to choose eight members was composed of the Minister and Vice-Minister of Education; a representative of each of the Ministries; one from the authorities of each province, Mongolia, and Tibet; one from each high institution under the direct control of the Ministry of Education; one from each National Library; one from each National Museum; two from the State schools in each province, Mongolia, and Tibet; one representing the Chinese residents of America, one of Japan, and two of the Straits Settlements; and twenty noted educators at the invitation of the Minister of Education.[21] Although the electors did, the candidates for election

---

[21] China Year Book, 1913, p. 386. This was the recommendation of the National Educational Conference, which met during 1912, as to the organization of the Central Educational Society. The law on the Central Educational Society was promulgated on the 29th of the 11th month of the first year of the Republic. See China Year Book, 1914, p. 502.

as representatives of the Central Education Association did not have to be members of the Association.

The Electoral College organized to choose the representatives in the Senate of the Chinese resident abroad consisted of one member appointed by each Chamber of Commerce formed in their places of residence by Chinese residing abroad. These Chambers of Commerce, however, must have secured the recognition of the Chinese Government. The representatives of overseas Chinese were required to have a knowledge of the Chinese language in addition to their other qualifications.

While the Senate was to be elected by a system of Electoral Colleges, the "Regulations" provided that the members of the House of Representatives should be chosen by the people. The plan adopted, however, resulted in an indirect election just as much as in the choice of Senators. There were two stages to the election. The first, in which all qualified electors took part, was called the primary election. Until a regrouping of administrative districts was made, the Hsien[22] were to constitute the electoral districts for primary elections, several Hsien being joined together to make up the final electoral district, of which there were several to each province. At the primary election fifty times the number of representatives to which the district was entitled were chosen. These constituted the electors in the final election.[23] So that, in fact, the

---

[22] For purposes of election hsien districts were places under the direct jurisdiction of Fu, Chihli-t'ing, and Chow; T'ing and chow. See Election Laws Ch. I Clause 10 China Year Book, 1913, p. 412.

[23] See appended table for illustrative case.

Kiangsu Province was alloted 40 Representatives.

Suppose—The province to be divided into eight final electoral districts and each final electoral district to be divided into 8 primary electoral districts.

On estimate of one per cent of population voting the province would have 230,000 qualified electors. (Approx. customs

members of the House of Representatives were chosen by an Electoral College of fifty times the membership of the House.

In the primary elections "any Chinese male citizen of twenty-one years or upwards, who at the time the list of electors is made up has resided in the electoral district for two years or more, and possesses one of the following qualifications, shall be eligible to vote for members of the House of Representatives: a) payment of a direct tax of $2.00 per annum or upwards; b) possession of immovable property of a value of $500.00 or upwards (except in the case of Mongolia, Chinghai and Tibet, where the possession of movable property of this value shall be sufficient to qualify as an elector) ; c) a graduate of an elementary or higher school; d) possession of an education equivalent to clause (c)."[23]

The Chief Controller of Elections was to be the highest ad-

estimate of population 1910, 23,980,000.)   230,000 ÷ 40 = 5750 electors to each representative.

Each electoral final district would contain 230,000 ÷ 8 = 28,750 electors.   28,750 ÷ 5750 (no. of electors to each Representative) = 5 representatives to be elected in each final electoral district.

There would be, therefore, 115 electors to each candidate in primary electoral district

3593.75 = number of electors in each primary district

3593.75 ÷ 115 = 31.25 candidates to be elected in each primary district.

31.25 × 8 (primary districts) = 250 candidates (making up electorate in final electoral district) × 8 (final electoral districts = 2000 candidates or electors who would have the selection of the 40 representatives for Kiangsu province.

NOTE—One per cent is generally accepted as a high estimate of the percentage of the population qualified and interested to vote. The figures throughout represent the author's calculations rather than published statistics.

[23] China Year Book, 1913, p. 411.

ministrative officer[24] of the province. He was to appoint the Controller for each final electoral district in his jurisdiction. The chief administrative officer of each primary district was to act as Controller in the primary elections. The Controller was to supervise the elections, pass judgment on the qualifications of voters, and take charge of all other matters connected with the election, such as preparing the ballot cards, and registration lists, appointing officials to take charge of the polls, prepare the list of successful candidates, etc.

It was necessary for a candidate to obtain "a number of votes equal to one-third of the sum produced by the division of the number of candidates to be elected in the district into the number of votes cast,"[25] in order to be elected at the primary election. In the final election the successful candidate needed to obtain a number of votes equal to one-half the sum produced by a similar division.

The first National Assembly elected under the provisions of the laws and regulations just discussed was controlled by the Kuo Ming Tang in both Chambers. That party had returned more than twice as many members as any other single party, and almost as many as all the others combined. It might be expected, then, that from the opening of the Assembly in

[24] In response to the question who the chief administrative officer was, the National Council decided that "in any province where, in addition to the Military Governor, a Civil Administrator has been specially appointed, such administrator shall be regarded as the 'Chief Administrative Authority' referred to in the Electoral Laws, but that in any province where no Civil Administrator has been appointed, and where there is only a head of the department of civil affairs, subordinate to the Military Governor, it is necessary to regard the Military Governor as the 'Chief Administrative Authority' referred to in the Electoral Laws." Pres. Mandate; Sept. 10. China Year Book, 1913, p. 423.

[25] China Year Book, 1913, pp. 416-17.

April 1913, the movement toward party government would continually grow in strength. As a matter of fact, however, the activity of the Kuo Ming Tang during 1913 brought about its overthrow, and made possible the establishment of autocratic government.

The aim of the revolutionary leaders had been to impose a parliamentary regime on the country in place of the Manchu rule, and the movement toward this end reached its height in the election of a radical Assembly. During the next year the influence of the 1911 revolutionists gradually declined, partly because of their own actions and partly because their activity was limited by the drastic measures taken against them by the government. The history of the next few years in China is marked by reversion to the old order of things, the return to the governmental conditions of the past under the influence of the idea that only through "strong man" rule could China hope to endure as a nation.

CHAPTER VII

The old Empress *D*owager, Tzu Hsi, had announced that the introduction of constitutional government would bring to an end all of the troubles of the State. The Manchus had tried it, and it had failed to save them, or to bring more settled conditions in the country. This was not held to discredit constitutionalism, however, for the failure was attributed to the insincerity of the Manchus and to the fact that they were aliens in China. The need of an effective and honest government under constitutional limitations was one of the arguments advanced by the revolutionists for the overthrow of the *D*ynasty. The revolution resulted in an unexpected change in the form of the government as well as the establishment of representative institutions, and under this new form constitutional government had been tried for a year without bringing the greater political strength and stability to the country that had been expected.

That government under the Nanking constitution had not materially bettered conditions was admitted by everyone, but the radical party claimed that this was due partly to the lack of a truly representative Assembly, in which, of course, it would have the controlling interest, and in part to the opposition of the President to the introduction of party government, concentrating the executive power in the hands of a Cabinet representative of and controlled by the majority party in the Assembly. The followers of Yuan Shih-kai and the conservative elements in the country, on the other hand, held that the failure of representative government in China was to be explained by the attempt to subordinate the executive to the legislative branch of the government. The point at issue was clear then. Should the Assembly continue to be the dominant branch of the government through a control of the executive, or should the Assembly be limited to criticism and the giving of advice, the power of interfering in the administration being withdrawn from it?

The National Assembly elected in 1913 was more nearly controlled by the Kuo Ming Tang, or radical party than by any other single organization,[1] and it might be said that the electorate had given its decision in favor of parliamentary government.[2] Naturally the Kuo Ming Tang members assembled in Peking in a jubilant frame of mind, prepared to resist every increased assumption of power by the President. This determination was strengthened by indications that the President did not intend to give up the struggle against parliamentary dominance.

Two months before the meeting of the Assembly the attempt was made partially to remove the work of framing the permanent constitution from the legislative branch of the government. Upon the receipt of a memorial submitted by many of the Tutuhs, the National Council was asked to pass a bill establishing a committee for the drafting of the constitution. This committee was to consist of eight representatives of the National Assembly, (or the Council if the Assembly had not yet been convened), six appointees of the Cabinet, two representatives of the Tutuh of each province, and one representa-

[1] "It had almost as many seats as all the other parties combined," says Millard. "Our Eastern Question," p. 63.

[2] The electorate of course must be understood as including only a very small proportion of the total population, in pre-republic China. Millard says only about 10,000 people (1/35 of 1 per cent) took part in the elections held and it is doubtful if many more participated in this election. See Millard, "Our Eastern Question," p. 54.

tive appointed by each of the provincial assemblies. The bill was rejected by the Council without even the formality of a discussion. But the proposal certainly indicated a desire on the part of the President to have some share in making the permanent constitution.

The next month (March) was marked by the murder of the leader of the Kuo Ming Tang, Sung Chiao-jen. The publications controlled by his party charged the government with the instigation of the assassination. It was said that Yuan hoped in that way to intimidate the party. While the responsibility for the murder has never been definitely placed, there is good ground for belief that the government was not entirely free from blame. Later developments would seem to place it as the first of a series of similar assassinations designed to remove the leaders of the opposition to the President. Whatever the truth of the charges made against the government by the Kuo Ming Tang leaders, this murder was not calculated to make more harmonious the relations between the Assembly and the presidential office.

In addition to the murder of Sung Chiao-jen and the attempted interference of the executive in the framing of the permanent constitution, the Kuo Ming Tang had a third specific grievance against the government—the definitive conclusion of the quintuple loan agreement before the Assembly had passed upon it. The hostility of the National Assembly to the President was manifested from the time of its convocation. The Kuo Ming Tang members let the President know that if he appeared in person formally to open the legislative body he would not be received in his capacity of provisional President, but could only appear as a private citizen! The presidential message, consequently, was transmitted through his secretary, but he in turn was denied permission to read it in person, being only allowed to present it.

The early sessions of both Chambers were taken up with the work of organization, election of officers, etc. Time was found, nevertheless, to call the government to account for the conclusion of the loan. Many of the sessions of the Assembly were marked by great disorder, the lack of internal harmony being clearly revealed. Instead of consolidating their position under the Constitution by a constructive attitude toward the problems of the day, the members of the Assembly limited their activity to the work of obstruction. While demanding the subordination of the President and Cabinet to the legislature, they failed to convince thoughtful people of their ability to carry on the administrative work that would have devolved upon them. If, during 1913, the National Assembly had attempted to supplant Yuan Shih-kai by demonstrating the fitness of an Assembly to exercise the large powers entrusted to that branch of the government by the Nanking Constitution; it might, conceivably, have been successful. But by blocking the work of administration by obstructive tactics, hindering all attempts at reconstruction and reorganization undertaken by the President whether good or bad, the National Assembly gave Yuan Shih-kai a reasonably good excuse for his subsequent attempt to overthrow parliamentary government.[3]

While the Assembly was occupied with its own quarrels. and with its criticism of the policy of the executive, Yuan Shih-kai was calmly proceeding to strengthen his position throughout the country. In pursuance of this end he began to replace the men in the provincial administrations who were hostile to him with his own friends. The President had the constitutional right to appoint and dismiss from office, so that

[3] This attitude caused the people to think of President Yuan as one who was trying to do something for the betterment of the country, while the Parliament wanted to prevent anything being done of a constructive nature.

nominally no exception could be taken to his action.   This was especially true of the first important change that he made. So far as the new provincial system had been worked out provision was made for a head of the Civil Administration who should be eventually the highest provincial official; and for a Military Governor or Tutuh.   In 1913 most of the provinces were controlled by the Tutuhs.   The Tutuh of Kiangsi province was a member of the Kuo Ming party, so that early in 1913 Yuan appointed a Chief Civil Administrator to relieve him of part of the administrative work.   The Tutuh, Li Lieh-chun, resented this limitation of his authority and prepared to resist the change by force.   On the surface the President was absolutely in the right in beginning to build up a civil administration by doing away with the military rule in the country.   But exception could be and was taken to his use of his constitutional powers to eliminate his strongest opponents in this way, while maintaining in office the Military Governors who were friendly to him.

No active steps were taken to make Li Lieh-chun recognize the authority of the Civil Administrator until June when he was ordered to vacate his post and come to Peking for reappointment.   Li gave up his office, but proceeded to Shanghai, and not to Peking.   The Vice-President, Li Yuan-hung, was then appointed acting Tutuh of Kiangsi in addition to the other posts which he held.   In July two other Kuo Ming Tang Tutuhs (in Anhui and Kuangtung provinces) were removed from office.

In justice to the President it can be said that not only was he strengthening himself by removing those hostile to him from control in the provinces, but that he was gradually restoring peace and order, and thus prosperity, to the country. Policies were being formulated and put into effect by which the troops were being gradually disbanded and returned to normal peaceful pursuits. Taxes were being collected again by official agents and paid into the national treasury, instead of being used for the support of the independent military chiefs. And while there were still a great many of the latter in the provinces, the administration being military in nature, yet the Tutuhs were being brought to recognize the authority of the President so that control was becoming more centralized.

All of this was being done independently of the Parliament. Peking remained a hotbed of intrigue, but a considerable part of the activity of the radicals had been transferred to the international settlement at Shanghai. There, under foreign protection, the opposition to Yuan Shih-kai became centered. This opposition rapidly assumed a revolutionary nature. The radical press began a campaign to undermine and eventually oust the President from his office. Secretly foreign aid was sought for revolution, and it was no secret that the Kuo Ming Tang leaders were preparing to reënact the scenes of 1911-12.

Yuan Shih-kai, with his agents everywhere, was fully informed of the progress of the movement. From the time of the growth of the revolutionary activity dates his use of assassination and terrorist methods in ruling the country. The more the activity of the radicals was extended, the more determined he became to complete the consolidation of his position in the provinces by removing possible enemies and by filling the high offices with his friends. Kiangsi being a strategic province, it was natural that he should attempt to oust Li Lieh-chun, a man of radical affiliations. He was fortunate in that his right and duty to appoint a Civil Administrator enabled him to accomplish his purpose, and at the same time permitted him to point out that he was only doing his duty by reëstablishing the civil authority.

Naturally this strengthening of his hand by the President was viewed with alarm by the Kuo Ming Tang and a series of small uprisings took place in the Yangtze valley. Finally, early in July, what is known as the Second Revolution broke out, when the ex-Tutuh of Kiangsi, Li Lieh-chun, attacked the forts at Hukow, and those forts declared their independence.[4] Many of the prominent leaders of the 1911 revolution were implicated in this movement. Proclamations were issued in the names of Huang Hsing, Chen Chi-mei and Dr. Sun Yat-sen calling upon the country to overthrow the traitor Yuan Shih-kai, and announcing the formation of a "punitive expedition" to Peking. The revolt was ill-timed however, and by September the situation was well in hand. "The rebellion" says Dr. Hornbeck, "was altogether premature, futile in its conception, an evidence of lack of statesmanlike qualities on the part of its leaders, and an indication that their much vaunted love of country was a cloak for personal self-seeking."[5] That is rather a severe indictment, but it is a just one. The whole struggle at Peking had developed into a quarrel over the control of the spoils. The majority of the members of the Parliament, the Kuo Ming members as well as the others, were struggling against the dominance of Yuan Shih-kai not solely or mainly because of their desire to preserve free government. In considerable part they were actuated by the desire to prevent the President from leaving them out in the

[4] This "declaration of independence" as a political move is very interesting. Men who have control of no territory and no army issue declarations of independence to protest against actions of the Central Government. Provinces declare their independence similarly, and several times there have been almost as many provinces "independent" of the Central Government, and not acknowledging any common control, as there are provinces in the Republic.

[5] "Contemporary Politics in the Far East," p. 43.

distribution of offices and the spending of the public money. Votes were for sale openly in Peking before the convocation of the Assembly,[6] and it was largely because the spoils were going to northerners instead of southerners that the Kuo Ming Tang so consistently opposed the government. Parliamentary government was desirable in the eyes of many political leaders because it created an opportunity for a greater number to participate in the disposal of patronage and the disbursement of the State revenue, than was the case under a monarchical rule.

The abortive uprising in the Yangtze valley was followed by an increased activity at Peking. The work of framing a permanent constitution for the Republic had been passed on to the National Assembly by the Council. After the overthrow of the revolutionists the Assembly took up this task in earnest, hoping to get it passed and accepted as the fundamental law of the land before Yuan Shih-kai had been able to make himself absolute master of the country. The President, on the other hand, was anxious to have his position confirmed by an election as permanent President. The section of the constitution dealing with the election and term of office of the President was first completed in order that the President might be elected and inaugurated on the date of the outbreak of the first revolution. Parliament was persuaded to take this action by an intimation that the Powers who had not yet recognized the Republic would give this recognition as soon as a permanent President had been chosen. The threat of possible foreign intervention was also used by the government in order to hasten the action of the Assembly.

[6] *Ibid.*, p. 42. As to this amenability of Parliament to bribery see also Weale, "The Fight for the Republic in China," p. 55.

The sixth chapter[7] of the new constitution dealt with the election and term of office of the President. Any citizen of the Chinese Republic, forty years of age, who had been a resident of the country for at least ten years was eligible for election. This election was to be by the National Assembly sitting as a National Convention. Two-thirds of the total membership of the Convention was necessary for a quorum, and election was to be by two-thirds majority. If, after two ballots, no candidate had secured the necessary number of votes, the third ballot was to be on the two names having the largest number of votes on the second ballot. A majority was sufficient to elect on the third ballot.

Little anxiety was felt as to the outcome of the election for the first permanent President of the Republic since the opposition to Yuan Shih-kai had been temporarily paralysed by the overthrow of the revolutionists in the Yangtze valley. Nevertheless three ballots were necessary before the final choice was made. The Vice-President on the first two ballots developed unexpected strength, preventing a two-thirds majority for the President. The third ballot, when only the two highest candidates could be voted for gave Yuan not only a majority, but the necessary two-thirds. His inauguration four days later was followed by the recognition of the Republic by the Powers who had not already taken such action. Secure now in his office for a period of five years the President was in a position to deal more firmly with Parliament.

On October 26th the Constitution drafting committee[8] finally passed the draft of the entire national constitution. The next step would have been the consideration of the draft by Parliament itself. However, other developments prevented

[7] Articles 56-57-58. See China Year Book, 1914, pp. 494-496. Entire draft given, pp. 490-499.

[8] This committee was composed of an equal number of numbers elected by and from each House of Parliament. It was

this, and as it for that reason, never went into effect it is not necessary to consider it in any detailed way. The underlying motive in the draft was the limitation of the executive and the concentration of legislative power and administrative control in the hands of the Assembly. No acts of the President were to be valid without the approval of a Cabinet Minister. The Cabinet itself was subordinated to the Assembly since the Premier could be appointed only with the concurrence of the popular Chamber, and the Ministers were to hold office only so long as they had the support of that body. State finances were controlled by the Assembly, although the government had the right to introduce an estimate of the expenses and revenues for the ensuing year. The provision was made also that the budget estimates could not be increased by the Assembly. In order to prevent any assumption of increased authority by the executive when the Assembly was not in session the draft permanent constitution created a permanent committee which was to continue in session throughout the recesses of the legislature and exercise all of the powers vested in that branch of the government, thus holding the President at all times under the active control of the Parliament.[9]

for that reason primarily representative of the ideas of the Kuo Ming Tang which was more nearly in control of this first Parliament than any other faction or party. The committee met in the Temple of Heaven, the work of framing a constitution containing ideas and principles new to China being carried on in the place peculiarly dedicated to old China. There it was that the Emperor, the "Son of Heaven," had in the past conducted the worship of Heaven and Earth, and there in the first days after the "Mandate of Heaven" had been taken from an Emperor and given to the people acting through their representatives, these representatives endeavored to frame an instrument of government that would consolidate control in the hands of the new organ, Parliament, the executive being subordinated to it.

[9] It should be remarked that during the period of framing of the draft constitution at this time, and its discussion, revision and

Yuan Shih-kai had made several attempts to secure modifications of the constitution while the committee was working on it, but his suggestions had been disregarded and his delegates refused a hearing. He took exception to the constitution as it was finally drafted because of the limitations imposed on the executive authority, and the creation of the committee of the National Assembly to watch ,over the administration. After the draft had been passed he called upon the high provincial officials for their opinion of it and for advice as to his action. The response was immediate. The draft constitution was denounced in a flood of telegrams from the provinces, and in some cases the dissolution of the Assembly was demanded.

Secured by his election as permanent President, and by the suppression of the rebellion against his authority, and assured of the support of the provincial officials, Yuan Shih-kai proceeded to take matters into his own hands. As a preliminary move, he ordered the dissolution of the Kuo Ming Tang[10] throughout the country on the ground that it was a seditious organization and had been implicated in the "summer revolution." The Kuo Ming members of the Assembly were deprived of their seats at the same time, by an executive mandate. Since their presence was necessary to secure a quorum, this act virtually brought about the dissolution of the Assem-

elaboration after the death of Yuan Shih-kai, the Assembly had the benefit of the gratuitous advice of many capable lawyers and political scientists, foreign as well as Chinese, and that the draft constitutions they prepared followed the French rather than the British or American systems. The French model was in general followed in drafting the constitution perhaps partly for this reason. Among those preparing such drafts may be mentioned Messers Piggott and Barrand.

[10] November 4, 1913. In this act he had the full concurrence of his Cabinet. Weale, "Fight for the Republic," pp. 55-56.

bly. Although the President was careful to make known his intention to preserve the Republic, he took no steps to have the Assembly brought up to its full strength by new elections, and it soon became evident that parliamentary participation in the government for the time being was ended.

After having successfully eliminated the Assembly, it might have been expected that Yuan Shih-kai would proceed to govern as a dictator without troubling about constitutional forms. But he chose the wiser course, of preserving the forms of constitutionalism, without however limiting his own supreme control.

Whether for effect, or because of a real desire for advice, he made use of the foreign constitutional and legal advisers to the government, asking an American, Dr. F. J. Goodnow, who held the post of legal adviser at that time for a memorandum discussing parliamentary conditions and procedure in China. It is worth while studying this document since it recommended several departures from the ideas of representative government which had prevailed during the first years of the Republic.

The first part of the memorandum was devoted to a consideration of the way in which representative government had developed in Europe through the exercise of the Royal prerogative. Thus the author showed that originally the parliaments were not dependent on popular will or choice, but were made up of representatives of the three predominant classes in the State—the Lords, the Church, and the Third Estate—summoned by the King's writ to advise in the government of the realm. In other words, the foundations of the present popular representative governments of Europe were laid while the State itself was organized practically as an absolute monarchy. Applying this to China Dr. Goodnow said: "Within the last two years, however, China has departed from her traditions and has attempted to establish a Republic. This attempt has been made, however, without any such experience as most European countries have had in parliamentary government. In other words, the attempt has been made to establish a Republic before the foundations have been laid for a parliament. . . . China is liable, if her position is not clearly apprehended, to pass through the same unfortunate experiences which have been characteristic of recent South American political life, and which find their most notable manifestation in the occurrences now taking place in Mexico."[11] The attempts at representative government in South American countries, he said, resulted in dictatorships with the continual strife and political disturbance incident to such regimes, and the same conditions would be produced in China because of her premature attempt to introduce popular government, unless representative institutions were adopted suited to the actual state and needs of the country.

All governments are founded upon interests in the State and not upon abstract theory. Thus China should undertake the establishment of a parliament representative of interests and not simply of indviduals. In that way the coöperation of the strongest classes would be enlisted in the effort to maintain a stable government. *Dr.* Goodnow suggested that the literary class, which had always been the governing class in China, should be given representation in the parliament, together with representatives of the landholding or agricultural class, the merchant class, and the provinces. The latter group would represent the interests of localities.

In order to obviate the difficulties of numerous and frequent elections, these representatives should be chosen mainly by appointment. Consequently, it was suggested that the

[11] *American Political Science Review,* November 1914.

President should have the right to appoint a certain number of the representatives, and the remainder should be appointed partially by the local assemblies, and in part by the chief administrative officers of the provinces. The memorandum suggested that the members appointed by the President should serve for long terms, and should continue in their appointments through dissolutions of the parliament. The idea running through the entire memorandum was that such an arrangement would provide a "safe" representative body for the immediate needs of the country, and that it would later develop into a truly representative assembly as new groups in the State reached a condition of political consciousness sufficiently pronounced to enable them to gain a representation in the government. The evolution of China's parliamentary system was to follow the lines of European development from an Assembly depending upon the Royal will to an Assembly founded upon the will of the people.

Yuan Shih-kai was a practical politician, concerned with the establishment of a government which could meet effectively the needs of the State. Furthermore, the fact had been repeatedly emphasized by a large group of Chinese, and by the foreign governments represented at Peking that the hope of China lay in the President. So that it is not to be wondered at if Yuan began to feel that the country could not exist without his strong hand at the helm. He had given the Parliament a chance to show what it could do, and it had failed to do anything. The sentiment of the country seemed to be behind him in his overthrow of parliamentary government. It is true that the "advices" he sought from the provinces and from officials generally, came for the most part from men who depended upon the President for their places, and who could be trusted to give acceptable advice. But in spite of that fact, it remains true that the sentiment of the people was just as truly reflected by these appointees of Yuan Shih-kai as if it had been given expression through some more popular agency. At the beginning of 1913 a radical majority had been returned to the Assembly, and yet, when that majority was deprived of power, the only protests came from those actually driven from office. The constituencies they claimed to represent remained silent.

In estimating the popular attitude toward the action taken by Yuan Shih-kai at this time, it must be remembered that he held a double mandate to reorganize the government—that which he held as the elected representative of the people, and that derived from the abdication edict of the Manchu Emperor, by which Yuan was given full power to establish a republican government suited to the needs of China. He had sworn to uphold the Republic, and, while the Assembly was dissolved, the Republic still existed. With that the people rested content.

The memorandum submitted by the Constitutional Adviser to the government laid down principles entirely in harmony with the President's own ideas of the needs of the State. The only thing that remained was to give effect to them in the most acceptable way. From the time of the dissolution of the National Assembly Yuan Shih-kai exercised dictatorial powers. But he was too astute a politician not to recognize the value of clothing his power in constitutional garb. The people wanted a representative government and at the same time they demanded a strong hand in that government. They wanted to reconcile oriental absolutism with western constitutionalism. So the President adhered to the forms of a constitutional government during the period immediately following his overthrow of the Parliament. When he departed from this line of procedure he paved the way for his own downfall.

His first act was to appoint an advisory Council to aid him

in the work of reconstituting the government. This Cheng Chih Hui Yi, or Political Council,[12] was made up of men of practical administrative experience, men of long service under the former *Dynasty* who had been trained in the same political school as Yuan Shih-kai. Working through the instrumentality of this Council the President proceeded to construct a constitutional system in which the executive was supreme, the representative assembly being more in the nature of an advisory than a controlling body.

The first recommendation made by the Political Council was that an elected Assembly be called into being, "which, being representative of the nation, would give constitutional sanction to the acts of the President."[13] The regulations for this assembly, the Constitutional Council, were so drawn up as to exclude from membership all except members of the old official and literati classes. Only men who had held an official post for at least five years, or were graduates of a law school, or holders of a degree higher than that of Chu-jen were eligible for membership. The electorate was limited to those over forty years of age who were officials, or held the rank of Chu-jen, or were graduates of provincial high schools, or possessed property to the value of $10,000. The Council was to consist of only fifty-six members. Its chief function was to revise the Provisional Constitution, and advise the President on any matters submitted to it.[14]

The Council was convened on March 18, 1914, and immediately addressed itself to the question of constitutional revision. Its work was soon completed and the revised constitution promulgated on May 1, 1914.

[12] China Year Book, 1916, p. 432.
[13] China Year Book, 1916, p. 433.
[14] *Ibid.*

The "Constitutional Compact," as the revised provisional constitution was called, was in the nature of a voluntary agreement by which the sovereign accepted certain limitations on his absolute freedom of action. Instead of a bicameral legislature, with executive as well as legislative powers, and a President and Cabinet accountable to the legislature, the Compact provided for a President who would "combine in himself all the powers of government"; a unicameral legislature with limited powers; and a Council of the nature of a Privy Council.[15]

All power over the administration was vested in the President, unlimited by any necessity to consider the wishes of other branches of the government. Thus he was empowered to prescribe and determine the organization of all offices, and to fix the duties of the officials; all civil and military appointments were to be made by him; he was made the commander-in-chief of the Army and Navy with the power to declare war and make peace, and to declare a state of seige; and he was the fountain of honor in the State. As the head of the State, diplomatic relations were controlled by the chief executive. Ambassadors and Ministers were to be received by him, and all treaty negotiations remained in his hands, with the exception that in case a treaty involved territorial change, or increased the burdens of the citizens, the concurrence of the legislature was required. This limitation was a direct benefit to the President since it forced him to share with the legislature the responsibility for making any change to which the people might be opposed. In addition to the powers vested in him as the head of the administration, the President was brought into direct contact with the legislative branch of the

[15] For translation of "The Constitutional Compact" see China Year Book, 1916, pp. 437-443.

government. He might initiate legislation and prepare the financial estimates for the consideration of the legislature. In time of emergency, executive ordinances were to have the force of law, but they must be submitted as soon as possible to the legislature for its approval. If this approval was withheld they were to become null and void.[16]

The Constitutional Compact further provided that the legislature should be convoked and all its sessions opened, prorogued or closed by the President. As has been stated, it was to be a single-chambered body, and was, in theory, elective. Its ordinary sessions were limited to four months, although they might be prolonged if the President felt the need for a more extended session; he also had the right to summon the legislature in special session. Its powers were similar to those exercised by the first National Assembly, which met in 1910. It was competent to discuss and pass bills, and the financial estimates, including the right to "discuss and pass or approve measures relating to the assumption of public debts, and to the contracting of other liabilities to the charge of the National Treasury."[17] But, as will be seen when we discuss the provisions of the Compact relative to finance, these rights were so limited as to give the executive an absolute control over the finances of the State. In addition to the above, the legislature could reply to inquiries from the President, receive petitions from the people, and initiate legislation equally with the President. It also might submit suggestions and opinions relating to legislation and other matters to the administration,

[16] For the promotion of the public welfare, for the execution of the statutes, or in pursuance of authority granted by statute, the President was empowered to issue, or cause to be issued ordinances, but no ordinance might alter a statute. Ch. III, art. 19.

[17] Ch. IV, art. 31 (3).

and had the right of interpellation, although such interpellations could not be so made as to censure the government. The President might refuse to answer questions put to him, if he felt that secrecy was desirable. Bills passed by the legislature were to be promulgated by the President, but if he disapproved of any measure it might be returned for reconsideration. On reconsideration, the bill had to be passed by a two-thirds majority, but even then the President did not need to promulgate it if he felt that it would harm either the internal administration or the foreign relations of the State. If the President withheld promulgation on the above grounds it must be with the concurrence of the Council of State. The President had the right, in concurrence with that body, to dissolve the legislature, in which case it was stipulated that new elections must be held within six months from the date of dissolution. On the other hand the legislature was empowered to impeach the President on charge of treason, but all danger to the President from this provision was removed by the fact that impeachment proceedings must have the approval of a three-fourths majority of a four-fifths quorum of the legislature. Yuan Shih-kai was determined to avoid the difficulties arising from a constant criticism of the government through impeachments, and yet felt it best to give the legislature the feeling that it had a weapon by which the form of the State might be preserved in case the President proved a traitor to republican institutions.

The other constitutions under which the government had been established at different times had made provision for a Cabinet to assume a measure of responsibility for the administration, but the Constitutional Compact marks a decided divergence from the former practice. The President, assisted by a Secretary of State, was given the sole responsibility for the administration of the government. The actual work of administration was to be conducted by the heads of the *De-partments*, acting, not as a body, but separately. The Secretary of State, the heads of *Departments*, and special delegates representing the President, were given the right to appear and to speak in the legislature, but could not be held accountable for their acts except through the President. They could be impeached only by the Board of Censors, and were to be tried, not in the ordinary Courts of law, but in special administrative Courts, which were to apply administrative law. Thus all control over the administration was removed from the representative branch of the government.

The ordinary Courts of law were to be composed of judges appointed by the President, and were given jurisdiction over civil and criminal cases, except where administrative officers or administrative provisions were concerned. Trials were to be conducted publicly, except where publicity was considered prejudicial to law and order or public morality, when secrecy might be observed. Thus secret trials such as had been objected to by the National Council in 1912 were provided for by law.

The legislature was given the constitutional right to pass on the estimates of the government, but certain estimates might be neither rejected nor reduced, unless with the consent of the President. These were: 1) those pertaining to the legal obligations of the State; 2) such necessary expenditures as might have arisen from the provisions of statutes; 3) expenditures necessary to carry out treaties; 4) expenditures necessary for the organization of the army and the navy. The Compact provided that all the old taxes and revenues should be continued unless changed by statute, and all new taxes should be imposed by statute. But when it is considered that the President determined the statutes through his power to refuse to promulgate bills passed by the legislature, it is apparent that final control over revenues was retained by the government. Furthermore a "continuing expenditure fund" was provided which was to embody appropriations extending over a period of years, and which could be used to meet special emergencies. After this fund was once voted the government had resources for which it did not have to account to the legislature. Then there was to be a reserve fund to be used to supply deficiencies in the estimates, or to meet requirements not otherwise provided for. In time of war or internal disturbance the President might make emergency appropriations, submitting them later to the Assembly for ratification. If the legislature should delay action on the budget, or should refuse to pass it the last year's estimates were to continue in force. The compact made provision for a Board of Audit, which was to go over the accounts, after which the receipts and expenditures of the year, with the report of the Board, should be presented to the legislature for approval.

Since the Constitutional Compact was provisional, one section of it was devoted to the procedure for framing a permanent constitution. That instrument was to be drafted by a committee not exceeding ten in number, appointed by the Council of State.[18] When the committee had completed its work it was to be submitted to the Council of State for examination and approval. After it had been accepted by the Council the constitution was to be submitted by the President

[18] This committee was actually appointed in July 1915. Its work, however, was interrupted by the agitation for a restoration of the monarchy, and the subsequent rebellion which finally brought the Kuo Ming Tang back into power. For a brief description of the membership of the constitutional drafting committee see *National Review* (China) for August 21, 1915.

to a National Convention for final adoption. Until the permanent constitution had been adopted the Constitutional Compact was to have the same force as the constitution.

In addition to the work of drawing up this Constitutional Compact, the Constitutional Council, or Conference, was given the task of framing the regulations for the Tsan Cheng Yuan (Council of State), the Li Fa Yuan (legislative assembly), and the National Convention which was ultimately to pass on the permanent constitution. Furthermore any question of amendment of the Compact was to be submitted to it. The Compact provided that amendment might be undertaken on a proposal of the President or a two-thirds majority of the legislature. In either case the proposal of amendment had to be sanctioned by a majority of three-fourths, of a quorum of four-fifths, of the total membership of the legislature. The actual work of amendment was to be undertaken by the Constitutional Compact Conference summoned by the President.

In May the Constitutional Compact Conference completed the regulations for the Council of State, and they were promulgated by the President on May 24. The members of the Council were to be appointed by the President, and, as it was actually constituted, the membership numbered seventy. The sole function of the Council of State was to advise the President on matters of State or such matters as he chose to submit to it. It was further empowered to offer suggestions to the President, but any memorandum embodying such suggestions had to be signed by ten members. The work of interpreting the constitution devolved on it also, as did the settlement of any disputes arising between the executive and the judiciary.

The Council of State met for the first time on June 20, 1914. For the time being it was to act as the legislative Assembly in addition to exercising its own advisory functions, and, as a matter of fact, the Council, with the President, constituted the government. Regulations for the legislature were drawn up and promulgated, but on one pretext or another its convocation was delayed. Since the members of the Council of State were appointed by Yuan Shih-kai that body was what might have been expected: a highly conservative group of men fully in sympathy with the aims of the President and completely under his control. China had indeed reverted to autocracy under a constitutional disguise!

The next step in the organization of the government under the Compact was the promulgation of the laws governing the Li Fa Yuan, or legislative council. This body was to consist of two hundred and seventy-five members elected indirectly, and holding office for a period of four years. Those qualified to serve as electors in the primary election[19] were men who had held or were holding the position of a high official; had graduated from an institution of learning not lower than a middle school; possessed immovable property to the value of $5000 or more, invested in commerce or industry. The qualifications for election in the primary election were the same as for electors except that they were moved up one degree.

---

[19] The double system of primary and final elections was followed in the provinces. The Central Electoral College consisted of residents of Peking who had rendered meritorious service to the country; or had been high officials; or were recognized scholars, or had certain other educational qualifications; or possessed property to the value of $10,000; or were members of the nobility or held rank in one of the eight Banner Corps. Overseas citizens with property to the value of $30,000 might vote in the Central Electoral College by coming to Peking. The Mongolian, Tibetan and Chinghai Electoral Colleges were made up of nobles of Princely or hereditary rank or title, or men otherwise distinguished.

Thus, in addition to the middle school education, the candidate was required to have continued his study in a high grade technical school. The property qualification was moved to ten thousand dollars, and the official must have held office for at least a year. The qualifications for membership in the legislative Council were placed even higher. Anyone might be elected who had rendered meritorious service to the State; who had been a high official for five years or more; who was an eminent or learned scholar; who had graduated from an educational institution not lower than a middle school after study of not less than three years, either in China or abroad, or who had an equivalent education; who had been a teacher in an institution not lower than a high grade technical school for three years or more; who had immovable property to the value of $30,000, or who had that amount invested in commercial or industrial enterprises.

These requirements followed closely *Dr.* Goodnow's suggestion that the official, literati and gentry classes, as such, should be represented in a single chamber legislature, thus constituting a representation of interests rather than of population.

It was intended that elections for the legislative council should be held early in 1915 but by that time other affairs of greater immediate importance held the attention of the government, and later developments precluded the idea of a convocation of such a body, so that, in fact, the promulgation of the regulations was as far as Yuan Shih-kai advanced toward the establishment of a semi-popular branch of the government.

At the request of the Council of State the Constitutional Compact Conference took up the question of the Presidential succession, and the Presidential Election Law was promulgated on *December* 29, 1914. This law is one of the most interesting documents of Chinese constitutional history. Instead of following western methods for presidential elections, provisions were made entirely unique to China. A candidate for the office of President had to be forty years old, and of twenty years residence in the country. The term of office was advanced from five to ten years. When the time for an election drew near the President was to write the names of three men as his nominees for the office on a plate of gold. This plate was then to be locked up in a casket, which was to be kept in a stone house in the residence of the President. The key to the casket was to be retained by the President, and the keys to the stone house were to be placed in the hands of the President, the Secretary of State and the chairman of the Council of State. On the day of the election a committee of ten was to be empowered to open the casket and the President was to make known the names of the candidates to the electoral college. The presidential electoral college was to be composed of fifty members elected from the Council of State and fifty from the legislative Council. In addition to the three names submitted by the President the electoral college might vote on the name of the President for reëlection. For purposes of election a quorum of three-fourths of the total membership of the electoral college was required. On the first ballot a two-thirds majority was necessary for election. If no one secured the requisite majority the two names standing highest on the list were to be voted on at the second ballot, when a majority was sufficient for election. In case, however, it should appear inadvisable to hold an election at the appointed time the Council of State might extend the term of office of the President for another ten years without the formality of an election. At the time of taking office the following oath was prescribed for the President-elect: "I swear that I shall with all sincerity adhere to the constitution and execute the duties of the President. I reverently swear."

The term of office of the Vice-President was to be the same as that of the President. At the time for a vice-presidential election the President was to nominate three candidates for the office. The form of election was the same as for the President.

The regulations for the National Convention which was to be convoked to pass on the draft of the permanent constitution were promulgated in March, 1915. But, owing to later developments, no attempt was made to give effect to them. The Convention was to consist of three hundred and thirty-five elected members; forty from the metropolitan district; two hundred and two from the provinces; nine from special territories; twenty-four from Mongolia, Tibet, and Kokonor, and twenty each from the legislative, judicial, and administrative offices. The Convention was to pass on the draft of the constitution submitted to it by the Council of State. It could only consider amendments to the Constitution on the proposal of at least forty members. Any amendments suggested must be submitted to the Constitution *D*rafting Committee, before being incorporated in the Constitution. The Convention was to meet in sessions extending over four months. If it did not reach a decision in that time it was to be dissolved and a new Convention elected.

At the time when Yuan Shih-kai carried out these measures concentrating power in his own hands there was no popular feeling against his action. The only strongly organized party of opposition had been broken up and its leaders driven from the country; the parliament, elected in theory by the people, had been dissolved; the Provisional Constitution had been amended out of existence by a body which was unknown to the Constitution; the provincial assemblies had been dissolved together with the local government bodies; a constitutional system had been inaugurated which reëstablished executive authority on practically the same basis as that upon which the authority of the Manchu Dynasty had rested. It would seem, indeed, that the entire work of the revolution of 1911, which had been represented as an expression of the popular desire to assume a share in the direction of political affairs, had been undone.

Upon what, then did the revolution accomplished by Yuan Shih-kai depend for its strength? Why was he able to bring about such radical changes without provoking an outburst too strong to be resisted? The answer to these questions involves three conditions which have already been touched upon. In the first place Yuan Shih-kai had a certain legal basis for his reorganization of the government. He had been commissioned by the retiring Dynasty to "organize with full powers a provisional republican government, and confer with the Republican Army as to methods of union."[20] His authority as the commissioner of the old regime meant more to one section of the country than any mandate he had received from the revolutionary organization at Nanking. He had sworn, it is true, to uphold the Provisional Constitution, but that did not preclude the possibility of making any changes in that instrument necessary for the good of the country. His legal right to institute changes incompatible with the Provisional Constitution was weakened by his statement before election that he considered the revolution as the source of his authority rather than the Abdication Edicts. But that did not prevent a great many of the people from looking on him as the successor to the old government in the same sense as the Ts'ing Dynasty

[20] Abdication Edicts, see above pp. 115-16.

had been successor to the Mings, and with the same right to make changes in the constitution of the State, provided he did not harm directly the everyday interests of the people.

The second factor to be considered is the fact that the ultra-liberal ideas of the southern revolutionary leaders had been tried, after a fashion, and found wanting. The Parliament, with its extensive powers, had not only failed to maintain itself against the constitutionally limited executive, but it had also failed to formulate any constructive policy which would have indicated its fitness to wield the powers given it even if it had been able to maintain its supremacy against Yuan Shih-kai. The case against the Parliament is presented by one of the most noted of Chinese scholars, Liang Ch'i Ch'ao, in the following words: "For more than twenty days it [the Assembly] could not elect a speaker, and over a hundred days elapsed before it was able to draw up rules and regulations for its own procedure. For a long time the absence of a quorum and the irregular attendance of the members became an almost everyday occurrence, and when there was a quorum the members quarreled with each other like a lot of old ladies from the country and behaved like naughty school boys. Before dispersing each day the members wasted half the day in wrangling about unnecessary things. With a salary of $6,000 per annum, none of the members seems ever to have given a thought for the benefit of the country. . . . We may have a great love for parliamentary institutions, but we love our country much more."[21] In the face of parliamentary incompetency the country was more than ready to respond to any attempt to restore a system which at least promised an efficient administration. The people were all the more recon-

[21] "Contemporary Politics in Far East," pp. 49-50—(citation taken from "The Justice," Vol. I, no. 15, July 1, 1913).

ciled to the change by the fact that the form of the Republic was preserved, and a certain appearance of constitutional sanction for the acts of the government was maintained.

The most important point to be remembered, however, is that the people of China have never felt that their daily lives were very greatly influenced by the central government. They paid their taxes, and they knew that it was possible for them to resist any great encroachments by the central authority on local prerogatives and customs. Further than that, what went on at Peking did not interest them very greatly. They lived their lives and were content to let those who wished to maintain themselves as part of the machinery of government carry on the administration. Naturally, the ones who made up the bureaucracy were the educated classes and the men of means. There was no hereditary nobility to make up the governing class and restrict it to its own membership. Education was made the basis for membership in the ruling class at a very early period of Chinese history, and every man who had money had a certain amount of education. So that the gentry and the literati formed one distinct class from which officialdom was entirely recruited. That there was no great jealousy of this class was due to the fact that membership in it was open to any one, and indeed many of the officials came from poor and humble surroundings. The revolution of 1911 had not overthrown the conception of the right of this class to wield the administrative authority. It had simply changed the organs of government so that instead of the administrative policy being formulated and directed by an absolute monarch it was given over to the control of an assembly which exercised the same absolute power as had the former monarch. Now Yuan Shih-kai, in effect, reversed the change made in 1911. Through all these shifts the administration was carried on by the same class, and the relation of the people to the central government had undergone no change. They saw the same officials functioning after Yuan had become the dictator as before; the condition of the country was not changed either for the better or the worse so far as they could see. Those interested in opposition had been driven from the country or temporarily silenced. And that national panacea—a constitution—had been preserved. It mattered little to the mass of the people whether the President or the Parliament had the supreme power until their selfish interests or local privilges were directly affected, or until they were otherwise stirred to action.

CHAPTER VIII

The monarchy movement of 1915-16 was but an incident, an interlude, in the constitutional history of the last few years. From one point of view it deserves but a bare mention in the story of constitutional development, but from another it throws so many sidelights on Chinese politics that it cannot be ignored. As we have seen, Yuan Shih-kai had taken all the necessary steps to consolidate his position as dictator in the Chinese Republic. He had replaced the Assembly elected under the Nanking Constitution with a body, the Council of State, so constituted as to be entirely subservient to himself. The Constitution itself, which had concentrated the supreme power in the hands of the Assembly, had been replaced by an instrument drawn up, under the supervision of the President, by a Conference of officials which based its authority on a presidential mandate. The Constitutional Compact not only combined in the President the supreme powers of government, but, together with the Presidential Election Law, made it possible for Yuan Shih-kai to retain the presidency as long as he wished to do so. All of this had been done with the passive acquiescence of all classes in the State. Any who showed a tendency to oppose the President were either forced to leave the country or were removed by imprisonment or assassination. Men like the Vice-President, Li Yuan-hung, of whose sympathy the government was doubtful, were concentrated in Peking on the pretext of giving advice to the executive, but in reality to keep them under the eye of the President. It seemed as though China, after four years of turmoil, had settled down for a few years under the rule of a "strong man" whose position was nearly impregnable, fortified as it was by the support of the Powers, and by the acquiescence of most of the gentry and literati.

The opening days of 1915, however, brought to China a more acute danger than any she has faced in modern times, not excepting even the danger to her national existence from the Russian policy in the North before the Russo-Japanese war. Less than six months after the outbreak of the great war in Europe, and its extension to the Far East by the action of Japan in driving German interests from Shantung province, while the attention of the western States was distracted from the non-European world, Japan suddenly served on Yuan Shih-kai a series of astounding 'demands' ranging from the disposition of the German holdings in Shantung to an agreement on the part of the Chinese government to allow Japan large administrative and police powers in China. These demands were presented out of a clear sky, when there were no oustanding questions under discussion by the two governments. Japan tried in vain to keep the world in ignorance of her action both by demanding secrecy on the part of the Chinese. and, when news of her action gradually leaked out, by at first denying that such demands had been made. When the fact of the negotiations had been so clearly established as to make denial futile, she denied that they were of such a nature as to endanger Chinese independence and territorial integrity. Finally she admitted the fact of Group V,[1] but insisted that that group had been presented not as 'demands,' but as material for friendly discussion.

[1] The demands were arranged in groups, one relating to Shantung, one to South Manchuria and Mongolia, etc. Group V consisted of the provisions designed to limit Chinese administrative autonomy.

The negotiations were prolonged until May when China was forced, under pressure, to agree to most of the least obnoxious of the rights and privileges desired by Japan. While forced to concede much., the Chinese government was able to safeguard the Republic's interests at the most vital points. This was due in large part to the diplomacy of the President; —to his skill in bringing the pressure of the other Powers to bear on the Japanese government, and in arousing the country to the danger of the situation.

Shortly after the conclusion, in May 1915, of the negotiations with Japan over these now famous 'demands' however, a feeling of unrest and uncertainty became marked in Peking. This rapidly crystallized into an agitation for the reëstablishment of the monarchical form of government in name as well as in fact, with Yuan Shih-kai as Emperor. What influence the Japanese question had in strengthening the movement will probably never be fully and conclusively established. The attempt has been made, through some unofficial documents, to establish the fact that Japan would have been glad to see China monarchical once more, providing the head of the State was amenable to Japanese influence.[2] This fact, it is said, was intimated to Yuan Shih-kai and he accepted the suggestion that the time was ripe for the reëstablishment of the Empire but refused to act as the tool of the Japanese government. Whatever the truth of this story of Japanese influence, it is certain that the Japanese demands influenced the course of events in another and more indirect way. President Yuan had conducted the negotiations with great skill, and, while forced to make concessions, had managed to check the Japanese at several points. His adherents could point to the fact that the

[2] See Weale, "The Fight for the Republic in China," pp. 123-148.

international situation was such that China must needs prepare against future activity of the Powers in the Far East.
The Japanese activity showed the necessity for preserving
strong government at home, and so long as there was an elective head to the State there was danger of internal commotion,
and thus of weakness, which would invite further foreign aggression.

Unquestionably the 1915 "demands" aroused an outburst of
patriotic feeling among the Chinese such as had not been exhibited for years. For the time being sectional feeling was
erased by the need for action against the common enemy.
This national patriotism was manifested in the organization
of societies for the protection of the country; in the boycott
of Japanese goods; and in subscription to the fund which came
to be known as the "National Salvation" fund. Schoolboys,
small farmers, the poorest of the coolies, officials, gentry and
scholars all contributed to this fund for the protection of the
country against foreign aggression. All parties rallied to the
support of the President. This unanimity of sentiment may
have caused Yuan Shih-kai to feel that the country would
support him if he should undertake to overthrow the Republic
and make himself the founder of a new Dynasty.

The first thing to be done in the furtherance of a movement
of any kind in China is to establish a society to conduct the
necessary propaganda. China is indeed the home of the "society" or "association"! The organization through which the
monarchists worked was called the Chou-an-hui or "Society
for the Preservation of Peace." The prime mover in the organization of the Chou-an-hui was Yang Tu, a member of
the Council of State, and an intimate of the President.[3] Num-

---

[3] See *National Review* (China), 15 January 1916. Article reprinted from *North American Review*, Dec. 1915.

erous other societies sprang up either in support of the movement or in opposition to it, but the Chou-an-hui was the organ
used to force the question on the attention of the country.
The President kept carefully in the background, always posing
as the defender of the Republic, but in reality directing and
controlling the whole movement.

Whisperings of possible change had been in the air for a
long time before an opportunity for direct action came. Shortly after the Chou-an-hui had became an active organization
Dr. Goodnow[4] returned to China for a visit. The administration took advantage of the opportunity offered to secure his
views on abstract questions of government. Dr. Goodnow
may have known of the agitation that was going on at the
time, but he certainly did not know that the President desired
to make use of his recognized position as an authority on questions of government in order to further the movement for a
restoration of the monarchy in China.[5]

In response to the request of the government he submitted a
memorandum setting forth his views in the abstract on the respective merits of various forms of government, and, further,
he applied these abstract decisions, reached by a study of the
political institutions of the West, to China. He said: "China,
owing to the folly of an absolute monarchical system, has ne-
glected the education of the masses, whose intellectual attain-
ments have been, consequently, of a low standard. Then,
there is the additional fact that the people have never had a

[4] Dr. Goodnow had been away on leave of absence, and was
still considered an "Adviser" to the government.

[5] There is no basis in fact for the charge made (see Weale,
"Fight for the Republic") that Dr. Goodnow returned to China
at the request of the government to advise it on the question of
the change in the form of the State. His visit was entirely unofficial, and when he left America he was unaware of the strong
movement on foot to restore the monarchy.

voice in the doings of their government. Therefore they have not the ability to discuss politics. Four years ago the absolute monarchy was suddenly changed into a republic. This movement was all too sudden to expect good results. If the Manchus had not been an alien race, which the country wished to overthrow, the best step which could then have been adopted was to retain the Emperor, and gradually lead him to a constitutional government. What the Commissioners on Constitutional Government suggested was quite practical if carried out gradually until perfection was reached. Unfortunately the feeling of alien control was bitter to the people, and the maintenance of the throne was an utter impossibility. Thus the monarchy was overthrown and the adoption of a republican system was the only alternative.

"Thus we see that China has during the last few years been progressing in constitutional government. The pioneering stage of the process was, however, not ideal. The results could have been much better if a person of royal blood respected by the people had come out and offered his services. Under the present conditions China has not yet solved the problem of the succession to the presidency. What provisions we have now are not perfect. If the President should one day give up his power the difficulties experienced by other nations will manifest themselves again in China. The conditions in other countries are similar to those obtaining in China and the dangers are also the same. It is quite within the bounds of possibility that the situation might threaten China's independence if internal disturbance should occur in connection with this problem and not be immediately put down.

"What attitude then, should those who have the good of the nation at heart, take under the present circumstances? Should they advocate the continuance of the Republic or suggest a change for a monarchy? It is difficult to answer these questions. But I have no doubt in saying that the monarchical system is better suited to China than the Republican system. For if China's independence is to be maintained, the government should be constitutional, and in consideration of China's conditions as well as her relations with other powers, it will be easier to form a constitutional government by adopting a monarchy than a Republic."[6]

But the memorandum went on to point out that three indispensable conditions must be observed before the restoration of the monarchy could be considered advisable. In the first place it must be certain that such a change as was contemplated had the support of the people and would not be opposed by the Powers. It must be made in such a way that there would be no uncertainty as to the succession after the death of the Emperor. And, finally, it must make definite provision for the progressive development of constitutionalism in China.

This, then, was the memorandum which the Chou-an-hui seized upon and used as a basis for its agitation for the restoration of the Empire. It was translated into the vernacular and spread broadcast throughout the country, together with a manifesto of the Society, based upon it. The Society spread rapidly in the provinces, most of the Military Governors becoming affiliated with it and lending their support to the movement. When the time was considered ripe the whole question was brought to an issue by a petition to the Council of State asking that the question of the form of government be taken under consideration. At the same time memorials and petitions poured in from the provinces. Petitions had been used to bring pressure to bear on the Manchus to secure limitations on their power, and now they were used to force the

[6] *National Review* (China), August 28, 1915.

executive to assume a greater authority and power.[7]   But with this difference, that the petitioners for a change back to the monarchy were men who held official positions under the government and who were interested directly, not in a limitation of the power of the central government, but in extending that power because it had been intimated to them that the President desired such action.   In other words, the whole "popular" agitation expressed through these petitions, and which finally caused the Council of State to take action, was carefully engineered from Peking by the henchmen of Yuan Shih-kai. Yang Tu, the ostensible head of the Chou-an-hui, was really only a tool in the hands of the President and his advisers. The real brain back of the movement, aside from the President, was Liang Shih-yi, the head of the Bank of China and a politician of no mean ability.

Instead of proclaiming the monarchy and trusting to force to overcome all opposition, a plan was worked out by which the people could have an opportunity to express their will as to the future form of the State.   Then, if opposition on the part of the Powers developed, the monarchists could point out the fact that it was the will of the people, and that since the people had voted for the change no internal disturbance need be feared.

On September 6, 1915 the President referred to the agitation for a reëstablishment of the Empire in a message to the Council of State.[8]   This agitation, he said, was incompatible with the position he held as President.   But instead of ordering all such talk absolutely repressed he went on to say that any question of a change in the form of the State was very

[7] It is claimed that the signatures to many of these petitions were forged.   *National Review* (China), 25 Sept. 1915.
[8] *National Review* (China), 10 September 1915.

important, and he recommended it to the careful consideration of the Council. After consideration, that body suggested that the National Convention, for which provision had been made in the Constitutional Compact and which was to be convened later in the fall of 1915 should be authorized to pass on the question of the monarchy. That would have meant a delay of several months, giving time for the opposition to the movement to unite and possibly prevent favorable action. Furthermore there was always the danger of foreign interference. So the Chou-an-hui requested the Council of State "further to discuss the question and to suggest the organization of another popular body with large and adequate powers, at an earlier date than the convocation of the National Convention."[9] This body should be empowered to consider the proposed change.

The Council of State lost no time in acting on this suggestion, and on October 6 passed "the Law on the Organization of the Convention of Citizen's Representatives."[10] Two days later this law was promulgated by the President. In submitting the law to him the Council stated: "In spite of the fact that we were reluctant to make any hasty proposals since we have already suggested methods and the Great President has also decided upon the procedure to follow, we cannot ignore the 'united appeal of the people' repeatedly uttered; and in consideration of the necessity of respecting the 'will of the people' this House has again brought up the subject for discussion. . . . The State is the State of the people, and the form of the State should be adopted or rejected according to the wish of the people; and as the will of the people is now for a speedy solution, it becomes our duty to yield to the desire of

[9] China Year Book, 1916, p. 483.
[10] *Ibid.*, pp. 483-4.

the people and place the question above everything else. . . . We therefore decide that the name of the body should be called the Convention of Citizen's Representatives, which shall be drawn from the members elected by the successful candidates of the primary election of the Citizen's Convention for the purpose of settling the question of the form of the State. In this way all the provinces, special administrative areas, Manchuria, Mongolia, Mohammedan regions and Tibet shall have representatives therein. . . . As the entire body of the country is in a state of exceeding haste to see the solution of the question of the form of the State, we hereby submit to you the text of the said law, together with the petitions and ask that the Great President shall speedily promulgate the same."[11]

The Convention of Citizen's Representatives[12] was to consist of 1834 representatives elected from the provinces, and special administrative areas; 32 from Inner and Outer Mongolia; 12 from Tibet; 6 from Chinghai; 24 representatives of the Manchu, Mongolian and Chinese Banners; 60 elected by the Chambers of Commerce; 30 representatives of the learned scholars; and 20 representatives elected by those who had done good service to the country. In the provinces and dependencies the election was to proceed from the point reached in the election of candidates for the National Convention. Thus the successful candidates in the primary elections were empowered to choose the representatives for the Citizen's Convention. The electorate was carefully restricted in all cases, and the election was put under the control of the high officials. Care was taken that the electors should act as desired by the government. Thus voters were required to sign their ballots.

[11] *Ibid.*
[12] China Year Book, 1916, pp. 444-446, for text of law organizing the "Citizen's Convention."

After the Convention of Citizen's Representatives had been constituted, the members were to have only one function—to vote on a question submitted to them by the government. This question was drawn up and passed by the Council of State, as the acting legislative body, and was then submitted to the President for approval, after which it was transmitted to the Superintendents of Election.

Absolutely no opportunity was afforded the members of the Convention for deliberation and discussion of the proposed change. They were to be simply the means of registering the will of the people at the dictation of the government. Careful instructions were sent to the Superintendents, who were all officials of the government, as to the exact procedure to be followed, so that there would be no chance of a slip.[13] The ballots were all printed in advance and marked in the proper way so all that the people's representatives had to do was to sign their names. In spite of the fact that care was taken to see that only "favorable" representatives should be elected, the actual voting on the question of the change in the form of the State was conducted in most cases under the eyes of policemen and soldiers, so that the necessity for affirmative action was kept continually before the voters in the Convention. As each vote was cast it was opened and scrutinized before the representative was allowed to leave the room. Under the circumstances it is little to be wondered at that the Convention of Citizen's Representatives decided unanimously for restoration of the monarchy. The result could well have been announced in advance.

The elections were completed and the vote taken in *December*, and, on *December* 11, the Council of State announced that the opinion of the country was in favor of a monarchy, and of

[13] See Weale, "The Fight for the Republic," ch. XI.

Yuan Shih-kai as Emperor. A petition was immediately sent the President asking him to ascend the Throne. He refused at first, because of his oath to support the Republic. But after being petitioned a second time he accepted, since the change had come from the people and he, as their servant, could not refuse to do their will.[14] Steps were immediately taken to prepare for the coronation in spite of the fact that "advice" had been tendered from several sources against the change of name for the government.

While the monarchists had been maturing their plans for securing the consent of the country to a reversion to the monarchical form of government, the opposition had not been idle. Signs of discontent with the proposed change had been manifested in many of the provinces. The office of a pro-monarchy paper in Peking had been bombed as a sign of disapproval of its activity. Notable scholars, led by Liang Ch'i Ch'ao had come out as opponents of the movement. Liang presented the case for the anti-monarchists in a very able pamphlet which was widely read throughout the country. As he said in the beginning in order to make his position clear, Liang Ch'i Ch'ao was not a radical Republican. In fact he had maintained consistently, since 1898, that constitutional government could be introduced into China best under a monarchical form of government. "Before I proceed with my argument," he said, "I wish to make plain two points. One is that I am not one of those reformers whose ears are their brains, and who are intoxicated with the doctrine of republicanism. I have, therefore, no partiality for the republican form of government nor any bias for or against other forms of government. . . . The second point is that I am not one of the veteran conservatives

[14] Translation of the mandates given, *National Review* (China), 18 Dec. 1915.

who lay so much stress on the importance of having a *Dynasty*. . . . If one wishes to consider the present situation of the country without bias or prejudice he must disregard the rise or fall of any particular family."[15] This statement of his position was certainly borne out by the facts. Liang Ch'i Ch'ao had been against the disenthronement of the Manchus in the first place, but after the Republic had been established he had come forward in its support. When Parliament had discredited itself he had seen the necessity for the establishment of a regime such as had been inaugurated under the Constitutional Compact. Therefore his arguments at this time carried great weight in the country. In his pamphlet Liang argued that the time had come when agitation for a change in the form of the State should cease, the Republic be accepted as a fact, and all efforts bent toward a reorganization of the government so as to give an efficient administration. The main thing was to get a workable organization and then consolidate and strengthen the country in order to secure peace and order, and prevent any foreign aggression such as had been undertaken successfully by Japan. He pointed out that Yuan Shih-kai had been given a term of office long enough to enable him to accomplish this work, and that provision had been made for his reëlection if it should be advisable for him to continue in office for more than the ten year term for which he had been chosen. At the end of twenty years surely the country would not be endangered by the necessity of choosing a new executive. All the possible arguments against a change in the form of the State were advanced in this pamphlet, which became to the opponents of the monarchical movement what Dr. Goodnow's memorandum had been to the advocates of a restoration.

[15] See Weale, "Fight for the Republic," ch. X,. for the complete text of this pamphlet.

In spite of the known opposition, the movement continued, however, until, as we have seen, its object had been attained. During the period from September until the death of Yuan Shih-kai the country was ruled under the iron hand of the military. Men who dared raise their voices against the change, or who were suspected of hostile sentiments were summarily arrested and executed if they remained under the jurisdiction of the government. It was only in the treaty ports where foreign protection was enjoyed that opposition to the President could be shown. This arbitrary suppression of all opposition accounts for the fact that the monarchists were able so completely to carry out their plans.

Another fact that Yuan Shih-kai was forced to consider carefully before allowing himself to be crowned as Emperor was the danger of possible foreign intervention. The Japanese had never been very favorably inclined to the Chinese Republic, and, as has been said, it was reported indirectly to the President that no opposition would be offered to a restoration of the monarchy. Many prominent Japanese statesmen had prophesied that the Republic could not have a very long life.[16] But the fact that it was Yuan Shih-kai who was expecting to make himself the Emperor changed the point of view of the Japanese. Since the time when Yuan had held the post of Chinese-Resident in Korea, where he had used his position to work against Japanese interests in that country, he had been little loved in Japan. During the whole of his official life he had come into conflict with the neighboring Empire in one way or another, so that it was a question from the very beginning whether Japan would sanction his elevation to the Dragon Throne. To offset the danger of possible Japanese

[16] See Count Okuma's views and Dr. Hioki's views as given in *National Review* (China), 10 Sept. 1915.

intervention, however, there was the hatred, in China, of Japan and things Japanese, engendered by the *D*emands. Intervention really might strengthen Yuan's position throughout the country and enable him to defy his old enemy.

The restoration movement was well under way before Japan took any open action. On October 28 Great Britain and Russia united with Japan, at the latter's request, in tendering advice to the Chinese Government opposing the establishment of a monarchy in China. They inquired what effect the change would have on the peace of the country, expressing the fear that a change in the form of the State would lead to widespread opposition, especially in the South where considerable unrest already was apparent. It was felt to be unwise to stir up trouble at a time when the international situation was so disturbed. All intention, however, of interference in the internal affairs of the country was disclaimed.

The Chinese Government replied that no danger was to be feared from an internal revolt against the monarchical change, and that it was more apt to cause trouble if the change was given up for a time at the request of the foreign powers. Preparations went on for the coronation in spite of the fact that advice counselling delay was again tendered, this time by Japan, Great Britain, Russia, France and Italy.

After the monarchy movement was well under way, everyone within the jurisdiction of the central government hastened to safeguard himself by going on record as favoring the change. Among those who submitted memorials favoring the overthrow of the Republic was a young Yunnanese who had been acting Tutuh of Yunnan province during the first revolution and after the establishment of the Republic. In January, 1915, this man, Tsai Ao, had been appointed *D*irector-General of the Bureau of Resurveying Cultivated Land, and had come to Peking to assume his new duties. Thus he was among the high officials who were under the surveillance of the President when the Imperial bee began to buzz. His later actions show that he sent in his memorial advocating change merely to quiet any suspicions which might be entertained of his loyalty to Yuan Shih-kai. He was next heard from in Yunnan province on *December 23*, when he united with other provincial officials in demanding that the Republic be restored. No answer being received, Yunnan province declared its independence and under the leadership of Tsai Ao prepared to resist the Central Government.

The reply that was finally made to the Yunnan telegrams is of interest because of its discussion of the threat of foreign interference, and its justification of the President's action in accepting the Throne and overthrowing the Republic which he had sworn to uphold. "The question whether the telegrams from Yunnan dated the 23rd instant are genuine documents or not has still to be ascertained. But in order to avoid misunderstanding we wish to reply to the principal points raised as follows:—The fact that Japan has together with Great Britain, France, Russia and another Government, tendered advice in a friendly spirit to China, requesting the postponement of the monarchical movement for fear that a hurried change might cause internal disturbance which would damage the commerce, life and property of their nationals—but with the distinct assurance that they have had no wish to interfere with our internal affairs—is not without precedent in the history of diplomacy. This, together with their declaration of watchful waiting, may be regarded as in the nature of approval; and recognition is in a fair way of being accorded. There is, therefore, no question of interference or disregard at issue. How can anyone fasten any blame on the government on such a pretext, seeing that the act was the friendly advice of the friendly Powers? On the other hand the responsibility must fall on those who consider such a friendly act as an act of intervention and thus cast an insult on the country.

"The Presidential mandate issued on the 11th instant contains the following passage": 'Keeping faith is of primary importance in connexion with the administration and protection of a country. When the Republic was first established I, the President, first took an oath before the Senate, promising to do my utmost to glorify the Republic. If I should set up an Imperial system for myself I should be violating my own oath, an accusation which I shall not be able to explain: I, therefore, request that another person be designated as the Emperor.'

"The Tsanchengyuan, in the capacity of the general representatives of the people, then replied that the taking of the oath was simply a formal undertaking by the Chief Executive of the Republic, registered strictly in his capacity as such Chief Executive, which office is itself based on the choice of the whole body of the people. The Chief Executive should follow the dictates of the people. If the people are for the Republic then the oath is valid, but if the people are for a constitutional monarchy the validity is consequently changed. Now the people are tired of the Republic and desire to have a monarchy. With the change of the form of government the position of Chief Executive no longer exists; hence the oath becomes null and void. . . . The change in the form of the government recently carried out was made by the unanimous decision of the officials and people according to legal methods. The unanimity of the will of the people can be seen through the fact that there was not a single dissenting voice. Even up till this day the telegrams from military and civil officials urging the President to ascend the Throne reach Peking in great numbers every day. The shouts of joy and congratulations are as irresistible as the force of the incoming tide. How could such manifestations take place unless the change has been made by the free choice of the people themselves."[17]

This justification offered for Yuan's acceptance of the Throne did not satisfy the Yunnan leaders and they prepared to defend the Republic by force. The strength of the Yunnan movement was very seriously underrated both by the Government and by students of the situation in the Far East. Thus one authority wrote: "It is scarcely to be expected that the rebellion will make great headway. In the first place the armed forces of the nation, especially the better trained troops of the North are under the absolute control of Yuan—to whom they are loyal. Nearly all the military governors in the provinces are either old followers or personal friends of Yuan; and the few exceptions are practical men and essentially conservative in disposition. In the second place, the principle of monarchical government fairly represents the political ideal of the people as a whole. Third, even his worst enemies concede that Yuan is the ablest man to whom the nation can look both for reconstruction within and for defense against what, after all, is the greatest menace to its liberties,—danger from without. . . . If Yuan's government is overthrown it will be by greater forces than those moving the rebellion in Yunnan."[18]

And yet, in a little more than three months after the outbreak in Yunnan the revolt had spread over South and Central

[17] Telegram sent by the Chenshih Tang and the Headquarters of the Generalissimo in reply to the telegrams from Yunnan oppoing the establishment of the Monarchy, *National Review* (China), Jan. 1, 1916.

[18] Hornbeck, "Contemporary Politics in Far East," pp. 99-100.

China; the northern troops had been unable to win any very decisive victories; the men on whom Yuan had absolutely relied for support deserted his cause one after the other, or pled with him to give up the monarchy; and it was pretty well established as a fact that whatever the people thought of the Republic, and however willing they were to submit to the absolute control of Yuan Shih-kai, they were not willing to sanction the restoration of the monarchy, with the succession passing in the course of time to an incapable like Yuan's eldest son, Yuan Ko-ting.

The Government felt with Yuan Shih-kai that "well trained troops will readily suppress the rebels on reaching the scene. A few ambitious leaders without popular support are engineering the rebellion. The voting shows that the public favors a monarchy."[19]

The indications were that this view of the situation was the correct one. No one knew just what the strength of the revolutionists was, or what support they could expect from the other provinces. Yunnan itself is in rather an inaccessible situation, so that it would take a long time to bring the forces of the North to bear effectively on the province, and thus test the strength of the rebellion. The officials in the other provinces had all supported the monarchy movement and there was no evidence of the fact that they had changed their views, or that they could not control the territory under their jurisdiction. It is not strange therefore, that the concensus of opinion predicted the ultimate triumph of the government. The only dissent from the general view as to the lack of opposition was expressed by the Japanese government when it advised a postponement of the change in the form of the State. The communique issued by the Japanese Foreign Office contained

[19] *Peking Gazette,* March 12, 1916.

the extremely significant statement that: "Although it would appear as if there were throughout the country no great opposition to the establishment of a monarchy, careful observation of the actual state of affairs in China based upon information possessed by the Imperial Japanese Government, shows that it is undeniable that such appearances are more superficial than real. The undercurrent of opposition is far stronger than would be imagined and a feeling of unrest is spreading to all parts of the country."[20]   Later developments served to prove the accuracy of the Japanese estimate of the strength of the opposition to the restoration of the monarchical form of government.

In the latter part of January Yunnan was joined by Kueichow province, its neighbor to the northeast. Kwangsi and Kuangtung provinces followed suit a short time later, declaring their independence of the central authority, and it was only with difficulty that the Peking government maintained itself in Hunan. As far as the actual military operations were concerned the revolutionists did not achieve any very notable successes. In fact it was in the face of military reverses that the movement against Yuan Shih-kai gained in strength by the addition of one province after another. During the first three months of 1916 Peking could point to the fact that it was gradually pushing the rebels from territory that they had occupied at the outbreak of hostilities. But it was not possible to cope with the disaffection and dissatisfaction that was invading one province after another. Just as the Manchus had been hurried in their reforms by the revolution of 1911, so the Emperor-elect tried to placate the country by showing his sincerity in the establishment of constitutional government, the necessity for which had been emphasized by Dr. Goodnow in

[20] See Weale, "Fight for the Republic."

his memorandum. The Legislative Assembly had not been convoked for various reasons, so now it was announced that immediate steps would be taken to establish the legislature provided for under the Constitutional Compact. In order that delay should be minimized the government suggested that the members of the Citizen's Convention should be called together to sit as the Lifayuan, since they had been elected by the people in almost the same way that members of the legislature were to be chosen.

The Council of State replied favorably to this suggestion. "A Lifayuan composed of members elected by the people ought to have been convened during the period of the Constitutional Compact. The need of such an organ is doubly urgent during this time when the Throne intends to start anew with the people. A mandate was issued last year in the twelfth month stating that the legislative organ would be established within a year. The desire of the people to see an efficient government at work is more earnest than ever, and in view of the need to respect the wish of the people and to reform the administration, the delay must not continue. The process of election to the Lifayuan, however, is exceedingly complicated and difficult, and it is impossible to expect the same to be carried through in a short space of time. In these circumstances it would be more practicable to treat the final election of the Citizen's Convention—already carried through in the provinces and all the special administrative areas in advance of the date fixed last year—as the final election for the Lifayuan. In pursuance of this policy the successful members of the final election of the Citizen's Convention shall be regarded as having been elected to the Lifayuan. The single balloting of the Special Central Electorate and the combined Electorate of Mongolia, Tibet and Chinghai, which have not yet been completed, shall be held at an early date for the purpose of electing members to the Lifayuan. In this way the legislature representing the wish of the people may be convoked within a short time."[21]

This sop thrown to the opposition did not serve to check the growth of the revolutionary movement, but was rather taken as an indication of weakness. During the early part of March, 1916, however, the government forces made considerable progress from the military standpoint, and it was felt that this offered Yuan Shih-kai and the monarchists a good opportunity to "reconsider" the question of the form of government, without appearing to have been forced to do so by the rebellion. The fact that reconsideration was felt to be necessary indicates that the early impression of the strength of the rebellion had been revised. From this time on Yuan devoted himself to preserving his authority in the country with the least possible loss of "face" to himself and his supporters.

During the whole of the monarchy episode he had left a loophole for escape by his declaration that he was acting against his better judgment, and was only giving in to the will of the people. That was the line he adopted in the mandate issued on March 22 cancelling the monarchy.

Yuan Shih-kai's "abdication" edict states in part: "Since the inauguration of the Republic troubles and disturbances have come in rapid succession, and I, a man of little virtue, have been obliged to shoulder the most difficult responsibility. Patriots of this country, who have cherished the fear of imminent dangers, have advocated the restoration of monarchy with the object of averting quarrels and securing permanent peace. Since the time of the second revolution our ears have been filled with their arguments; but from time to time I have

[21] *Far Eastern Review,* March 1916.

discouraged their movements. However since last year the circumstances have been greatly changed and I have been unable to suppress their opinion. They have unanimously said that 'unless a constitutional monarchy be introduced, the existence of the Chinese nation will never be preserved.' . . . "As the sovereign authority of the Chinese nation is lodged with the whole body of the people of the country, I could not raise any opposition when the question was finally settled by the whole body of Citizen's Representatives. However my heart could not be at ease if I should ascend the Throne by breaking my oath of inauguration and disregarding principle and faithfulness. I showed my sincerity and modesty by refusing to accept the post of honor. But the said Yuan insisted that the oath of the Chief Executive was based upon the position he held at that time, but that as the condition changed he should follow the will of the people. Hence I could not make any further excuse on account of the grave responsibility forced upon me. However in order to satisfy temporarily the public desires I proceeded with the preparatory works, and no actual steps were taken. After the outbreak of the trouble in Yunnan and Kueichow, I promulgated a mandate ordering that the preparatory works should be delayed, and that no more petitions requesting the enthronement should be transmitted to me. Then I promulgated another mandate hastening the convocation of the Lifayuan with the hope of ascertaining as soon as possible the real opinion of the people, and devising some means to relieve me of the difficulty. . .

"Through misunderstandings the present trouble has arisen. My sincerity has not been sufficient to move the heart of the people, and my understanding has not been able to read the signs of the times. It is the lack of virtue on my part, and therefore I have no right to blame others. . . .

"I hereby declare that I still recognize that the memorials and documents transmitted to me through the acting Lifayuan in connection with the request for enthronement are inconsistent with the present condition of the country. The bill passed on the 11th day of the 12th month of last year on the recognition of monarchy is hereby cancelled, and the State *Dep*artment is hereby instructed to return to the acting Lifayuan all the petitions urging enthronement from the provinces and special administrative areas, so that they may be returned to the original petitioners to be destroyed. All preparations for the restoration of monarchy are hereby stopped. Thus I hope that by imitating the repentence and remorse of the ancients, the love and grace of heaven will be received. We will cleanse our hearts and thoughts, so that trouble will be averted and the people will obtain peace and tranquillity."[22]

The revolutionists, up to the cancellation of the monarchy, had been fighting for that very end. But when they had achieved their original purpose they changed their demands to include the complete elimination of Yuan Shih-kai from participation in public affairs, and also the punishment of the leaders in the monarchical movement. Instead of being placated by the cancellation edict they regarded it as a sign of weakness. For that reason the months following the restoration of the Republic were taken up with the agitation for the removal of the President. Very little fighting occurred during the period, but several provinces declared independence and the independence of the other provinces was not cancelled. Both sides endeavored to find a basis of compromise which would serve to reunite the country. While nothing short of the re-

----

[22] *Far Eastern Review,"* March 1916. The italics are the author's. See also translation given in *Peking Gazette,* March 23, 1916.

tirement of the President would satisfy one section of the South, another group expressed its willingness to see the President retain his office, provided his authority in the government was made merely nominal. This suggestion was accepted by the President and he proceeded to form a Cabinet.

An edict promulgated on April 21 stated that the failure of the President to bring about a stable condition in the country was due to the lack of a responsible ministry. "Examining the root of this failure I find that it has been due to the absence of a Cabinet and the consequent lack of direct responsibility. The fact that I have merely assumed the appearance of an unlimited control of all the powers of the State has been the cause of dissatisfaction on the part of the people."[23] The Secretary of State was therefore authorized to take control and organize a government "with the Ministers of the Metropolitan Ministries as members thereof *who are to be mutually responsible to and for one another.*"[24] This was to be the first step in the formation of a responsible Cabinet.

The actual organization of the Cabinet was provided for in a mandate issued simultaneously with the above. The Cabinet was to consist of the Secretary of State and the heads of departments. The Secretary of State was to be the head of the administration, and all laws and mandates were to receive his countersignature before becoming effective. All affairs of State were to be decided by the Cabinet members meeting as a body.[25]

The only question was to whom the Cabinet was to consider itself responsible. Yuan Shih-kai was still strong enough to control any assembly elected under the provisions of the Con-

[23] *Far Eastern Review,* April 1916, p. 428.
[24] *Ibid.,* pp. 428-429.
[25] *Ibid.,* p. 429.

stitutional Compact, and it was to be feared that the members of the Cabinet, including the Secretary of State, would act at the dictation of the President. The responsibility of the Cabinet might mean no more than it had during the few months just preceeding the revolution of 1911 when the Manchus nominally conceded the principle of responsibility by creating a figurehead Cabinet.

The question of settlement had narrowed down, then, in May 1916, to the future of Yuan Shih-kai. The independent provinces were almost unanimous in the demand for his withdrawal from public life. The Military Commanders in the Northern provinces wished him to retain office, although favoring a responsible Cabinet government, such as had been established by the edict of April 21. They pointed out that the control of the administration had been transferred from the President to the Cabinet under the direction of Premier Tuan Chi-jui, and that the Secretary of War had assumed control of the army so that Yuan was rendered powerless. They also pointed out that if the President were removed from office it might open the way for mutinies of the troops, and a general looting of the northern cities, since the soldiers of the northern armies were more loyal to their chief than to the State.[26]

The balance of power between these two opposed groups was held by the leaders in the middle provinces. The question of the day was what position would be assumed by Fêng Kuo-chang, Tutuh of Kiangsu province, whose influence was supreme in the lower Yangtze region. He held office under appointment of the Peking government, and the northerners af-

---

[26] This seems rather inconsistent with the argument that Yuan had been rendered powerless by the transfer of control over the army to the Secretary of War. But political necessity frequently overrides consistency in Chinese politics.

firmed his absolute loyalty to Yuan Shih-kai. The South, on the other hand, claimed that at heart he was an anti-monarchist and in sympathy with the revolt against the overthrow of the Republic.

The first statement of Fêng's position came on April 26. In a lengthy memorial to the President he discussed the situation in the country. But his statement left his attitude toward the retention of the President in office still indeterminate.

Finally, his hand was forced by the government gathering together its forces in the loyal provinces to secure a declaration of terms from the independent provinces. General Fêng Kuo-chang then suggested to General Ni Shih-chung and General Chang Hsun that they should meet to discuss their future action. This meeting, held at Hsüchowfu, the stronghold of Chang Hsun, resulted in the despatch of a circular telegram to the provinces asking them to send delegates to Nanking with full powers to discuss terms of peace. At the same time eight fundamental questions were suggested for the consideration of the Conference. These embraced the position and future status of both the President and the Vice-President; the question of the constitution of a parliament; the revision in some particulars of the Constitution, until a permanent constitution could be adopted; the question of the National finances, which were in a very serious condition; the question of the army control and disposition; the qualifications and standing of both military and civil officials; the future treatment of the advocates of monarchy—whether they should be killed or simply sent into retirement; and, finally, the question of party members in Parliament.

This whole programme was construed in the South as an indication of General Fêng's desire to substitute his own for Yuan Shih-kai's control of the country. The southern leaders responded by the establishment of an independent government with Canton as the capital. TheVice-President, then virtually a captive in Peking was named as the President of this new government, and all its acts were promulgated in his name. This step consolidated the northern military leaders in opposition to the South, and it looked as though a definite break would be made between the two sections of the country.

In spite of developments in the North and the South, the promoters of the Conference at Nanking, who had volunteered their services as mediators between the two sections, proceeded with their activities. The first indications were that they expected to use the Conference as an instrument for the retention of Yuan. On May 13 it was stated[27] that the three Generals concerned had telegraphed the President to that effect, only stipulating that he should hand over all military, executive and legislative power to the Cabinet, and assure the mediators personally of his sincerity in giving up the power. If he did this they declared their readiness to urge the southern leaders to cancel the demand for the retirement of Yuan Shih-kai from political life.

When delegates finally assembled at Nanking it was found that the independent provinces were not represented, and they refused to send delegates until the President gave assurances that he would give up his office. Yuan at this time stated that he was perfectly willing to go into retirement, providing he could be convinced that trouble would not follow. "I assure you that I have not the least desire to linger at my post, nor am I unwilling to yield power and position."[28] But so long as the President retained control of the northern capital, it was impossible to prove to him that the troops would not

[27] *Far Eastern Review,* May 1916, p. 480.
[28] *Far Eastern Review,* May 1916, p. 483.

mutiny immediately after his controlling hand was removed. It only remained to see what action the Conference would take, even without the representation of the independent provinces. Meetings were held on May 19 and 20, and it was apparent from the first that the delegates themselves were undecided. "Some were in favor of retaining Yuan Shih-kai, other advocated Li Yuan-hung, while a section desired an election for President as soon as possible. This group was willing to allow Yuan to retain his post until a Parliament could be called and an election be held."[29]   After discussion it was decided to inform the South that the Conference favored the retirement of the President, but felt that definitive action should be taken only by a Conference representative of all the provinces.

During May three hitherto loyal provinces declared their independence of the Peking government. This fact, together with the action taken by the Nanking Conference, made it impossible for the supporters of the President to continue to hold out. Provision was made for his departure from the country, and the parliamentarians prepared to reassume control of the government. With this in view members of the old Parliament assembled in Shanghai. The Military Government which had been set up in Canton issued a manifesto declaring in part: "Since the Parliament is the most important organ provided for in the Provisional (Nanking) Constitution and from which all laws have their origin, how shall we be able to reorganize our administrative affairs if the restoration of the Parliament is further delayed. We hereby notify the members of the National Assembly and call on them speedily to formulate a programme for the convocation and a meeting place of the Parliament so that all unsettled questions may be

[29] *Far Eastern Review,* May 1916, p. 484.

settled without delay, and all the organs called for by law may soon be organized."[30]

The members of the Parliament who had assembled in Shanghai also issued a call to all who had held seats in the old Assembly. "In consequence of Yuan's rebellion, the righteous troops have risen against him. The whole country has joined the movement like the sweeping wind; and a settlement of the general situation is at hand. . . . Yuan continues to show defiance behind the barricade of strong arms and to make use of his bottomless cunning and capacity for intrigue. The disturbances cannot be suppressed unless the foundation of the country be at once consolidated. We, members of the Parliament—albeit we have been intrusted by the people with our duties—have not been able to discharge the same during the last three years owing to the unlawful action of Yuan. At this time of extraordinary national crisis, it is our duty to meet in accordance with law. Article 20 of the Provisional Constitution provides that the Senate may have full freedom to call, hold or adjourn meetings. Article 28 provides that the Senate shall automatically dissolve when the National Assembly is inaugurated; and the functions of the Senate shall be fulfilled by the National Assembly. It is thus seen that the National Assembly is empowered to call, hold and adjourn meetings. In order to meet the demands of the necessities of the situation, we have been holding meetings in accordance with this provision; and over two hundred members have now reached Shanghai for this purpose. We have now the honor to issue this formal summons to all the members of the National Assembly, except those who are accomplices in Yuan's rebellion, to report at Shanghai not later than June 30. A

[30] *Far Eastern Review,* June 1916, p. 20.

suitable place will then be fixed for the resumption of the sessions of Parliament."[31]

Since Peking had finally agreed that Yuan should retire, the South gave up its demand for his punishment equally with the other members of the monarchical party. The southern leaders guaranteed him a safe departure from the country in return for his promise that the Metropolitan troops would preserve order after he left. The American legation also promised asylum to the defeated autocrat.

But, after all, the final decision rested neither with the North nor the South. On June 5 all the terms of settlement had been agreed upon. But on June 6 a higher hand intervened and death claimed the right to settle the dispute. It was the unanimous feeling throughout China that nothing more opportune could have happened. So long as he lived Yuan Shih-kai would have been able to make his influence felt in the country, either directly or indirectly. He might have been as much a thorn in the side of the government as Dr. Sun Yat-sen has been since his retirement from the presidency in 1912 in favor of Yuan Shih-kai. It was truly said that "Yuan Shih-kai, late President of China, has earned warmer expressions of gratitude from all classes of his fellow countrymen by his death than by any or all of the acts of his official life."[32]

After his death the last mandate of Yuan Shih-kai, sanctioned by him as he was dying, was promulgated. By this mandate the executive authority was transferred to the Vice-President, Li Yuan-hung, in accordance with Article 29 of the Constitutional Compact. The mandate was as follows:

"The Min Kuo has been established for five years. Un-

[31] *Far Eastern Review*, June 1916, p. 21.
[32] *Far Eastern Review*, June 1916, p. 10.

worthily have I, the Great President, been entrusted with the great task by the citizens. Owing to my lack of virtue and ability I have not been able fully to transform into deed what I have desired to accomplish; and I blush to say that I have not realized one ten-thousandth part of my original intention to save the country and the people. I have, since my assumption of the office, worked in day and thought in the night, planning for the country. It is true that the consolidation of the country is not yet accomplished, the hardships of the people not yet relieved, and innumerable reforms are still unattended to. But by the valuable services of the civil officials and the military men, some semblance of peace and order has been maintained in the provinces and friendly relations with the Powers upheld until now. While on the one hand I comfort myself with such things accomplished, on the other hand I have much to blame myself for. I was just thinking how I could retire into private life and rest myself in the forest and near the springs in fulfillment of my original desire, when illness has suddenly overtaken me. As the affairs of the State are of the gravest importance, the right man must be secured to take over charge of the same. In accordance with Article 29 of the Provisional Constitution which states that in case the office of the Great President should be vacated for certain reasons, or when the Great President is incapacitated from doing his duties, the Vice-President shall exercise power and authority in his stead, I, the Great President, declare in accordance with the Provisional Constitution that the Vice-President shall exercise in an acting capacity, the authority and power of the Great President of the Chung Hua Min Kuo.

"The Vice-President being a man of courtesy, good nature, benevolence and wisdom, will certainly be capable of greatly lessening the difficulties of the day and place the country on the foundation of peace, and so remedy the defects of me, the

Great President, and satisfy the expectations of the people of the whole country. The civil and military officials outside of the capital, as well as the troops, police, and scholars and people should doubly keep in mind the difficulties and perils of the nation, and endeavor to maintain peace and order to the best of their ability, placing before everything else the welfare of the country. The ancients once said: 'it is only when the living do try to become strong that the dead are not dead.' That is also the wish of me, the Great President."[33]

[33] *Far Eastern Review*, June 1916, p. 21.

CHAPTER IX

Li Yuan-hung, the new President of the Republic, had become a national idol since the revolution in 1911. He alone of the prominent leaders had the trust of all sections of the country, and of all classes. It was not any great brilliancy of mind or of achievement that made the country welcome General Li to the presidency so much as his constancy of character and honesty of purpose. What was needed in the new head of the State was the capacity for unselfish and disinterested service. He must be a man who would allow free play to the parliamentary party and yet keep parliamentary activity within reasonable bounds in order to prevent a recurrence of the conditions which had paved the way for the overthrow of Parliament by Yuan Shih-kai. On the other hand it was necessary for the President to have the support of the military leaders, the so-called Pei-yang party, and reconcile them to the limitation of administrative control by legislative action. Li Yuan-hung was a military man, but a firm believer in the elimination of the military from control over the administration. He was therefore not the first choice of the military men for President. But he was the one distinctly military leader who could command the support of the South, and he had a strong constitutional claim to the succession from his position as Vice-President. To have passed over General Li and opened the office of President to general competition would have led to the practical disruption of the Chinese State. There were factions among the military party of the North, centering around the acting Premier, Tuan Chi-jui, and the Yangtze Viceroy

Fêng Kuo-chang, and the South was similarly divided. Both sides were agreed on the proposition that only in the person of the Vice-President could the two sections be held together. So the death of President Yuan brought General Li Yuan-hung into office as a moderator between the two sections of the country.

That the New President's task was to be no easy one became apparent from the outset. The situation was essentially the same as when Yuan Shih-kai became President at the time of the establishment of the Republic. In response to the demand of the South Yuan had created a Cabinet during his last days in office. The Premier, Tuan Chi-jui, was one of the military party, so that the North controlled the executive branch of the government, just as in 1912. The Parliament had reassembled in Shanghai, as has been noted, but had not established itself yet as a part of the Peking government. The first question that arose, naturally, was the exact status of constitutionalism in China. What was to be the distribution of power between the two branches of the government?

If the Constitutional Compact was to be regarded as the fundamental law, the Shanghai parliamentarians had no legal status since they had been elected under the provisions of the original (Nanking) constitution. Furthermore any assembly that should be elected would have very little power so long as the Constitutional Compact remained in force.

On the other hand, if the Nanking Constitution should be revived the condition would be reversed, the executive being subordinated to the Parliament. Since the North controlled the executive at the time of the downfall of Yuan Shih-kai, and this control was continued through the transfer of the presidential powers to the Cabinet, the revival of the Nanking Constitution was demanded by the "independent" provinces as one condition preliminary to their return to allegiance. Tuan Chi-jui the Premier opposed this demand as long as possible on the ground that since both constitutions were only provisional, it was advisable to continue under the existing instrument until a permanent constitution could be framed. His argument ran as follows: "The [revised] Provisional Constitution of the 3rd year has been in force for some time and has been repeatedly quoted as the standard for administration. If it be blotted out by one single sentence, all the laws of the nation may be similarly shaken. . . . Others say that the Provisional Constitution of the 3rd year derives its origin from the Provisional Constitution Conference and the Provisional Constitution Conference had its origin in the Political Council, and since all the members of the Council were appointed by the Government, they could not be considered as a legally constituted organ and consequently to revive the Provisional Constitution of the 1st year is tantamount merely to the cancellation of an old mandate. But this is also impossible. The reason why the people are not satisfied with the Provisional Constitution of the 3rd year is because the organ which made this law had its origin in a mandate. How then can we toler-ate the idea of reviving the Provisional Constitution of the 1st year? . . . A mistake has already been made some time ago. How can we repeat the same mistake this time? I do not see why the people want to follow an example which they know to be wrong. If it is to be held that a law can be restored by a mandate, why then cannot it be cancelled by a mandate also? A law then can be restored today and cancelled tomorrow."[1]

Before a reply could be framed to these arguments the government was forced to an unconditional surrender. Fighting

[1] *Far Eastern Review*, October, 1916, pp. 176-177.

was reported as continuing in Kuangtung province, and the whole country was disturbed by bands of marauders and insurrectionaries. So long as the power of the government was questioned in the provinces which had declared independence it was impossible to bring order out of the existing chaos. If Tuan had been hoping that the southern leaders would recede from their advanced position as a result of the telegram setting forth his views, he was immediately undeceived. In the midst of the controversy over the constitution, the Chief Commander of the Yangtze fleet wired to Peking declaring his independence of the Central authority.[2]

This new declaration, together with the fact that none of the provinces had cancelled their independence, forced Tuan Chi-jui to reconsider the question of the constitution. On June 29 a mandate was issued providing for the convocation of the old Parliament and the revival of the Nanking Constitution, "in order that the will of the people may be satisfied and the foundation of the country consolidated."[3] The Premier not only gave in to this demand for the reconvocation of Parliament and the revival of the Nanking Constitution, but met all of the other demands of the South including the one that the monarchist leaders should be punished.

Parliament was summoned to meet in Peking on August 1, and was formally opened on that date, in spite of the opposition of some of the members who wished to transfer the seat of government to Shanghai. In order to get the constitutional machinery in operation again it had been decided to treat the entire period from the time of the dissolution of Parliament

---

[2] "The Navy will not obey the orders of the Ministry of Navy in Peking until the restoration of the Provisional Constitution of the 1st year of Min Kuo, the reassembly of Parliament, and the formation of a responsible Cabinet." *Ibid.*, p. 177.

[3] *Ibid.*, p. 177.

in 1913 until its meeting in 1916 as an interregnum.[4]   Thus the members were to serve their full terms during the period when the Nanking Constitution was in active force.   If this view had not been taken it would have been necessary to hold new elections immediately since the term of the members of the House of Representatives and a number of the Senators had expired during the dictatorship.

While the Constitutional Compact was in force the Parliament had no legal position, but when the first Provisional Constitution was revived the Cabinet which had been formed under the authority of the President was placed in the same position.   The Premier, however, was confirmed in his position by the joint action of both branches of the legislature, and the Cabinet nominations which he submitted were accepted.   It seemed as though an "era of good feeling" had dawned in Peking, and that, by the coöperation of the President, the Cabinet, and the Parliament, the necessary reform and reorganization of the government might be effected.   The situation in the provinces was still unsettled, but after the inauguration of the President and the meeting of the Parliament the "declarations of independence" had been cancelled, and where there was unrest it was due to the presence of unattached soldiery preying on the country, or to individual struggles for supremacy in the provincial government, as in Kuangtung province.

This apparent harmony was however not to last long.   No sooner had the Parliament reassembled than the Military Chiefs began to assume a dictatorial position toward the government.   Among the appointments made to Cabinet positions was that of T'ang Shao-yi as Minister of Foreign Affairs. The opposition to Parliament concentrated its attack on the

[4] The foreign "Advisers" Dr. Morrison (British), Dr. W. W. Willoughby (American), and Dr. Ariga (Japanese), advised that this view of the monarchical period be adopted.

new Foreign Minister before he had even assumed office.   In September a Conference of the military leaders was held at Hsüchow the stronghold of the old Manchu supporter Chang Hsün.   This Conference claimed the right to be consulted by the government before any steps of importance were taken and it demanded the resignation of T'ang Shao-yi, accusing him of a desire to overthrow the Premier.   This organized attack made on T'ang caused him to delay at Tientsin on his way to assume office, and finally forced his resignation.   He made his resignation a protest against the illegal interference of the military in the affairs of the government, intimating that some of the high officials in Peking were implicated in the campaign against his assumption of office.   As a matter of fact, the Premier took no steps against the Hsüchow Conference, which went so far as to organize a "Union of the Provinces" with the avowed purpose of interference if Parliament should "under any pretext create disturbance or take up an unconciliatory attitude toward the provinces."[5]   This whole question of dictation to the government by such an unconstitutional and illegal body as assembled at Hsüchow later assumed such importance that it led to a complete overturning of the government.   For that reason its more detailed consideration must be postponed.[6]

From the time of the resignation of T'ang Shao-yi as Minister of Foreign Affairs, the relations of the Premier, Tuan-Chi-jui, with Parliament were strained.   For a long time it proved impossible to fill the vacant position in the Cabinet. Lu Chêng-hsiang was first nominated by the Premier, and then Wang Ta-hsieh, and both names were rejected by Parlia-

---

[5] *Peking Gazette*, September 22, 1916.

[6] *Infra*, ch. X, especially pp. 234-235; note p. 234 for a discussion of the Peiyang military party and its influence.

ment. Finally the veteran statesman Dr. Wu T'ing-fang was suggested and his nomination was confirmed by both Houses. In spite of his great age Dr. Wu accepted the post of Foreign Minister in order that there might be a head to that Department at a time when many delicate negotiations were in progress with foreign nations.[7]

The confirmation of Dr. Wu as Foreign Minister did not end the conflict between the Cabinet and Parliament. Other nominations to Cabinet positions were rejected; the loan policy of the government was continually criticised; constant inter-pellations were addressed to the government concerning the ad-ministration of the country; and there was a growing tendency to heckle members of the Cabinet when they were forced to appear in Parliament.

It is hard to apportion the blame for the strained relations existing between the different branches of the government. Certainly no one branch was entirely responsible. Parliament showed again most of the tendencies which had weakened its control over the government during the first months of the Republic: a disposition to talk and do nothing; to obstruct the work of administration and reorganization needlessly; and to censure the Cabinet for acting on its own initiative when it was found that no direction of policy was forthcoming from Parliament. Parliament wished to feel that it held the con-trol, but refused to exert itself to assume the responsibilities placed upon it as the controlling and directing organ.

On the other hand the Premier was partly to blame for the opposition to his policies in Parliament. The Constitution

[7] Discussions were going on between France and China con-cerning the attempt of the former to extend her "concession" at Tientsin, and between Japan and China over a fracas between Chinese and Japanese at Chêngchiatun. Japan took the oppor-tunity presented to advance in another guise some of her 1915 Demands.

provided a way by which the Cabinet could assume the direction of affairs in the legislative body—the Ministers having the right to appear and explain their policies to the members of Parliament. But from the first Tuan Chi-jui looked
upon a legislature as an unnecessary evil in government.
Following the lead of Yuan Shih-kai, he tried to carry on the
administration without consulting the wishes of the representatives, only appearing before them to ask their consent for
work already undertaken. When a Cabinet position was to be
filled no attempt was made to discover the wishes of Parliament and then make an acceptable appointment. The nomination was made first and its acceptability discovered later when
action was taken in Parliament. In some cases, without doubt,
an entirely unacceptable candidate was brought forward with
the expectation that after he had been rejected Parliament
would be willing to accept the real candidate of the government. It is true that the opinion of one of the parties[8] was
usually ascertained and its support secured, but that party,
which was really that of the government, was in the minority
in Parliament so that its support meant little.

The differences between the legislative and executive
branches of the government went much deeper than any disagreement over specific issues. The conflict was a renewal of
the struggle which had been waged since 1911 between the old
Manchu bureaucracy which had survived in the persons of
the military leaders making up the Pei-yang party, and which
controlled the army of the North, and Young China in the
persons of foreign educated Chinese and all those who had
led in the opposition to the unprogressive Manchu government.
Since the leaders of the latter group were almost all from
South and Central China the issue really lay between the North

[8] The Chin Pu T'ang.

and the South. The northerners, whatever else may be said of them, were men of experience in administration, while the southerners, although not all young men, were still theorists without great practical experience. They were impatient of the restraint imposed by the conservative old officials, and the latter, accustomed to the subserviency of the young, found it difficult to make use of the knowledge and ability of men who knew how things were done in England, France and America, and wished to make of China a political replica of those countries. Mutual distrust and suspicion also was responsible for much of the antagonism between the two sections. This distrust manifested itself in the government through the executive going its own way irrespective of Parliament, and that body constantly feeling itself slighted and standing on its dignity in small matters as well as more important ones. Peking was a hotbed of intrigue and corruption. Unsubstantiated charges and countercharges were made, and, instead of both sides meeting issues on their merits, calumny took the place of reason in discussion.

One of the few hopeful indications of the growing ability of the Chinese to conduct parliamentary proceedings in an orderly manner came in connection with the election of a Vice-President to fill the place left vacant by the elevation of Li Yuan-hung to the presidency. The members of Parliament were by no means unanimously agreed that it was necessary to elect a Vice-President before the expiration of the presidential term, when both places would have to be filled. There were several candidates for the position and it was feared, in view of the already strained relations between the executive and legislative bodies,—the military party and the advocates of civil government free from outside interference —that to proceed with an election would be to precipitate a governmental crisis. This was especially feared because of the suggested candidacy of the Premier. The question was argued in an orderly manner, however, in the Assembly, and it was finally determined not to delay but to elect the Vice-President to serve during the unexpired term. Tuan Chi-jui announced several times that he was not to be considered a candidate for the office, but in spite of his statements many expected that he would figure prominently in the election. Aside from Tuan, the principal contestants were General Fêng Kuochang, the Viceroy of Kiangsu province, and General Lu Yungting, former Tutuh of Kiangsi province. General Lu was supported by the extreme radicals.

According to the Presidential Election Law[9] which also regulated the election of the Vice-President, the election was to be by the two Houses of Parliament sitting as the National Convention. Two-thirds of the membership of the Assembly was necessary to constitute a quorum, and election was to be by a three-fourths majority. If no decision was reached after two ballots, however, the third ballot was to be on the two candidates who secured the most votes on the second ballot. A majority vote was sufficient to elect on the third ballot.

The two branches of the Assembly met on October 30 in joint session and proceeded to ballot for the Vice-President. The election of General Fêng Kuo-Chang seemed assured from the outset. On the first ballot he secured more than half of the total number of votes cast, but not the required three-fourths. The second was equally indecisive, but he was elected on the third when the voting was limited to the two highest competitors, Fêng Kuo-chang and Lu Yung-ting. On the first and second ballots a number of scattered votes were cast,

[9] This section of the permanent Constitution had been passed in 1913 before the dissolution of Parliament.

some of the members seemingly regarding their work with little seriousness.[10]

On the whole the result of the election was well received throughout the country. The new Vice-President had close connections with the military party, but he had refused to identify himself with it in its attempts to dictate the policy of the country since the death of Yuan Shih-kai. While he had supported Yuan in his overthrow of parliamentary institutions, he had partially redeemed himself in the eyes of many of the people by his attempted mediation between the North and the South just before the death of the President, At least he had shown a certain political foresight in breaking away from Yuan before his own political career had been ruined by his connection with that statesman. Another vital consideration in its bearing on the outcome of the election was the important strategic position held by General Fêng on the lower Yangtze. It was much safer to have him interested in defending the government than to give a grievance which might cause him to use his influence to stir up trouble in an unsettled region.

The *Peking Gazette* gives us an interesting comparison between the election of the Vice-President and the choice of a President in 1913. "Everybody remarked on the contrast between this election and the election for the late President Yuan Shih-kai. In 1913 the House of Parliament was surrounded by many cordons of armed soldiery and the gates were blocked by troops to prevent any of the M.P.'s escaping during the proceeding. Looking over the walls surrounding the House, one saw plainly the many troops with fixed bayonets peering into the Parliament building, for what everyone

[10] Among others, votes were cast for K'ang Yu-wei and General Chang Hsün. See *Peking Gazette*, Oct. 31, 1916.

was free to imagine for himself.   Yesterday only a handful of soldiers patrolled the streets to direct the traffic.   With the exception of parliamentary guards in full uniform and about half a dozen military police there was nothing unusual about the policing of the occasion.   People, including the M.P.'s, moved about freely and the spectators were not subjected to close scrutiny as if they were assassins.   The Republic is indeed among us!   In perfect harmony with this promising atmosphere was the very orderly conduct of the members of Parliament."[11]

A second and more important task to which the Parliament addressed itself was the framing and adoption of a permanent constitution for the Republic.   This had been undertaken by the first Parliament elected, and its task had been almost completed at the time when the Kuo Ming Tang members had been driven from Peking by Yuan Shih-kai.[12]   The President had objected to several provisions of this first draft of the permanent constitution, so that it had been thrown into the wastepaper basket when he made himself the dictator.   Yuan Shih-kai, in his turn, had undertaken the work of providing China with a permanent constitution, appointing a commission to draw up an instrument acceptable to him, but the monarchy movement prevented anything of value being accomplished by this commission.

As soon as Parliament had assembled in Peking after the collapse of the monarchy movement it took up the work of constitution framing at the point reached in 1913.   The basis of discussion was the draft permanent constitution presented in that year.   A Conference on the Constitution[13] was organ-

[11] *Peking Gazette,* October 31, 1916.
[12] The draft of the constitution prepared by the Constitution Drafting Committee had been submitted for the action of the Conference on the Constitution.
[13] The two Houses acting in that capacity.

ized for the consideration of the provisions of that draft with a view to amending it rather than substituting an entirely new instrument.[14]

The fact that it had already received the tentative approval of the members of Parliament[15] in its main outlines did not prevent a serious disagreement as to the final form in which it should be cast. Political changes during 1914-15 had brought about new party alignments. The events of the same years had shown the necessity of adapting the fundamental instrument of government to conditions as they existed in China rather than merely incorporating in it the most advanced political ideas of the West. Yuan Shih-kai and the representatives of the old mandarinate had condemned the draft constitution of 1913 as unsuited to the immediate needs and capacity of China because of the excessive powers vested in the Assembly and the consequent limitations placed on the executive branch of the government. The Constitution Drafting Committee had refused to hear the views of the President and the men who had been engaged in the practical work of administration. The constitution drawn up, for that reason, while admirable in theory for the government of a democratic State, lacked the adaptable nature of an instrument which had resulted from a compromise between new ideas and old practice.

The events of the year 1913 had served to discredit political parties and party action in China. The Kuo Ming Tang had been condemned for its connection with the summer revolution of that year, and later many of the Chin Pu Tang supporters had fallen into disgrace because of their support of

---

[14] This conference met in the Temple of Heaven, alternating its sittings with that of Parliament as a legislative body.

[15] It had been sanctioned by the drafting committee composed of 60 members, 30 chosen by each House of Parliament.

Yuan Shih-kai. But where there is room for difference of opinion on political issues party groupings will result.

The regrouping of the members of Parliament after their return to Peking came as a result of the differences over the provisions of the permanent constitution. Party grouping in the main followed the old Chin Pu Tang and Kuo Ming Tang lines. On constitutional questions Parliament was divided into four main groups, each consisting of several smaller ones. These were 1) the "Constitution Discussion Society" which was made up principally of old Kuo Ming Tang adherents; 2) "the Constitution Research Society," a Chin Pu Tang group; 3) the Constitution Deliberation Society, composed of deserters from both the Kuo Ming and the Chin Pu Tangs; and 4) the Constitution Mutual Discussion Society" consisting of members from Shantung, Chihli, Tibet and Mongolia, who were neither radicals nor conservatives, but who merely fell in line with the majority, whatever that happened to be.

The strongest clash between the different groups came over the discussion of the provincial system. This chapter of the constitution had been omitted from the draft prepared in 1913. The issue concerned the relation of the provinces to the Central Government. One party[16] desired to see the provincial system practically freed from the control of Peking, the provinces being in effect self-governing States united only for the regulation of their mutual interests. Under this de-centralized system the Governor of the province would have been an elected official responsible partly to the Central Government and partly to the provincial assembly.

The other extreme was presented by those who demanded that the province should be only an administrative area, the officials being appointed by the President and subject to his

[16] The Kuo Ming Tang.

direction and control.[17]   Between these two extreme groups were the moderates who favored granting a large degree of autonomy to the provinces, but giving the President a restricted right to appoint high provincial officials.

Under the Manchu regime the Governor had been appointed by the Emperor and no high provincial official was allowed to serve in his native province.   With the outbreak of the revolution the provincial governments were largely self-constituted. Sometimes the Governor held office in virtue of an election by a provincial assembly or other local organization.   In most cases however he was simply a noted revolutionary leader holding office because of that fact.   A notable departure from the old Manchu practice lay in the fact that the Governors were frequently natives of the provinces.   After the establishment of the Republic most of these men were confirmed in their positions as Tutuhs or military Governors.[18]   Later, attempts were made to replace them by civil Governors.   Yuan Shihkai used his right of appointment to fill these high provincial posts with his own friends and supporters, in some cases going back to the Manchu idea that no official must serve in his native province.

The way in which the former President had made use of his right to appoint provincial officers to strengthen himself had convinced many people that the safety of the country depended upon limiting this right.   If the party in control of the Parliament had also controlled the executive it is probable

[17] This was, in effect, the position taken by the Chin Pu Tang members.

[18] In addition to the Tutuh, and the civil Governor where one had been appointed, there were, in many of the Provinces, the irresponsible military chiefs holding no official position in the provincial administrative system, but maintaining themselves by force of arms.

that this fear of the presidential use of the patronage would not have been so strong. As it was, the executive could control the major part of the country by appointing his adherents to provincial office. Yuan Shih-kai had been successful in securing himself as dictator largely for that reason, and while he ultimately failed to maintain himself it was due to the fact that he went beyond the point where his own appointees would lend him their support. Consequently there was good reason for this conflict over the manner of appointment of the Governors.

In addition to the fear of presidential appointment there was another reason to be urged in favor of the province itself making a choice of its chief officers. In the past the people had been little concerned with the personnel of the administration. They seldom knew personally the officials over them with the exception of the lowest in the scale, the district magistrate, and he was usually transferred before coming into intimate relationship with the people of his district. At least he was not a native of the place. The result was that the officials did not know the local needs and customs as well as if they had been natives of the province or of the district. If, under the new system, the right to choose provincial officials was given to the local assemblies they would undoubtedly select some man well known in the province, and with an intimate knowledge of the local customs and traditions, to serve as Governor or in other high office. This would bring about a more intimate relationship between the people and the government and help to pave the way for a true representative system in the national as well as in the local administration. A similar result would follow from the proposal to allow the local assemblies to nominate two candidates for the position of governor, one of them a native and the other a non-resident of the province, the President of the Republic making a choice between the two men nominated. By giving the people even an indirect influence in determining their higher rulers, the much vaunted democracy of China would be extended gradually from a direction of village affairs to a control over the entire provincial system and the national administration.

On the other hand this suggested enlargement of provincial control might easily lead to disruption of the State. The tendency had always been to put local advantage before national interest, and this had been held in check only partially by the old method of absolute appointment of officials by the Central authority and holding them responsible for the administration of their province or district. The provincial official, while responsible to Peking for carrying out the policy of the Central government, had been forced, even under the old regime, to consider the effect of that policy on local opinion. This had resulted in the lack of uniformity of administration in China which has already been noted. If the Governor depended on the provincial assembly for his election, or even for confirmation after appointment by the central executive, the administration would tend more than ever to consider local interests and prejudices rather than national needs. The State, instead of being unified, would become a confederation of States. The advocates of provincial autonomy favored making the country a Federal Union, pointing to the United States as the model to be followed. But there is this important difference between China and the United States to be borne in mind. In the United States the necessity of establishing an intimate relationship between the individual and the Federal Government was seen from the first, while in China the Central Government has never exercised a direct control over the individual. In the collection of taxes, for example, national needs were met by assessments on the provinces as such, rather than by levies on the people directly. Therefore any de-centralized system that should be established would be more comparable to the condition of the states under the Articles of Confederation than to the Federal Union formed in 1789.

Furthermore, all of the proposals for appointment by the assemblies, or limitation of the presidential appointing power, meant an extension of the elective system beyond the choice of representatives to watch over and control the administration. This would introduce the element of uncertainty and unrest into the provincial administration which was feared in national politics because of the periodic election of a President. It might lead to conflict between rival contestants for provincial office, keeping the provinces in a state of perpetual turmoil. However, this argument cannot be pressed too far because the Chinese are much more accustomed to compromise in such cases than to carry the controversy to the point of open conflict.

From the international point of view there could be but one answer to the question of the form in which the provincial system should be cast. All past experience both in China and other countries has been that foreign relations can be most satisfactorily carried on under a centralized system of administration. Treaty engagements made must be uniformly carried out in all parts of a country. China has suffered repeated humiliation in the past because of the variation in carrying out treaty provisions in the several provinces. This international factor is one that cannot be disregarded in a country like China where the Powers hold a peculiarly favored position. The future of the State depends on the ability of the Central Government to avoid entanglements in foreign relations. If the establishment of provincial autonomy would weaken the control of Peking in the conduct of foreign affairs, then, even at the expense of less popular participation in the government, the decision should be in favor of a centralization of authority.

The discussion over the provincial system went on without a decision being reached. Several times it seemed as though an acceptable basis of agreement would be found but all of the compromises suggested failed to bring the two extremes together. In addition to the differences over the appointment of the officials, there was the added question of whether the provincial system should be included in the constitution or should be established by ordinary legislative enactment. If it became a part of the constitutional law it would be very difficult to adjust it to conditions as they changed from time to time, or to remedy any defects that appeared when it was put into actual operation. On the other hand, if it was promulgated as an ordinary law it could be changed too easily, it was felt, and for that reason would be liable to constant experimentation. The division on this latter question was along the same party lines as on the actual provisions of the provincial system.[19]

The other important point of difference that arose in the discussions of the Constitutional Conference was whether Confucianism should be made the State religion. All were agreed that the doctrines of Confucius should be used as the basis for instruction in ethics in the schools, but many felt that it was unwise to insert a specific clause in the constitution to that effect. The old conservatives were supporters of the idea, but

[19] The Kuo Ming Tang members advocated the inclusion of the provincial system while the Chin Pu Tang and the military leaders opposed it. The Chin Pu Tang finally agreed to its inclusion if definite provision was made for the appointment of the Governor by the President.

after much discussion, and the expression of opinion from the provinces, the clause was omitted from the constitution.

While Parliament was working over the draft of the permanent constitution the usual spring housecleaning in Chinese politics was approaching. The draft of the constitution had been rushed through its third reading by the drafting committee in 1913 to forestall a threatened overturn of Parliament by Yuan Shih-kai, and in the spring of 1917 it was necessary to push the permanent constitution through the second reading for a similar reason. The Constitution as it passed the second reading in the Constitutional Conference was published in July after Parliament had been driven again from Peking —this time by the action of the northern military leaders. Very few changes were made in the draft by the Conference. No agreement had been reached on the provincial system, so that it was omitted from the Constitution. The principal change made was in the elimination of the chapter in the draft providing for a permanent parliamentary committee to sit during recesses, keeping the government under the supervision of Parliament during the whole year. This was the provision that had been objected to in particular by Yuan Shih-kai when the terms of the draft had been made known. Aside from that change only a few alterations in wording had been made. Thus the wording of the clauses providing for a responsibility of the Cabinet to Parliament was altered to make certain that there would be no misunderstanding of what was meant.[21]

The government of the Republic of China, if this permanent Constitution as drawn up by Parliament becomes effective, will be that known as parliamentary or responsible rather than the American or presidential system. Entire control over the administration is vested in the Assembly. It is given

[21] Articles 75 and 81.

the right to interpellate the Ministers, and to pass a vote of want of confidence in the Cabinet. All legislative power is concentrated in Parliament, together with control over national finances. On the other hand, the Cabinet is given the right to appear and defend its policies, and to introduce legislation, so that it will almost inevitably tend to assume the direction of the administration, instead of acting simply as the creature of Parliament. While the Cabinet is made responsible to the body representative of the electorate it is safeguarded from subserviency through the power given it to dissolve Parliament after a vote of want of confidence, instead of itself giving up office. While the executive power is vested nominally in the President, the Constitution provides that the real direction shall be in the hands of the Cabinet. It will, of course, depend largely on the personality of the incumbent of the office what influence the President will have in the administration. President Li Yuan-hung was by no means a negligible factor in the government during his term of office, although he left the direction of affairs to the Premier. As a mediator between the various factions in Parliament, and between Parliament and the Cabinet, he filled a very necessary place in the machinery. Form the standpoint of power, however, the important position was that of Premier rather than that of the President, and this will be increasingly true if the permanent constitution comes into force, and the machinery of government runs more smoothly.

CHAPTER X

In the last chapter brief mention was made of the continued interference of the military leaders in the conduct of the civil government. After the death of Yuan Shih-kai the only check on the absolute power of Parliament lay in the constitution of the executive. Li Yuan-hung, as President, did not attempt to assume the dominating position which had been Yuan's by virtue of his personality and ability. President Li accepted the subordinate position given the President under the Nanking constitution, and based all of his acts on a desire to do nothing that was not strictly constitutional. The real executive power, however, descended to the Premier acting at the time of Yuan Shih-kai's death. It was from the Cabinet rather than the President that active opposition to parliamentary control developed. While nominally the President was the head of the administration, the constitution provided that all of his acts must have the countersignature of a Cabinet Minister. So long as the President was the strongest man in the executive branch, and possessed of the most influence in the country, he could keep the Cabinet subject to his dictation, so that the right of countersignature could not be used as a check on his actions. The Cabinet formed in the summer of 1916 was not of President Li's choosing, however, but was a legacy from the preceding administration. When it received the confirmation of Parliament, the direction of the administration became vested in the Premier, Tuan Chi-jui, instead of the President.

Tuan was recognized as one of the strongest of the military leaders, and he came into office under the influence of the same ideas that had dominated Yuan Shih-kai, his old leader. It was inevitable that he should rebel sooner or later against parliamentary interference in the administration just as Yuan had done. The only question was whether he could maintain himself in the conflict. In a struggle against Parliament Tuan Chi-jui lacked the prestige that had been so great a factor in the early successes of Yuan Shih-kai in the same contest. More important still, he had not succeeded to the position of acknowledged leader of all factions of the military and conservative parties. He could not be depended upon absolutely to control his own supporters, and this fact weakened him for any possible struggle within the government itself. Knowing that others were desirous of supplanting him as the chief Minister of State Tuan tried to maintain his hold on the militarists with one hand and on Parliament with the other. The consequence was that, eventually, he lost control of both.

In the autumn of 1916 the Military Governors of the provinces, following the precedent set by the Vice-President, Fêng Kuo-chang, who had tried to settle the conflict between the North and the South by a mediating Conference, held a Conference at Hsüchow under the auspices of Chang Hsün. Lacking a leader to whom they acknowledged a common allegiance, the Military party[1] attempted to formulate and enforce a policy of opposition to parliamentary control by means of conference action. They succeeded in preventing T'ang Shao-yi

---

[1] The northern military party (Peiyang party) was not a definitely organized group but was made up of those military men who actually controlled troops either under governmental authority or without it, and the Tutuhs of most of the northern provinces. They thought in terms of the old rather than the new since most of them had been members of the old officialdom.

from taking his place as Minister of Foreign Affairs, and they formed a theoretical "Union of the Provinces" which was really a union of the Military Governors of several of the provinces. Article two of the Regulations of the Union stated: "The Union is organized for the purpose of preventing the desperadoes from monopolizing the powers of the government. If Parliament should, under any pretext, create disturbance or take up an unconciliatory attitude towards the provinces, the Union will meet and consider a plan to make a unified fight (in a punitive sense) against Parliament."[2]

Tuan Chi-jui was accused at the time of using this Conference to coerce his opponents in the government. It might be suspected, however, that he was not in entire sympathy with the movement towards a military dictation which might easily undermine his authority equally with that of Parliament. That he did not take action against the Conference was probably due in part to his sympathy with its anti-parliamentary bias, and in part to a realization of his inability to exercise a control over the Tuchuns.

As a matter of fact nothing except words came from this first Hsüchow Conference, although there was the ever present possibility of the words leading to action. The Military Chiefs of the North continued to keep in communication with each other during the remainder of the year but with the passage of time less fear of their dictation was felt. They were far from united among themselves, several aspirants to the leadership of the group striving to make good their respective claims. In this disunion lay the greatest hope for a peaceful development towards parliamentary government in China. The opening months of 1917, unfortunately, provided a new

[2] *Peking Gazette,* September 22, 1916.

issue, and one that finally brought the struggle of the military faction against Parliament to a crisis.

On the ninth of February 1917, China joined the United States in sending a note to the German Government protesting against the extension of submarine warfare. This step was followed by the severance of diplomatic relations a month later, when no satisfactory reply had been received. In taking this action the executive and legislative branches of the government worked in practical harmony. Just before it was finally determined to break off relations, it is true, President Li refused to sanction the decision which had been reached by the Cabinet in favor of such action. The temporary breach between the President and the Premier was healed almost immediately, however, and at the same time the question of supremacy in the executive was settled in favor of the Premier.[3] When the Cabinet decision was submitted to Parliament for its approval the House of Representatives sustained the contemplated action by a vote of 331 to 87, and the Senate voted to support the government by a majority of about 150. It seemed that the possibility of war against another State would have the effect of reconciling the various factions in Chinese politics, and thus produce a beneficial internal effect.

When the breaking off of diplomatic relations had no effect in bringing about a modification of German policy, the government was forced to contemplate the third step—an actual declaration of war. There was considerable opposition to this

[3] Because of presidential opposition to his policy, (the President insisting upon his right to declare war and make peace), Tuan Chi-jui resigned and left Peking for Tientsin. The President and the high officials, however, all urged him to resume office, and he finally consented to do so after President Li had promised him a free hand for his war policy. See *Far Eastern Review*, March 1917, "China Breaks with Germany," for summary of the controversy.

in many quarters on the ground that China had nothing to gain by war with Germany, and had much to lose by becoming her active enemy. It was necessary, in order to counteract this feeling, that the government should be able to show substantial advantage to China from joining the Powers at war with the German Empire. To this end negotiations were commenced with the representatives of the Entente Powers at Peking. The Chinese desired that the country should be released temporarily from the payment of the Boxer indemnity; that a revision of the tariff provisions should be undertaken in the interests of China; and that the provision of the Boxer protocol prohibiting the movement of Chinese troops in the vicinity of Tientsin, and that permitting the maintenance of foreign troops in the Legation quarter of Peking, should be cancelled. The Chinese Government, in return for these concessions, agreed to assume only two responsibilities towards the Entente: 1) the supply of primary materials; and 2) assistance in respect of labor.[4]

Before he had received a favorable reply from the Powers, the Premier gave Parliament to understand that he was assured of substantial concessions along the lines indicated if China joined the Entente. The negotiations dragged on, however, without any decision being reached, and interest in the war issue declined throughout the country. As interest lessened the majority of the government in Parliament decreased. It soon became apparent that the unanimity of the different departments extended only to the question of war with Germany, and that opposition was steadily growing even to the war policy of the Cabinet.[5]

[4] *Far Eastern Review,* April 1917.
[5] German influence was steadily at work on Parliament and the people trying to stir up opposition to the war policy in every possible way. For instance, in Tientsin, maps showing the extent of

In order to divert attention from the unsatisfactory condition of the negotiations, Premier Tuan resorted to the expedient of asking the advice of the country. If it could be shown that a unanimous public sentiment favored war, he would have that to urge as a reason for the favorable action of Parliament, irrespective of possible concessions from the Powers. To aid in the manufacturing of this sentiment Tuan summoned to a conference some of the Military Governors.[6]

From the time this conference met the question of war became more a matter of internal politics than of foreign policy. The Military Governors assembled in Peking late in April, and the attention of the country was immediately centered upon their activities. The different views of the conference were set forth in the *Far Eastern Review* as follows: "The majority of the Pekingese find the fact that Vice-President Fêng Kuo-chang and General Chang Hsün have instructed their delegates to vote for war, much more interesting than the percentage of increase in the Customs Tariffs which the allies may or may not concede. The radical press sees an ominous military plot behind the calling of a military conference and airs the opinion that the Premier is preparing to force war upon a peace-loving and peaceably inclined people by a display of military power and cohesion among the big military chiefs. The press which supports the Peiyang (Military) party on the other hand heralds the gathering as an honest attempt to probe the collective sentiment of the nation before entering upon a

the German conquests since 1914 as compared with the successes of the allies, were put up on the walls of the houses. Sun Yat-sen, T'ang Shao-yi and their followers also tried actively to frighten Parliament into opposition to the war policy.

[6] The Conference was scheduled to meet April 16, but did not meet until "sometime after the twentieth." *Far Eastern Review,* May 1917.

campaign against the 'common enemy of neutral nations' and in support of the abstract right of weak nations to life, liberty, and the pursuit of happiness."[7]

The Conference decided unanimously in favor of war without waiting for concessions from the Entente. Further delay was deprecated since China had already "lost face" with the Powers by her procrastination. On May 1 several of the Tuchuns called upon the Premier and communicated the views of the Conference to him. He, in his turn, reported their decision to Parliament which immediately declared itself in favor of war.[8] After the President had given his assent to the policy it remained only to secure the passage of a declaration of war through the Assembly.

When the bill was submitted to Parliament it was felt that the government would have a sufficient majority to insure its passage. In spite of this fact no attempt was made to rush it to a decision. The Cabinet members and the Military Chiefs occupied themselves in entertaining the members of Parliament, hoping to make the passage of the bill doubly certain. It was just at this time[9] that a mob demonstration in favor of war took place outside the Parliament building. This unfortunate demonstration was blamed on the Premier, who was accused of attempting to coerce Parliament into a support of his policies. The majority of the Cabinet resigned in the storm that followed, and Parliament refused to take any action on the war bill until a new Cabinet was constituted. The opposition press demanded the resignation of Tuan Chi-jui and the choice of a new Premier as well as a new Cabinet. Tuan however held to his position and demanded action by

[7] *Ibid.,* p. 460.
[8] May 7, 1917.
[9] May 10, 1917.

Parliament on the question of war. The whole matter was postponed by the Assembly on the ground that there was no Cabinet to carry out the necessary war measures in case Parliament passed the bill. This amounted to a vote of want of confidence in the government, and, logically, should have been followed by the resignation of the Premier.

A new phase of the struggle was inaugurated on May 20, when the Military party came to the aid of the Premier, demanding the dissolution of Parliament. Up to that time the issue had been whether or not Parliament should declare war on Germany. The Tuchuns, however, changed the issue, basing their demand for a dissolution of Parliament on the objectionable nature of certain provisions of the draft permanent constitution. "What has greatly shocked us," the Tuchuns stated in their petition, "is the passage of a number of articles of the draft constitution by the Constitution Conference at the second reading and those approved by the committee meeting the other day. Among these articles one reads that when the House of Representatives passes a vote of lack of confidence in the Cabinet Ministers, the President shall either dismiss the Cabinet or dissolve the House of Representatives, but the said House must not be dissolved without the approval of the Senate. Another states that the President can appoint the Premier without the countersignature of Cabinet Ministers. The third provides that any resolution passed by both Houses of Parliament shall have the same force as law."[10] The petition then went on to lay down the principle upon which parliamentary government is based, that in case of conflict either the Cabinet must resign or appeal to the country in a new election. The check on the absolute power of Parliament, which lay in the right of dissolution, was lost, it was claimed, in the draft per-

[10] Translation, *Far Eastern Review*, June 1917, p. 499.

manent constitution, since the House could be dissolved only with the consent of the Senate, a body constituted in much the same way as the House, and with the same interests to defend.

After discussing the defects in the Constitution and commenting on the manner in which the meetings of the Constitution Conference had been conducted, the petition stated that the dissolution of Parliament was necessary for the best interests of the country. "An examination of the past experience of other countries shows that the making of the constitution should not be left in the hands of the Parliament. If China wishes to have a good constitution there is no other method except to attack the problem at the root. If the whole thing be not completely wiped out, soon the second reading will be completed and once the text is settled the third reading will only result in alterations in wording. It will then be impossible to alter the spirit of the law."[11]

Instead of dissolving Parliament at the request of the Military party the President, on May 23, surprised the country by the dismissal of the Premier. *Dr.* Wu Ting-fang was appointed acting Premier[12] and the name of Li Ching-hsi was submitted to Parliament for confirmation as successor to Tuan Chi-jui.[13] The approval of Parliament was given by a large majority in both Houses.[14]

[11] *Far Eastern Review,* June 1917, p. 499.
[12] Dr. Wu was then Minister for Foreign Affairs.
[13] Li Ching-hsi was an Anhui man and a nephew of the famous Li Hung-chang. He had held various high positions under the Manchus, having been Governor of the Yun-kwei provinces in 1909. Li was an intimate friend of Yuan Shih-kai and politically must be classed as a conservative militarist. For chronological sketch of Li Ching-hsi's life see: China Year Book, 1916, p. 529.
[14] House of Representatives, 388 votes for and 56 against; Senate, 166 for and 25 against.

After the dismissal of Tuan Chi-jui the Tuchuns assembled in conference at Hsüchow. The Conference decided to oppose the formation of a Cabinet by Li Ching-hsi, but intimated that it would not oppose a government headed by Wang Shih-chen, the Chief of the General Staff. General Wang, however, refused to consider the position, although Li agreed to give way to him. This first move by the Hsüchow Conference was followed almost immediately by reports that the Military Governors of Fengtien and Anhui provinces had declared independence of the Central Government. Fukien, Chekiang, Chihli, Shantung, and Hupeh, all of them under the control of members of the Peiyang party were reported as also having joined the revolutionary movement.

In spite of the reported action of the provinces, President Li Yuan-hung reiterated his determination not to dissolve Parliament. "I cannot sanction the dissolution of Parliament. The provisional Constitution does not provide for any such drastic action," he said on May 21.[15] From that time on, nevertheless, as the revolutionary movement gained greater headway, the President showed signs of weakening. While emphasizing his determination to do nothing unconstitutional he did everything possible to conciliate the Peiyang party. The Military Chiefs refused to consider anything short of an absolute dissolution of Parliament, and the earlier reports of revolt were confirmed by telegrams declaring independence.

If the President had taken a decided stand against the Tuchuns at the outset, the situation might have been saved. Instead of ordering steps to be taken against them he wasted time attempting to conciliate them by considering every suggestion made for filling the post of Prime Minister. The first man he appointed, Li Ching-hsi, was a conservative, and a man

[15] *Far Eastern Review,* July 1917, p. 529.

allied with the Military party. He refused to come to Peking to assume office, or to attempt to form a Cabinet in opposition to the wishes of the revolting Tuchuns, showing clearly that he could not be relied upon to act against them in case of necessity.

Being unable to form a government acceptable to both Parliament and the rebellious Governors, President Li took a step which, in the light of the past history of the Republic, is almost inexplicable, unless it is to be explained by the assumption that the President was willing to do anything to end the crisis. On June 1 a mandate was issued calling upon the notorious and infamous General Chang Hsün[16] to come to Peking to mediate between the Tuchuns and Parliament. General Chang had been only a thorn in the side of the Government since the first revolution. He was well known for his desire to see the monarchical regime restored under the Manchu *Dynasty*, and had no sympathy with democratic government under any guise. The first attempts at dictation by the Military party in the fall of 1916 had been made under his direction and at his instigation. This was the man who was called upon by the President of the Republic of China to mediate at a time of grave crisis—he who had been a practical outlaw, maintaining himself by the strength of his personal army for almost eight

---

[16] Chang Hsün, a Kiangsi man, had been raised to high office by the Empress Dowager Tzu Hsi. He had been appointed as commander-in-chief for the Manchus in Yunnan and later in Kansu. In 1911 he was commander-in-chief of the Kiangnan forces, with headquarters at Nanking. He remained faithful to the Manchus to the very end. The abdication of the Manchus found him occupying important points along the Tientsin-Pukow railroad, where he maintained himself by sheer force. Yuan Shih-kai secured his support for the monarchy movement by appointing him Field-Marshal and High Inspector of the Yangtze provinces. For fuller description of his life see: China Year Book, 1916, pp. 500-501.

years! It seems strange that the President, who above all others in the country had always declared his faith in constitutionalism and parliamentarianism in China, should have called upon a virtual brigand to settle a constitutional crisis. The mandate summoning General Chang Hsün to Peking deserves reproduction as an interesting document: "Chang Hsün, the Tuchun of Anhui, has, in a telegraphic message, given his views of the present situation in words at once earnest and sincere. On account of my lack of virtue and ability as well as the fact that my prestige is insufficient to command respect, some of the officers whose duty it is to defend the country, have joined together in hostile demonstration. Events have turned out to be against my wish and I am smitten by regret and remorse. Chang Hsün, *who is highly meritorious and respected as well as public spirited and patriotic,* is requested to at once come to Peking in order to confer with us regarding the affairs of the State. I believe confidently that he will be able to save the dangerous situation by coping with the difficulties. In earnest longing I wait for his arrival."[17]

Chang Hsün accepted the task laid upon him, but did not go to Peking immediately as he had been asked to do. The revolting Tuchuns had established themselves at Tientsin as the headquarters for operations against Peking. A provisional military government had been formed and many prominent anti-parliamentarians were to be found there. Tuan Chi-jui himself, after his dismissal from office, had taken up his residence in Tientsin. General Chang, therefore, stopped at Tientsin to get the views of the leaders there before going to Peking to take up his work of mediating. He arrived in Tientsin on June 7, and did not leave for the capital until a week later.

[17] *Far Eastern Review,* July 1917, p. 537. The italics are the author's.

After interviewing Tuan Chi-jui, Li Ching-hsi and others, General Chang showed what could be expected of him as a mediator. On June 8 he made the statement that the whole difficulty was practically solved. "I have wired to the President to dissolve Parliament, and I will go to Peking on Sunday to finally settle matters"[18] were his words. In other words mediation and dictation were synonomous to him.

The wavering attitude of the President became more pronounced after Chang Hsün's message reached him. Instead of continuing to stand firmly on the constitution he began to seek middle ground between giving in to the Militarists and Chang Hsün entirely by dissolving Parliament, and defying them to do their worst. The southern provinces assured him of their support, both moral and military; but Yunnan, Kueichow, Kuangtung and Kuangsi looked very far away when compared with Chihli, Shantung and the revolting provinces.

The first real intimation given the parliamentarians that President Li might fail them came when he suggested the possibility of Parliament dissolving itself by reason of a continned lack of a quorum. While this appeared to the President as the best way out of the dilemma, it did not appeal with great force to the majority of Parliament. Even before the President suggested this step, however, it had occurred to the members of the Yenchiu-hui (Chin Pu Tang). That party had assisted the President to overthrow Parliament in 1913, and it now aided the revolt of the Tuchuns by its members absenting themselves from Parliament. The Chin Pu Tang members published a statement in support of the Tuchuns, expressing disapproval of certain articles of the proposed constitution.

[18] *Ibid.*, p. 538.

The six points which "tended to create disturbances and revolutions" in the future were laid down as follows: "1) The system of Parliament has not been improved and its organization has not been definitely fixed; 2) when any decision of the Houses is returned by the government for reconsideration the ordinary method of voting will be employed to make a final decision; 3) the mandate dismissing the Prime Minister does not require the counter-signature of Cabinet Ministers; 4) the partiality shown in the provisions of the right of 'vote of want of confidence' and that of power to dissolve the House of Representatives; 5) the bills passed by the Houses shall become the Laws of the Nation; and 6) the provincial system has been hastily provided for in the constitution."[19]

In addition to refraining from attending the meetings of the Constitution Conference, and thus making action on the constitution impossible, the Chin Pu Tang members considered the advisability of resigning from Parliament in a body, making it impossible for it to function because of a lack of a quorum. This action was considered as early as May 24. If those members resigned there would be no necessity for a formal dissolution of Parliament, since many of the Kuo Ming members were beginning to leave Peking in fear of being forcibly detained and imprisoned. Parliament, however, refused to dissolve itself formally in order to help the President out of a bad situation.

After Chang Hsün's advice, the President became convinced that he had no alternative to the issuance of a mandate dissolving Parliament and ordering a new election. It is not necessary here to discuss the play and counter play of forces working on him before he reached a final decision and issued

[19] *Far Eastern Review,* July 1917, p. 529.

the mandate.[20] His continued vacillation showed the President to be what the *Far Eastern Review* well called him, "an idol with feet of clay."

Having established himself as the dictator to the President, Chang Hsün left Tientsin, arriving at Peking on June 14 with a large force of his own "army." The immediate result of the dissolution of Parliament was the "cancelling of independence" by the revolting Tuchuns. At the same time it became evident that the seat of trouble simply had been transferred from the North to the South, which now threatened to take up arms in defense of the constitution and Parliament.

Li Ching-hsi consented to assume office when Chang Hsün requested that he do so, and commenced the almost hopeless task of forming a Cabinet. The warning from the South caused little alarm since the military strength of the Tuchuns was available to crush any revolt.

The *Peking Gazette* summarized the gains from the revolt of the Tuchuns as follows: 1) dissolution of Parliament; 2) "borrowing" of funds from government railways; 3) "boosting" of Chang Hsün; 4) dissolution of a provincial assembly in Fukien; 5) formation of a Cabinet without the approval of Parliament (not yet completed); 6) isolation of the Chief Executive; 7) return of monarchist propagandists (not yet completed); 8) destruction of the provisional Constitution and the part of the permanent Constitution which has passed the second reading; 9) the creation of a Council of Elder Statesmen (not yet completed); 10) the creation of a bogus legislature for the making of a new constitution (not yet completed); 11) creation of a new Parliament in violation of the existing laws (not completed); 12) wholesale suppression of democratic elements (fairly complete).

[20] June 13.

Before the new Premier had an opportunity to form a government worthy of the name, and before sentiment in the South had definitely crystallized either for or against the new conditions in Peking, the world was treated to what became eventually an amusing spectacle. It had been known for a long time that General Chang Hsün desired nothing more than an opportunity to restore the Manchus to power. His loyalty to the former rulers of China is the one redeeming feature of his entire career. At various times since the death of Yuan Shih-kai it had been rumored that he was contemplating action against the Republic. Thus for a time the various conferences at Hsüchow were reported as favoring Manchu restoration, and when he reached Tientsin on his way to Peking as the "official" mediator, it seemed certain that General Chang would attempt some drastic action against the Republic. He stated definitely, however, that he was interested only in the dissolution of Parliament, and had given up all idea of reinstating the former Dynasty. This decision was apparently reached after he had learned that the Military leaders would not support him in any such movement.

The ease with which he became established as dictator in Peking, however, evidently caused him to over-rate his strength and influence. Whatever caused him to change his mind and attempt his scheme, the fact is that he did reach the conclusion that the time was ripe for the Restoration. On July 1, as the result of a midnight resolution, the Manchu Dynasty was declared restored to the Throne, Peking was placed under control of the military forces of General Chang, and China for a few days became a monarchy.

As if by magic the old 'Dragon' flag of the Manchus was substituted for the flag of the Republic in all parts of Peking. Edicts were issued by Chang Hsün, in the name of the Emperor, notifying the people of the change in their allegiance, and preparations were made to defend Peking against any forces that the anti-Manchu party might be able to muster. General Chang had his own troops with him, and it was upon them that he placed his chief reliance. They had gained a bad name as ruffians and fighters without ever having been called upon to engage in battle against regular troops, and it was this name that terrorized the people of Peking and its vicinity when their leader first came to act as 'mediator'. The appearance of his troops as much as anything else, helped to lend the air of comic opera to this restoration attempted by Chang. For example they were all required to retain the queue as a reminder of the good old days of the Manchu supremacy, and the different divisions wore various colored uniforms, the most picturesque being a vivid blue. In addition to their military force, the Manchu adherents seemed to rely on a general passive acceptance of the change, both by the people and the Tuchuns, after it had been definitely effected. But in that expectation the event proved that they were grievously in error.

When the fact of Chang Hsün's *coup d'état* became known the Tuchuns merely restated the object of their 'punitive expedition,' directing it against the new monarchy. Tuan Chijui took supreme command of the forces and by the middle of July had made himself master of the situation, defeating Chang Hsün and forcing him to seek refuge in the Legation Quarter of the city. This effort to dislodge the monarchists involved some little fighting, but it, again, was of the comic opera variety. Foreigners in Peking regarded it as so little dangerous in character as to permit them to go out on the wall of the city to observe it as an interesting spectacle. There was really much more danger to spectators than to the actual participants in the fighting. Chang Hsün's army exhibited all of the weaknesses of mercenary troops in the face of actual danger, coming over in large numbers to the army of the Republic until the 'Empire' was defended by only a faithful but stupid few. Thus the would be King-maker learned when it was too late that the conservative militarists were as distinctly anti-monarchical and anti-Manchu as they were opposed to Parliament.

One beneficial result of the short-lived monarchical restoration was the final elimination of Chang Hsün as a factor in Chinese politics. Another was the temporary union of all factions in opposition to the Manchus. The constitutionalists could not act against the Tuchuns when the latter were fighting to uphold the Republic instead of to overthrow it. The futility of a continued strife which only opened the way for control by such men as Chang Hsün must have been apparent to both sides. Had the struggle against the monarchy continned long enough to allow of active participation by the South it is entirely possible that the temporary sinking of differences in the face of the common foe might have resulted in a permanent healing of the breach. The fighting was over, however, before the constitutionalists could take part, and, as a matter of fact, their coöperation was not sought by Tuan Chi-jui. The overthrow of the monarchy was wholly the work of the Peiyang party, and left it, in union with the Chin Pu Tang, in substantial control of the government.

President Li Yuan-hung had been successful in gaining a refuge in the Japanese Legation when the restoration was proclaimed, and from there he requested the Vice-President, Fêng Kuo-chang, to act in his place, and also authorized Tuan Chi-jui to resume office as Premier and form a Cabinet.[21] Later

[21] The text of the telegrams may be found in the *Far Eastern Review* for August 1917, pp. 608-609.

he announced his intention of retiring forever from political life. His last political act was an announcement of this intention and a plea to the country to sink all differences and work unitedly for the good of China.

In order to forestall any recognition of the monarchy by the Powers, Tuan appointed an acting Minister for Foreign Affairs[22] before he left Tientsin to take charge of the Republican army. At the same time, when the former Minister for Foreign Affairs, Dr. Wu Ting-fang,[23] learned of the *coup d'état* undertaken by Chang Hsün, he left the North hurriedly and established himself at Shanghai as the Minister for Foreign Affairs. By taking this action he, too, hoped to prevent a recognition of the monarchy. The effect was, however, to emphasize again the differences between the North and the South.

After the republican forces had regained control of Peking the Premier undertook the formation of a Cabinet. Here again was presented a possible opportunity of uniting the constitutionalists and the militarists. If recognition had been given the former equally with the latter in the construction of the government harmony might have been restored. No attempt was made in this direction, unfortunately, and the first list of Cabinet members contained only militarists and members of the Chin Pu Tang. This was true also of the Cabinet as it was finally constituted.[24] The Peiyang party felt that

[22] Mr. Wang Ta-hsieh.

[23] Dr. Wu had offered his resignation several times, but it had never been accepted.

[24] The Cabinet as constituted by July 17 was as follows: Premier and Minister of War, Tuan Chi-jui; Navy, Admiral Liu Kuan-hsiung; Foreign Affairs, Wang Ta-hsieh; Interior, Tung Hua-lung; Finance, Liang Ch'i Ch'ao; Communications, Tsao Ju-lin; Justice, Lin Chang-min; Commerce, Chang Kuo-han; Education, Fan Yuan-lien. One member, the Premier, was a member

this was an opportunity not to be lost for strengthening itself in control. This was evidently also Tuan's opinion. In justification of his Cabinet appointments the Premier said that the great source of weakness in the past had lain in coalition Cabinets which could not harmoniously administer the government. Now the opportunity was presented of eliminating the southern party and entering upon a harmonious administration, and this opportunity should not be lost. He may have been influenced also by the recollection of the opposition always shown him by the South.

The southern leaders took the constitution of the Cabinet as a direct challenge and the old struggle was resumed. Even before the shortlived monarchy, Kuangtung province had declared itself self-governing, although not independent. The difference lay in the fact that it still recognized Li Yuan-hung as President and the Parliament as being in existence. After the resignation of the President and the succession of Fêng Kuo-chang to the office as the head of the military government which controlled the North, the movement for separation of the South from the North gained headway. Many chronic revolutionists such as Sun Wen came to Canton and the formation of a government there was begun. Parliament was endeavoring to function from Shanghai so that for an interval the country was triply divided. Finally the members of Parliament in Shanghai went to Canton, and the permanent division of the country under two governments appeared imminent. The permanency of such a division, however, depended on the lack of ability of the northern government to

of the Peiyang military party, and the others were members of the Chin Pu Tang, or more nearly in sympathy with it than with the constitutionalists of the South. Some were known for their support of the 1915 monarchy movement.

bring the South under its authority, or of the southern government to extend itself over the North. The issue was definite.

The government at Peking, headed by Tuan Chi-jui was recognized by the Powers as the legal government of China and was dealt with as such when the question of war with Germany was again revived. A proclamation was issued on August 14 declaring a state of war to exist between China on the one hand and Germany and Austria on the other. It seemed very much as though a country at war with itself was only adding to its burdens by undertaking a foreign war. But to take such a step meant getting the solid support of the Entente Powers behind the Peking government. The 'value of this support was recognized by the Canton government which protested that it alone had the power to declare war and make peace, since those powers were vested in Parliament by the constitution, and the Parliament, so far as it could be said to be in existence, was in the South. The constitutional issue, under the circumstances, did not appeal to the Powers as a valid reason for not working with the most powerful element in the State, and the one in control of the administrative machinery of most of the provinces.

From the time of the overthrow of General Chang Hsün the internal history of China has been the story of the struggle between the North and the South, first of all, and in the second place between various factions in the North. Fêng Kuo-chang succeeded to the office of President, but he did not leave his post in the Yangtze valley to assume office in Peking until the latter part of July. The experience of Li Yuan-hung who also had left a high provincial position to go to

Peking, served as a warning to the new President.[25]   From his position at Nanking as Viceroy of Kiangsu province Fêng Kuo-chang could exert a great influence on the country. While there he had his army to aid him, and he had control of a region of great importance to both the North and the South.   In Peking, separated from his immediate supporters, he would be constantly in danger of losing all direction of affairs.   The South held out every possible inducement for him to join the constitutionalists in their fight against Tuan Chi-jui and the northern Generals, but the North appeared the stronger to him for he finally went to Peking, accompanied by a bodyguard, to assume office.   Before he would consent to leave Nanking, however, he made sure, so far as possible, of a continued control of the Yangtze.   He insisted that one of his supporters[26] be made Viceroy of Kiangsu province, and another be appointed to fill the vacancy in Kiangsi.[27]   One of his friends was already in control of Hupeh province, so that these appointments assured to President Fêng continued control of the Yangtze valley.

Both the President and the Premier aspired to the leadership of the Peiyang party[28] and their rival aspirations eventu-

[25] While at Wuchang and supported by his troops General Li had exercised a much greater authority than when in Peking and separated from the soldiers loyal to him.   After Yuan Shih-kai persuaded him to come north, he was practically a prisoner until he succeeded to the presidency, and even then, as has been seen, he was only able to make himself felt by siding with one party or the other.

[26] Li Hsun, Tutuh of Kiangsi province.

[27] Made by the transfer of General Li Hsun to Kiangsu.

[28] The Peiyang party, it may be noted, was divided into two factions, the Chihli faction of which General Fêng and his adherents had control, and the Anhui faction dominated by General Tuan Chi-jui.   General Ni Ssu-chêng who was leader in the movement to overthrow Parliament was an Anhui man.

ally led to conflict in the government. This conflict developed first over the question of the steps to be taken against the constitutionalists. The Premier desired to take active military action while the President's policy was rather one of conciliation. Tuan had allied himself with the Chin Pu Tang, finding it impossible to eliminate from influence both the political parties. He made this alliance with the expectation that through the Chin Pu Tang he would be able to control the Parliament which all agreed eventually must be elected. The President, in order to have similar party backing, wished to conciliate the South, in order to control the Kuo Ming Tang members who would certainly represent that section of the country. This fact helps to explain his desire to conciliate rather than coerce the South.

It is futile to attempt to give a clear and coherent account of Chinese politics during the last months of 1917 and the first months of 1918. The summaries of political conditions in the current weeklies and monthlies rightly headed their accounts "The Chinese Political Fog," "The Muddle in Chinese Politics," etc., etc. Fighting went on intermittently between the North and the South without either side gaining any distinct advantage. Tuan Chi-jui, as the leader of one faction of the Peiyang party insisted on strong measures being taken, while the President as the leader of another faction nullified all such action.

After he perceived that the President would not support him in his efforts to check the southern forces Premier Tuan insisted on resigning. For a time no one could be persuaded to undertake the task of forming a new Cabinet. Finally General Wang Shih-chen accepted the Premiership, with the policy of peace with the South through negotiation. The peace policy eventually had to be given up. Reports from the South were not encouraging, and the Tuchuns finally took matters in their own hands, announcing that either Peking would have to give up all idea of compromise with the constitutional· ists or they would carry on the war independently of the Central government.   Three of their leaders were thereupon authorized to conduct the war, and peace talk was at an end for a time.   Matters went from bad to worse in the contested provinces as well as at Peking.   In the provinces desultory fighting continued simultaneously with peace discussions, and neither had any real effect.   In Peking the President had lost control of the Peiyang party,[29] and its real leader, Tuan Chi-jui, refused to resume office.

In the latter part of February 1918, a definite agitation for peace was begun, the Chinese Chambers of Commerce and all business interests supporting the movement with enthusiasm. At this time, however, the three Manchurian provinces were federated under the leadership of General Chang Tso-lin, who moved a large force into the metropolitan province and announced his intention of going to the aid of the northern forces.   This brought all talk of peace to an end in the North. Tuan Chi-jui came back to office as Premier with the solid support of the Northern Tuchuns, and a vigorous campaign was undertaken against the South.   For a time, again, it looked as though the two sections would be brought by force under one government.   But the North did not prove strong enough to extend its power to the provinces in the far South, or to maintain more than a precarious hold on the middle provinces.

From the strictly constitutional point of view there is but

[29] Li Hsun developed a policy and a following of his own, attempting to play the same game that President Fêng had formerly—to preserve the neutrality of the Yangtze provinces—thus holding the real balance of power between the North and the South.

little of interest to record. The pretence of constitutionalism and parliamentarianism was maintained in the North. The South, of course, claimed to be struggling to preserve the constitutional regime in China. But while the old Parliament reassembled at Canton nothing of a constructive nature was done in the South to advance the course of constitutional development.

In the North, in order to maintain the pretence, Tuan Chi-jui, the Premier in the fall of 1917, summoned an Assembly for the purpose of framing an acceptable law for the election of a new Parliament. The Law was promulgated by the President February 17, 1918,[30] and under it a Parliament was elected in time to proceed to the election of a President in the autumn of 1918.

The new Parliament consisted of two chambers, the Senate and the House of Representatives. The members of both Houses were elected by a system of electoral colleges. The qualifications for electors were 1) educational; 2) property, shown either by the payment of direct taxes or by ownership; 3) service as an official. The qualifications for electors of Senators were higher than for electors of members of the House of Representatives, but were of the same nature. In order that Parliament might be more easily controlled the membership of both Houses was reduced, and the representation of the provinces reapportioned, strengthening the hold of the Northern provinces and assuring a quorum for action in case the South did not choose to elect representatives.

The first task to which the new Parliament at Peking addressed itself was the election of a new President of the Republic. Previous to the election, the Tuchuns, or Military

[30] The text of the law is published in the *Far Eastern Review,* July 1918, pp. 296-303.

Leaders of the North, met in Conference at Tientsin to consider the question of the presidency and the vice-presidency. Fêng Kuo-chang was a military man and a leader of one faction of the military group, but because of the continued breach with Tuan Chi-jui, the leader of the other faction, it was felt to be inadvisable to continue him in the presidency. The one man who seemed to command the support of both factions was Hsü Shih-ch'ang, a representative of the old regime, but a man of administrative experience and of great capacity.[31] Accordingly he was elected by Parliament on September 4 as the successor to Fêng Kuo-chang.[32]

The position of the new President was a difficult one. No one recognized more clearly than did he the necessity for peace and harmony in the country, both because of internal needs and because of the international situation. That the Powers wished for an adjustment of the internal difficulties was emphasized by President Wilson in his message of congratulation to President Hsü. "This is an auspicious moment," he said, "as you enter upon the duties of your high office, for the leaders in China to lay aside their differences and guided by a spirit of patriotism and self-sacrifice to unite in a determination to bring about harmonious coöperation among all the elements of your great nation so that each may contribute its best effort for the good of the whole and enable your Republic to reconstitute its national unity and assume its rightful

[31] Member of the Grand Council from 1905 to the Abdication, and, after the resignation of the Regent in 1912, one of the Grand Guardians of the infant "Emperor."
During the 1915 Monarchy movement he had been given the title of one of the "Four Friends of Sung Shan" (Yuan Shih-kai). He was a "sworn brother" of Yuan Shih-kai.
[32] After considerable squabbling it was found to be impossible to elect a Vice-President.

place in the councils of nations."[33]   The international view of the necessity for peace was further emphasized from time to time by the Allied Ministers in Peking.

But while President Hsü Shih-ch'ang realized the necessity for peace he was not unaware of the forces with which he would have to contend, both in the South and in Peking, in his effort to restore harmony and unity to China.   A permanent peace for the country depended and depends on the abolition of military government in the provinces.   This could be accomplished only by the gradual elimination of those who had been ruling China since the dissolution of Parliament by Li Yuan-hung in 1917.   This was ostensibly for what the South was fighting.   But in actual fact the southern provinces were just as truly ruled by the military as the northern.   Consequently there would be an opposition in both sections of the country to any settlement that meant the limitation of the power of the Tuchuns.

While the President had been raised to that office by the northern Tuchuns he did not by any means command their absolute allegiance.   Whether in or out of office Tuan Chi-jui remained always a factor to be considered.   In the Cabinet Tsao Ju-lin commanded considerable support, because of his party following and his great natural abilities.   The President, then, had to prepare the way in the North before he could undertake peace discussions with the South.   He waited, watched, and worked until November 16 when a presidential mandate was issued ordering the northern soldiery to stop fighting and return to their original posts.[34]   Following this declaration of an armistice steps were taken to bring about a Conference between the Military Government of the Southwest and the

[33] *Far Eastern Review,* November 1918, p. 460.
[34] *Far Eastern Review,* Dec. 1918, p. 505.

Peking Government with a view to discovering a basis for peace and reunion.   The absolute victory of the allies in Europe as indicated by the armistice of November 11 undoubtedly reacted on the military in China, causing them to support Hsü Shih-ch'ang in his peace move.

This idea of a conference had been advocated by both Chinese and foreigners for a long time, and several concrete suggestions as to a basis for settlement had been advanced.   The one most worth consideration was that put forth in an analysis of the situation by W. W. Willoughby, former Legal Adviser to the President.   In brief he suggested that "there be constituted a joint or Conference Committee composed of a small number of members from each of the Canton and Peking Parliaments, this committee to agree upon the terms of new laws for the organization and election of a new National Parliament, these laws thus agreed upon to be enacted, without amendment, by both Parliaments, and, under them, a new Parliament could be elected, whereupon the Parliaments now sitting at Peking and Canton would go out of existence.   Prior to this the Canton Parliament might elect Hsü Shih-ch'ang as President of the Republic, or after the convening of the new Parliament that body could elect Hsü to the Presidency.   Thus would be brought into existence a government the constitutionality of which neither side could or would be disposed to assail."[35]

Such a Conference, to discuss the points at issue and reach a settlement, was finally constituted and assembled at Shanghai.   It is not necessary, even were there space, to discuss the controversies between the two sides prior to the meeting at Shanghai.   Chu Chi-chien was appointed Chief delegate of

[35] Published in *Far Eastern Review*, November 1918, pp. 433-436.

the Peking Government while T'ang Shao-yi headed the delegation representing the Military Government of the Southwest.

The first question taken up by the Conference involved a questioning of the sincerity of the North. T'ang claimed that the terms of the second armistice agreement were being violated by a continued advance of the northern forces in Shensi province. This question caused a temporary suspension of the Conference until the southern delegation was satisfied that the fighting had entirely stopped.

At the same time the southern delegation demanded that the Peking Government discontinue the War Participation Board of which Tuan Chi-jui was the head, and disclaim any intention of accepting further advances from Japan for the services of that Board.[36]

But the rock on which the Conference finally split, and this in spite of repeated advices from the allied Ministers not to let anything prevent a consolidation of the country under one government, was the demand of the South that, as a preliminary to peace, the mandate issued by Li Yuan-hung dissolving Parliament should be cancelled. This was the fifth of eight points submitted to the Conference by T'ang. There was agreement on the other seven.[37] When the North refused to give in on this point both delegations resigned and returned, the one to the North, the other to the South.

The course of the internal Conference was influenced greatly by the Paris Peace Conference when it announced its

[36] This Board had been established to direct such military aid as China might furnish her allies in Europe. A Japanese loan was to finance such participation. Advances on the loan had been made, and Japan suggested her readiness to complete the loan. The Southern objection was based on a fear that the money would be used to finance a resumption of internal warfare.

[37] *North China Herald* (Weekly ed), May 17, 1919, p. 412.

decision on the Shantung question. A widespread agitation sprang up throughout the country to prevent the Chinese representatives from signing the treaty, and this agitation reacted directly on the Government at Peking which was held accountable for the actions of the members of the Chinese delegation to Paris. A Cabinet crisis was precipitated which resulted in the elimination of the most strongly pro-Japanese member of the Cabinet, Tsao Ju-lin.

What the future will bring forth it is hard to say. The anti-Japanese feeling in China if it develops far enough may conceivably make possible a union of the provinces for the purpose of protection against external aggression. In all parts of the country there is a continuation of the demand for the resumption of the Conference and a settlement of the internal question.[38] If popular sentiment is sufficiently aroused against the militarists so that their opposition to any solution of the difficulty would be removed, peace would not be long delayed, and it would be possible to recommence an orderly constitutional progression.

[38] It has been reconvened but up to the present time, 1920, January, has not worked out a plan of settlement acceptable to both the North and South.

CHAPTER XI

From an oriental despotism to a limited monarchy; from monarchy to republicanism and back to monarchy for a day before the restoration of the Republic; from a parliamentary Republic to a division into two States, each ruled by a group of irresponsible military chiefs, with the Parliament a dummy rather than a board of control; such have been the political mutations in China during the past twenty years. After tracing constitutional development in modern China, seemingly we come back to our starting point, semi-irresponsible government—certainly we do not find such a logical and ordered development into a democratic State as seemed to be indicated by the events of 1911-1912.

That these twenty years of development have not been productive of good not even the most severe critic of China would venture to say. The education of the people politically, while it has not proceeded very far, has been substantially begun. Valuable reforms have been instituted in legal procedure and the administration of justice; there have been the necessary experiments with foreign institutions so that the process of adapting them to the peculiar needs of China is well under way; and in spite of change, there has been retained in the political organization the agency through which eventually the democratic voice of China will make itself heard. Because parliamentary control is for the present lost, the value of the successive acknowledgments of the necessity of a Parliament to satisfy the people should not be underestimated.

China has always been classed as a democratic country, and

very properly so, by those who have appreciated the control exercised by the people over the local administration, and the respect necessarily shown by the government, both central and provincial, for local customs and wishes. The right of revolution was recognized both in theory and practice, and was a powerful weapon in the hands of the people for the preservation of their freedom from a too autocratic power. It was this element of democracy in China which caused observers to expect too much from her in the transformation years after the outbreak of the revolution. Proceeding from a local self-government, it was felt and predicted that China would escape the years of toil and experimentation incident usually to the change from autocracy to democracy. That there has been much confusion, unrest, and even retrogression is not to be wondered at if one stops to consider some of the reasons of a fundamental nature for the apparent failure of representative democracy in China.

The necessity for a period of preparation and readjustment was recognized more clearly by the dynastic rulers of China than by the revolutionists who were bent primarily on one thing, the elimination of the Manchus, and only secondarily on the solution of the problem of popular control of the government. Because of this recognition of unreadiness, and of course also because of their own necessity, the Manchus strove for a nine year period of development and gradual change before the actual promulgation of a constitution and the election of a Parliament. What might have been accomplished in these nine years it is of course impossible to say, since the revolutionary ferment denied any breathing space to the Government. The leaders of the revolution were of foreign education in many cases, or had received the rudiments of a western education in foreign maintained schools in China. They felt themselves able to give the people the intelligent direction and guidance that would be necessary after the transfer of sovereignty from the Emperor to the populace. Their belief would seem to have been, not in popular government itself, but in a government by the qualified few in the interest of the unqualified masses. Thus from the beginning there was a very extended limitation of the right of the suffrage, by various kinds of qualifications. This would certainly constitute a recognition of the lack of preparation of the people to participate in the government of the country, even while the doctrine of popular sovereignty was being preached.

The self-constituted leaders of the uneducated masses styled themselves the "Young China" party. That many of them had received a thorough education in western universities or in Japan is undeniable. But those who studied in the United States, England or France were studying the operation of political institutions foreign to China in the setting natural to the institution and the student naturally found it difficult to visualize them in a Chinese environment. The tendency was for him, the longer he was absent from his country, to overestimate its advancement, and to think of China in western terms. Consequently he could not see that what might have been of proven worth in another country might not be adapted to the needs of China. Where the student had received his education in Japan he had seen an imitation of English parliamentary government rather than its complete adaptation to the needs of the Oriental country. Furthermore even in so close a neighbor as Japan, conditions were very different from a Republican China. The Manchus were able to and did draw on Japanese experience in their attempt at a solution of the constitutional problem; the founders of the Republic had different needs to consider. Thus a study of constitutional government in Japan would not give the student an adequate knowledge of the problems which have to be faced in a Republic and of the manner of solution of these problems in China, the first Oriental Republic. From the standpoint of training, then, these new aspirants to leadership in China had to study in the school of practical experience before they could hope to solve the problems facing the country. In many cases they had no experience in actual administration prior to the revolution. They were theorists who found it difficult to divorce themselves from theory for the sake of expediency.

Many of the old regime came into the service of the revolution after it had manifested its strength; but because of their training in the old school they were able to give only a lip-service to the new institutions and ideas. Concerned only with practical considerations of administration they found it difficult to work in harmony with the "New China." But since they were the holders of administrative posts and were men of experience in practical politics the revolution found it necessary to avail itself of their services, even though mistrusting the sincerity of their professed belief in the principles of the revolution. They entrenched themselves in the executive and administrative services where the ground was most familiar to them, while "Young China" concentrated its efforts on a control of Parliament, which it intended to make the supreme organ of government. This brought the new into the conflict with the old regime that has prevented the orderly operation of a constitutional government.

The essence of parliamentary government is that the Assembly should act as the body representative of the people, carrying out their wishes through legislative act. One problem of representative government is the devising of ways in which the Parliament shall truly speak for the nation and not for itself alone—the establishment of a continuing connection between the electorate and its agents. In order that the people shall effectively control the government through Parliament they must be sufficiently interested in national affairs to follow the work of the government carefully and intelligently. Because representative government demands this political interest in more than local affairs, John Stuart Mill says that in many cases a people prepared to carry on the work of local government well may be entirely unfitted for the operation of a representative government. The history of China during the past few years assuredly illustrates the truth of his statement. For generations the people of China had effectively controlled the local government. But this very control had done much to unfit them for the control of the national democratic government established in 1912. They were not accustomed to look beyond the provincial boundaries even where they had looked that far abroad. They had no thought for national needs and problems. That was left for those who made a business of government,—the literati and bureaucracy. Even in time of war sentiment was localized. Thus, while the British were hammering on the gates of Peking, they were appealed to by the Chinese at Shanghai for aid against the Taiping rebels. Again, in time of flood, each province looked out for itself without thought for the needs of its neighbors. Instances of this lack of national feeling and thought might be endlessly multiplied. When the people then were expected to supervise the work of national government and administration they had no intelligent conception of the problems faced. The years since the revolution of 1911 have been remarkable for the development of a national feeling among the people in the provinces, a development which will ultimately make possible the successful operation of a representative government in China.

Even though the people had been ready to assume the direction of the government the organization of the Empire presented a problem which up to the present time has proved impossible of solution. Under the Manchu Dynasty while China had been outwardly a unified State, actually there was more nearly a union of independent provinces in the person of the Emperor. Practically each Governor or Viceroy had been the ruler of his own province. In many respects the Empire might be compared to the old Roman Empire. Peking had extended its sway over the country step by step, appointing its agent to rule the province, but leaving him to his own devices so long as the tribute was paid. The national revenues were not derived by a direct levy on the individual so much as by assessment which might be collected according to the wishes of the inhabitants. The Central control was not manifested to the people except through an alien soldiery and an alien officialdom. This soldiery was for a two-fold purpose: to manifest the power of the Emperor and to afford protection to the people in return for the contributions they made to the Imperial treasury. The officials, not being indigenous to the locality were regarded as the representatives of a foreign power, and were forced ultimately to deal with the people through their own representatives. So far as the Peking Government was concerned, until the foreign impact of the last century, if the contributions came in regularly from the provinces, and there was no evidence of disaffection which might be directed against the Imperial authority, the provincial authorities were the rulers in their own jurisdiction. The distribution of powers territorially inclined strongly toward the provinces.

With the presentation of the new problems brought by the presence of foreigners in the country, and with the attempt to introduce foreign institutions, the Manchus faced the alternative of either making themselves the leaders of a Federal Union of the provinces or of uniting the government under a centralized direction from Peking. In the last years of their rule they made the decision for centralization and began to interfere more and more in provincial affairs. This was especially shown in the movement to nationalize railway construction and operation. But this attempt to centralize was one factor in the ultimate overthrow of the *Dynasty* since it brought into opposition the "gentry" in all of the provinces, who might otherwise, through fear of revolutionary ideas, have been led to align themselves with the representatives of the established order.

The Republic, when it faced the same problem, decided in favor of centralization, just as the Imperial authorities had. This decision, in its turn, made for dissension and factional strife in the new government, and for opposition in the provinces to every attempt at centralization.

In addition to the problem presented by the traditional independence of the provinces, the Manchu rule had left the Republic with another problem which yet remains to be solved before China can expect peace and order. The provincial governments had been under a double direction; the civil administration represented by the Governor, and a coördinate military control. The necessity of maintaining an alien rule was of course responsible for the introduction of the military element in the government. Each military governor had his own forces which were responsible to him and for whose conduct he was responsible to the central authorities. Thus instead of there being one national army recruited from all over the country and paid from the Imperial treasury directly, there were separate armies in the provinces, separately maintained. So long as the commanders of these forces were Manchu they were held under the direction of the Emperor because they stood or fell with him. With the outbreak of the revolution, however, the control of these forces, together with the forces recruited for the purpose of revolution passed into the hands of Chinese commanders. Thus the way was paved for Tuchun control in the provinces simultaneously with parliamentary control in Peking.

When the military administration made necessary for a time by the revolution was not immediately replaced by a superior civil administration, with a nationalization of the army, the framework of an extra-legal government of a very pernicious character was provided. The assertion of this extra-legal authority depended upon one thing, force, and it had to be given consideration or be destroyed. There was no middle ground. Since it was not destroyed at the beginning it has gradually become more and more assertive, with each indication of its strength, until finally it has come to control not only the provincial governments, but the central government itself. Conditions at Peking were responsible in part for the ultimate triumph of the Tuchunate, for there was going on at the capital the struggle between Parliament and the executive for control. The Tuchuns naturally aligned themselves with the executive, and were used by it in its struggle with Parliament, only to find that it had invoked a force which ultimately overshadowed it.

Aside from the purely internal factors responsible for the failure of representative government in China, the outside world, and particularly Japan, must bear a share in the responsibility. Properly used the influence of the Powers might have brought strife to an end long before this. Improperly used it has made possible the long continued civil war which has been raging intermittently since 1911.

Consider the situation in 1911 ! The Imperial treasury was empty, and the outbreak of the revolution deprived the Manchu government of great sources of revenue. An empty treasury meant that no money was available for soldiers and munitions for use in quelling the rebellion, unless it could be obtained by foreign loans. On the other hand the revolutionists were equally in need of funds, in spite of the fact that they had the revenues of most of the provinces south of the Yangtze upon which to draw. Four alternatives presented themselves to the foreign governments. Either they could allow their nationals to make loans indiscriminately to both sides; they could restrict them to the aid of the de jure Imperial government, in which case the revolution would have been a failure from the outset because of a lack of funds; the Powers might have permitted their nationals to make loans only to the revolutionary government, which would have amounted to active intervention against the established and recognized authorities; or aid might have been denied to both parties equally. To have adopted the first course would have meant the prolongation of the strife indefinitely. Aid to the Imperial government exclusively was objectionable to the Powers because of the reactionary and the anti-foreign disposition of that government, a disposition that had been modified since 1900, but only because of necessity. Aid to the revolutionists in order to promote the overthrow of a government with which the Powers were at peace would have been undesirable both from the standpoint of international law and ethics. The last alternative, then, was the one adopted, a "watchful waiting"; as little active participation as possible under the circumstances, with, however, a decided leaning toward the South manifesting itself. The result of this policy was a compromise of the question, by the elimination of the Dynasty on terms favorable to the Manchus, and the establishment of the Republic, but with the North, in the person of Yuan Shih-kai, in control of the executive, while the South controlled the legislature.

After the establishment of the new government the Powers through the Six Power Group prepared to finance it through the initial difficult years of its existence. There has been much criticism of the policy of restricting loans to the Group, but on the whole it was the wisest thing to do under the circumstances. Without such restriction the entire resources of the country might have been alienated by an indiscriminate borrowing on the part of the individual provinces to meet their immediate needs.

The outbreak of the great war in Europe had an unfortunate reaction on the relation of the Powers to China in that it made Japan the sole Power of the group in a position to make advances to China to meet her pressing needs, the United States having withdrawn from the Consortium after the political change in this country in 1913.

When the monarchy movement came in 1915 the South and West immediately sprang to arms to defend the Republic. The Powers, however, continued to treat with the Peking government as the rightful authority in China. This continued recognition was of substantial advantage to Yuan since it gave him a source of revenue that might otherwise have been denied. Advances continued to be made on the loans contracted, and the funds thus gained were used largely for the purpose of putting down the rebellion. But while Japan, as the representative of the Four Power Group, made advances to Yuan and thus enabled him to maintain his hold on the government, she was accused of lending aid equally to the South, both in money and munitions.

This same accusation has been brought against her more recently during the struggle between the North and the South for control. A vast number of loans, some large and some small, have been made to the Peking government, and the South has also, though to a lesser extent, looked to Japan for material support. This has made possible a continuation of the division between the two sections for a longer period of time than would have been possible had the policy of 1911 been followed. Count Okuma, as early as 1905, said openly that a strong, united China constituted a menace to Japan, and, since 1914 his countrymen seem to have followed him in that belief, to the extent of aiding both parties to any quarrel that arose in China, thus keeping that country in a state of perpetual turmoil.

From this it does not follow that Japan should bear the blame for the failure of the Chinese to stabilize conditions in their country. Her policy, both in loaning money, and in acts of aggression on China have made it much more difficult for the Chinese to reconcile their quarrels, but the fundamental reasons for the failure of the new form of government set up in 1912 are to be found in China herself.

With conditions as they exist today where is the ground for hope in the eventual establishment of a democratic government in China? Can the Chinese be expected to work out a solution of their problems for themselves? How can the other Powers render the most service in the stabilizing of conditions in China?

Professor W. W. Willoughby, former Legal Adviser to the President, has suggested a plan for the reconciliation of the two sections of the country. In brief, it is that the Conference at Shanghai, representative of both the North and the South, should be empowered to draw up laws for the election of a new Parliament. These laws would then have to be accepted, without alteration, by both the Peking and the Canton

Parliaments. Thus the new Parliament would have an un-questioned title from both contestants for power. Then the Canton government should elect Mr. Hsü Shih-chang, who has already received an election in the North, to the presidency of the Republic. This would not be asking too much of the South for he commands the respect of both sections of the country. If this should not be done, then the new Parliament could give the necessary validity to his title. If the election of the new Parliament were under the proper supervision, Chi-nese if possible, foreign if desired, it should represent the entire country, uniting in its membership the various factions that have been at loggerheads for so long.

But that would not entirely meet the needs of the situation. It would do no more than restore the country to its condition in 1912. There would remain the problem of the Tuchunate, and the problem of financing the new government until it could meet its own needs. These two problems might be solved simultaneously. The old Consortium for the purpose of loaning money to China has been revived at Paris. It pre-sents a means of utilizing the financial strength of the Powers for the purpose of setting a united China on her feet financial-ly, just as the Five Power Group was used in the early days of the Republic. If a comprehensive loan could be made suffi-cient to provide for immediate administrative expenses and to consolidate all of the foreign obligations of the Chinese Re-public in one international loan the pressing needs of the gov-ernment would be taken care of, and the danger of financial control by one Power obviated, without an indiscriminate pledging of the resources of the country. But in order that the experience of the past few years should not be duplicated, any comprehensive loan to China should be made under con-ditions that would provide for the adequate supervision of the *expenditure* of the funds actually turned over to the government. A large part of the moneys recently advanced to the government has been diverted to the personal needs of the official, either as "squeeze," or as out and out appropriation of public funds. The latter could be prevented by parliamentary auditing of accounts, but it is not unreasonable to think that a good deal of "squeeze" might be overlooked and condoued by any Chinese supervisory board, while it would not be under foreign supervision. With such an oversight of the public expenditure the Powers would be able to deprive the military chiefs of the subsidies from the Central government which have enabled them to maintain their forces and thus their grip on the country, and it would only be a question of time until they would be entirely eliminated as a factor in Chinese politics.[1]

On the surface this would look like a betrayal of China to the exploitation of Western capital. This would not necessarily follow, however, for it could be only a temporary expedient at the best, to tide the country over the present emergeney. She will have to borrow to finance herself in any case, and it is obviously much better for her to borrow from a group of Powers than from any one Power, or from a number of States acting independently the one of the other. She will need the money not only for administrative needs but for industrial development as well, and experience has shown that only through a supervision of expenditure can there be assurance that money loaned for development projects will not be diverted to other needs.

[1] This would certainly follow if the revenue services of China were to be put under foreign administration to prevent the maintaining of these "personal armies" by the collection of the taxes, thus not only enabling the military men to pay their troops but depriving the Central Government of large sources of income.

In any case the world cannot afford longer to ignore China. She constitutes a problem today just as she has for the past twenty years, and a problem that may prove to be the cause of another world war. The international complications in the Far East can be adjusted most naturally by an honest attempt to aid China in the settlement of her internal difficulties, and this can best be done, from present indications, by some action similar to that outlined above.

APPENDIX ONE

Nine Year Programme of Constitutional Preparation.[1]

First Year, 1908-09.
  a—Organization of Provincial Assemblies.
  b—Issue of Local Administrative regulations.
  c—Issue of census regulations.
  d—Issue of regulations for financial reform.
  e—Establishment of a Bureau for the reform of the Manchu system, particularly as regards the treatment of Bannermen, and the fusion of Manchu and Chinese.
  f—Preparation of elementary lesson-books for teaching reading.
  g—Preparation of books for general reading.
  h—Revision of the Penal code.
  i—Drafting of Civil, Commercial and Criminal laws.

Second Year, 1909-10.
  a—Inauguration of Provincial Assemblies.
  b—Issue of Regulations for the National Assembly.
  c—Elections for same.
  d—Organization of Local Administrative Councils.
  e—Taking of census of whole Empire.
  f—Investigation of Provincial Budgets.
  g—Reform of Metropolitan Official system.
  h—Drafting of Civil Service Examination regulations, and of regulations for official salaries.
  i—Issue of regulations for Judicial Courts.
  j—Organization of Judicial Courts.
  k—Drafting of new Criminal Laws.
  l—Organization of Elementary Schools.
  m—Inauguration of modern constabulary system.

Third Year, 1910-11.
  a—Inauguration of the National Assembly.

[1] China Year Book (1912), pp. 361-63.

b—Local administrative system to be extended to townships.

c—Report by Viceroys and Governors on census in provinces.

d—Consideration of Provincial Budgets.

e—Drafting of local tax regulations.

f—Endeavor to carry out Provincial Budgets.

g—Reorganization of Provincial Official system.

h—Issue of regulations for Civil Service Examinations.

i—Establishment in all Capitals and Treaty Ports of Judicial Courts (Shenpanting).

j—Issue of new Criminal Laws.

k—Extension of primary education.

l—Organization of Police in hsiens.

Fourth Year, 1911-12.

a—Organization of system for auditing government accounts.

b—Investigation of the Budget for the Empire.

c—Issue of Government tax regulations.

d—Enforcement of Civil Service and Official Salaries regulations.

e—Establishment of Judicial Courts in Fu's.

f—Organization of elementary Schools in all townships.

g—Organization of Rural Police.

h—Consideration of the revised Commercial, Civil and Criminal Laws.

i—Extension of Local Government system to townships.

j—Investigation of the census.

Fifth Year, 1912-13.

a—Local Government system to be carried out this year.

b—Issue of new Metropolitan and Provincial Official systems.

c—Judicial Courts in all cities, towns and townships must be in working order this year.

d—Extension of elementary education.

e—Extension of Police system.

Sixth Year, 1913-14.
  a—Endeavor to carry out Budget for the whole Empire.
  b—Organization of Judicial Courts to deal with political matters.
  c—Complete organization of all judicial Courts in the provinces.
  d—Inauguration of Village Courts.
  e—Enforcement of new Criminal Laws.
  f—Issue of Civil and Commercial Laws.
  g—Police forces shall be established this year in all towns and villages.

Seventh Year, 1914-15.
  a—Strict adherence to the Imperial Budget.
  b—One per cent of the population should be able to read and write in this year.

Eighth Year, 1915-16.
  a—Budget for Imperial Household.
  b—Abolition of all distinction between Manchu and Chinese.
  c—Organization of a Statistical Department.
  d—Enforcement of new Civil and Commercial Laws.
  e—Organization of Police throughout the Empire to be completed.
  f—Two per cent of the population should be able to read and write in this period.

Ninth Year, 1916-17.
  a—Issue of Constitutional Laws.
  b—Issue of Imperial House Laws.
  c—Issue of Parliamentary Laws.
  d—Issue of regulations for the election of an Upper and Lower House.
  e—Elections for the Upper and Lower Houses.
  f—Preparation of Budget for the following year for discussion in Parliament.
  g—Organization of a Privy Council and of Advisory Ministers.

h—Five per cent of the population should be able to read and write in this period.

As a result of the agitation for an early convocation of the national Parliament a "Revised Programme of Constitutional Preparations" was issued, shortening the period of preparation by three years. The "Revised Programme" can be found in the China Year Book (1912) p. 376.